nd his successors bestowed on Winchester, London
merged in 1066 as the place where Duke William
accepted and where it was essential for him to stage his
he strength of Rory Naismith's narrative derives from
f the disparate sources needed to understand London's
ccess. The author's deep knowledge of the complexities
on coinage is matched in this book by an acute sense
tance of the recent archaeological discoveries that have
the city took shape within, and beyond, and then again
cient Roman walls. Anyone who loves London – that
overflowing river" (which is probably the ancient meaning
– will want to buy this superb book.'

Henrietta Leyser, Emeritus Fellow and Former Lecturer in History,
er's College, Oxford, author of *A Short History of the Anglo-Saxons*
d of *Beda: A Journey Through the Seven Kingdoms in the Age of Bede*

be Saxons is the first comprehensive treatment of Anglo-
don. Rory Naismith ranges widely across archaeology,
d written sources – showing an impressive command of
b-disciplines in the process – to piece together a fresh
the early medieval metropolis. Engagingly written yet
ive, this is everything a history book should be!'

Levi Roach, Senior Lecturer in Medieval History,
University of Exeter, author of *Æthelred: The Unready*

A Fellow of the Royal His
Lecturer in Medieval British
earlier books include *Money a*
which in 2013 won the Best
Society of Anglo-Saxonists.

King Alfred
nonetheless
needed to be
coronation.
his mastery
developing s
of Anglo-Sa
of the impor
revealed how
within its a
"place of the
of its name)

H
St Pe
an

'Rory Naismith in his new book
extraordinarily diverse range of e
with many unfamiliar details a
in Roman Britain, and extends I
England in 1066. By virtue of its
at the hub of a network of roads
throughout the Anglo-Saxon period
at the centre of events and was ren
of commerce. From the foundation
Westminster Abbey, Dr Naismith at
reader through all the city's twists an
bringing to life a rich supporting cast
English and Danes. This is an origi
early London.'

'Citadel of
Saxon Lor
coinage an
multiple s
picture of
authorita

Simon Keynes,
of Angl

'No one can know yet to what degree I
of England's capital. But Rory Naismitl
Saxon London is a reminder of how —
fered during its first millennium, and th
to contend – it survived such that poss
key to power during the Norman Conqu
the first century, deserted by the Romans
outdone by Ipswich in the seventh, and c
metropolitan status of Canterbury and Yor

Citadel
of the
Saxons

The Rise of Early London

RORY NAISMITH

With all best wishes ~

Rory

I.B.TAURIS
LONDON · NEW YORK

Published in 2019 by
I.B.Tauris & Co. Ltd
London • New York
www.ibtauris.com

Copyright © 2019 Rory Naismith

ISBN: 978 1 78831 222 6
eISBN: 978 1 78672 486 1
ePDF: 978 1 78673 486 0

A full CIP record for this book is available from the British Library
A full CIP record is available from the Library of Congress

Library of Congress Catalog Card Number: available

Text design and typesetting by Tetragon, London
Printed and bound by CPI Group (UK) Ltd, Croydon, CRO 4YY

I long to go through the crowded streets of your mighty London, to be in the midst of the whirl and rush of humanity, to share its life, its change, its death, and all that makes it what it is.

Bram Stoker, *Dracula*

Contents

List of Maps and Figures

Maps

Figures

Abbreviations

ANS   *Anglo-Norman Studies.*

ASC   *Anglo-Saxon Chronicle.* This is the modern term for a group of Old English chronicles covering the period 60 BC–AD 1154. The eight principal surviving manuscripts are traditionally referred to using the letters A–H, with substantial variations among them, though all descend from a compilation made c.892. When there is no substantive variation, the year alone is given (a second year in brackets indicates the year given at a time of chronological dislocation in the chronicle). For translation, see *The Anglo-Saxon Chronicle: A Revised Translation*, trans. Dorothy Whitelock, David C. Douglas and Susie I. Tucker (London, 1961).

ASE   *Anglo-Saxon England.*

ASSAH   *Anglo-Saxon Studies in Archaeology and History.*

ASWrits   *Anglo-Saxon Writs*, ed. F. E. Harmer (Manchester, 1952).

BCS   *Cartularium Saxonicum: A Collection of Charters Relating to Anglo-Saxon History*, ed. Walter de Gray Birch, 3 vols (London, 1885–99).

CantCC   *The Charters of Christ Church, Canterbury*, ed. N. P. Brooks and S. E. Kelly, 2 parts (Oxford, 2013).

CantStA   *Charters of St Augustine's Abbey, Canterbury, and Minster-in-Thanet*, ed. S. E. Kelly (London, 1995).

Chert   *Charters of Chertsey Abbey*, ed. S. E. Kelly (Oxford, 2015).

DOE   *Dictionary of Old English* (University of Toronto: www.doe.utoronto.ca/).

EHD   *English Historical Documents*, vol. 1: *c.500–1042*, ed. Dorothy Whitelock, 2nd ed. (London, 1979).

EHR   *English Historical Review.*

EME   *Early Medieval Europe.*

GDB   Great Domesday Book. References are to folio number in *Domesday Book*, ed. John Morris et al., 35 vols (Chichester, 1973–86), but many other editions are available.

Glast   *Charters of Glastonbury Abbey*, ed. S. E. Kelly (Oxford, 2012).

HE   Bede, *Historia ecclesiastica gentis Anglorum* (*The Ecclesiastical History of the English People*).

K   *Codex Diplomaticus Ævi Saxonici*, ed. John M. Kemble, 6 vols (London, 1839–48).

LondStP   *Charters of St Paul's, London*, ed. S. E. Kelly (Oxford, 2004).

MGH   Monumenta Germaniae Historica.

PAS   Portable Antiquities Scheme (www.finds.org.uk).

Pet   *Charters of Peterborough Abbey*, ed. S. E. Kelly (Oxford, 2009).

RIB   R. G. Collingwood and R. P. Wright, *The Roman Inscriptions of Britain* (Oxford, 1965). See also R. G. Collingwood and R. P. Wright, *The Roman Inscriptions of Britain 2: Instrumentum Domesticum*, ed. Sheppard Frere and R. S. O. Tomlin (Oxford, 1990–5); R. S. O. Tomlin, R. P. Wright and M. W. C. Hassall, *The Roman Inscriptions of Britain 3* (Oxford, 2009); and romaninscriptionsofbritain.org.

S   P. H. Sawyer, *Anglo-Saxon Charters: An Annotated List and Bibliography* (London, 1968).

SCBI 1   Philip Grierson, *Sylloge of Coins of the British Isles 1: Fitzwilliam Museum, Cambridge: Ancient British and Anglo-Saxon Coins* (London, 1958).

SCBI 16   C. E. Blunt, F. Elmore Jones and R. P. Mack, *Sylloge of Coins of the British Isles 16: Norweb Collection: Ancient British and English Coins to 1180* (London, 1971).

SCBI 63   Anna Gannon, *Sylloge of Coins of the British Isles 63: British Museum. Anglo-Saxon Coins I. Early Anglo-Saxon Gold and Anglo-Saxon and Continental Silver Coinage of the North Sea Area, c. 600–760* (London, 2013).

SCBI 64   Hugh Pagan, *Sylloge of Coins of the British Isles 64: Grosvenor Museum, Chester. Part II: Anglo-Saxon Coins and Post-Conquest Coins to 1180* (Oxford, 2012).

SCBI 67   Rory Naismith, *Sylloge of Coins of the British Isles 67: British Museum, Anglo-Saxon Coins II: Southern English Coinage from Offa to Alfred c. 760–880* (London, 2016).

SCBI 69   Tony Abramson, *Sylloge of Coins of the British Isles 69: the Abramson Collection: Coins of Early Anglo-Saxon England and the North Sea Area* (London, 2018).

Sel   *The Charters of Selsey*, ed. S. E. Kelly (Oxford, 1998).

TLAMAS   *Transactions of the London and Middlesex Archaeological Society*.

WBEASE   *The Wiley-Blackwell Encyclopedia of Anglo-Saxon England*, ed. Michael Lapidge, John Blair, Simon Keynes and Donald Scragg, 2nd ed. (Chichester, 2014).

Timeline

		London	England
43	ROMAN LONDON		Roman invasion of Britain
60/61		London destroyed in Boudicca's revolt	
180s–220s		London's city walls built	
c.410			End of central Roman rule in Britain
456	EARLY ANGLO-SAXON LONDON	Britons supposedly retreat to London after defeat in Kent	
597			St Augustine's Christian mission reaches England
604		Foundation of St Paul's Cathedral	
c.670	LUNDENWIC	Beginning of substantial settlement of *Lundenwic*	
679			Battle of the Trent between Mercia and Northumbria
735			Death of the Venerable Bede
764		Fire in London	
793			First known viking raid in England
796			Death of Offa, king of the Mercians
798		Fire in London; Coenwulf proposes archbishopric of London	
801		Fire in London	
829			Ecgberht of Wessex temporarily conquers Mercia
842		Viking raid on London	
851		Viking raid on London	
865			Arrival of viking 'great army'
872		Viking army takes winter quarters at London	
877			Vikings take over and settle eastern part of Mercia

Year	London	England
883	Confrontation with vikings at London	
886	Alfred's restoration of London	
893	London serves as base in campaign against vikings	
895	Londoners participate in campaign against vikings	
899		Death of Alfred the Great
911	London passes from Mercian to West Saxon rule	
c.914	First reference to Southwark in *Burghal Hidage*	
937		Battle of *Brunanburh*
939		Death of Æthelstan
962	St Paul's Cathedral destroyed by fire	
975		Death of Edgar
982	Fire in London	
994	Viking attack on London	
1012	London venue of key meeting and tribute payment; Archbishop Ælfheah killed at Greenwich	
1016	London at centre of conflict between Edmund Ironside and Cnut	Death of Æthelred II
1017	Cnut has Eadric Streona killed in London	
1018	London forced to pay £10,500 in tribute	
1035		Death of Cnut
1051	Earl Godwine and his sons flee meeting at London to go into exile	
1052	Earl Godwine and his sons return to London	
1065	Consecration of Westminster Abbey church	
1066		Death of Edward the Confessor; Battles of Stamford Bridge and Hastings; Norman Conquest of England

LUNDENBURH

Preface

This book was written for several reasons. First and most important among them is my long-standing interest in the Anglo-Saxon history of London and other English towns. Second, when I began to teach a course on medieval London at King's College London in 2016, I was prompted to articulate my understanding of the subject in a coherent way. Third, although there is a dauntingly impressive line-up of books already in existence on London and its past, few of these have focused on the early Middle Ages, and I wanted to come at the subject from a different angle: one which combined archaeological and other material sources, but was primarily written from the point of view of a historian, and explained why the city developed in the way it did, and what made it different from others.

The opportunity to write this volume came at the invitation of Alex Wright, and it was shepherded through production by Sara Magness. They and the whole team assembled by I.B.Tauris have been supportive and friendly from start to finish. Gesche Ipsen provided expert and sensitive copy-editing. Isobel Thornley's bequest to the University of London and the Department of History at King's College London both kindly provided grants to support the costs of reproducing images. I am also grateful to a number of friends and colleagues who kindly read through some or all of the book, and responded with constructive comments: John Clark, Andrew Reynolds and Levi Roach. Fruitful discussions about the early history of London, or specific questions arising from it, have fed into this book as well, and for these I am thankful especially to David Bates, Alex Burghart, Susan Kelly, Victoria Ziegler and all the students at King's who have taken 5AAH3001, 'London from the Romans to the Middle Ages'.

Last but not least, I was as always helped and supported at every turn, and in every way, by my wife, Brittany Schorn.

*

In what follows, dates for kings and bishops normally refer to periods in office, not lifespans. The symbols 'x' and '*' are used occasionally to refer (respectively) to an unknown but specific point between two dates, and to words in reconstructed languages (such as 'proto-Brittonic', the ancestor of Welsh, Cornish and Breton) which are not actually recorded in any surviving source.

A note is also required on words in medieval languages. Names are represented in their generally accepted modern form; so, Æthelred II rather than Æthelræd, Alfred the Great rather than Ælfræd, and so on. Quotations from texts are normally translated into Modern English, with the original included only when it is of particular significance to the point at hand. In such cases spellings follow the source as edited, meaning that there is no absolute consistency: where 'w' is used in the preferred modern form of a word, for example, medieval texts in Latin or Old English might offer 'u', 'v', 'uu' or 'vv' instead. 'Old English' refers to the language of the Anglo-Saxons. A few letters used in Old English (and also Old Norse, the language of the vikings) have fallen out of use: 'Æ/æ' (known as æsc) represents a vowel between a and e, similar to that of 'cat'; 'Þ/þ' (*thorn*) represents an unvoiced 'th' sound, as in 'thistle', while 'Ð/ð' (*eth*) is a voiced 'th', as in 'though'.

Finally, a word on references to London itself. In this period its status did not conform neatly to modern urban categories. *Londinium* (i.e. Roman London) is generally referred to as a 'city', following modern scholarly usage; so too is its successor, the walled settlement extending from Ludgate Hill to the Tower. This usage also conforms to the traditional British definition of a city as anywhere with a cathedral. The seventh- to ninth-century trading settlement that grew up to the west of the Roman walls is, for the sake of clarity, usually referred to as a 'town'.

INTRODUCTION

> The sea-reach of the Thames stretched before us like the beginning of an interminable waterway. In the offing the sea and the sky were welded together without a joint, and in the luminous space the tanned sails of the barges drifting up with the tide seemed to stand still in red clusters of canvas sharply peaked, with gleams of varnished sprits. A haze rested on the low shores that ran out to sea in vanishing flatness. The air was dark above Gravesend, and farther back still seemed condensed into a mournful gloom, brooding motionless over the biggest, and the greatest, town on earth.
>
> Joseph Conrad, *Heart of Darkness*

The London that the sailors approach in *Heart of Darkness* lurks just out of sight, beyond an eerie and murky stillness. Conrad's waterborne perspective on the city – imagined from a vantage point on the winding Thames – creates a sense of distance, and even unfamiliarity. There might be a vast metropolis near at hand, but while bobbing on the waves waiting for the tide to turn, it seems a million miles away.

Of the many celebrated representations of London in literature, this one is especially apt in setting the scene for the early Middle Ages. London in the age of the Anglo-Saxons is at once very familiar and far removed. It occupies the same space as modern London, and provides many of the names for areas and streets that have persisted down through the centuries. In that sense its legacy is very much still with us. Yet the foundations laid in the first millennium have been built over and around so many times that this chapter in the city's history lies buried deep in a way that those of more recent times do not. While St Paul's evokes Wren's London, or the Tower and Westminster the city of the later Middle Ages, Anglo-Saxon London is not reflected in any monuments that still stand today. Like Conrad's London, it sits in a well-known landscape but hovers just out of our grasp in the shadows.

The aim of this book is to venture into those shadows and trace the development of London between the end of the Roman city in the fifth century and the Norman Conquest of 1066. The contrast in the state of the city at these two points could hardly be more extreme. In the fifth century, London was an empty shell. Once the leading urban centre of the Roman province of Britain and one of the greatest cities in the northern part of the empire, it had fallen victim to the empire's structural disintegration. By the middle of the fifth century it lay overgrown and abandoned, a pale reflection of what it had been. An altogether different impression would have been made on anyone visiting the city around the time of the Norman Conquest. By contemporary standards, it was one of the largest and most important settlements in northern Europe. It was where the kingdom's leaders gathered and did business, a market for the finest craftsmen and richest merchants, and a draw for settlers from far and wide. In a word, it was again a city – a huge, thriving one.

If Anglo-Saxon London was essentially a new city, it nevertheless wore old clothes. It owed much to its Roman predecessor, beginning with the stout walls built c.AD 200, which helped keep London and its defenders safe from many attacks, especially in the ninth, tenth and eleventh centuries. The Anglo-Saxon settlement was also still known by a derivative of the name *Londinium* that had become attached to the Roman town on the north bank of the Thames. But the caesura of the post-Roman centuries cut a deep gash in the city's history. When London began to be resettled around AD 600, its character had changed dramatically. It was no longer the base for province-wide administration; instead, it was the bishopric for the East Saxons, and a budding hub of commerce, founded by enterprising merchants who travelled North Sea trade routes. These two functions, growing up in parallel, were reflected in a changed physical layout. London's commercial focus had shifted west of the Roman walls to what is now Covent Garden, Aldwych and the Strand. For about two centuries, London was a twin city: the Roman defences sheltered St Paul's Cathedral and possibly some other prestige buildings amid the ruins, while the bulk of the population lived and did business in what was known as *Lundenwic*, the new western settlement.

Lundenwic characterises the first half of London's Anglo-Saxon revival; the second half is often given the shorthand name *Lundenburh*, 'London-borough', or fortress London. Viking threats combined with economic pressures led the inhabitants of the old Strand settlement to relocate back into the Roman walled city in the ninth century, and a new community gradually took shape there. It emerged as a key stronghold in the struggles of Alfred the Great (871–99) against the vikings, with a strong sense of communal identity that set it apart from other towns of the period and led it to dominate the surrounding area. However, London's growth gathered pace swiftly in the decades around A D 1000, as it became a key military stronghold, centre of royal government and populous commercial hub. The city of this period was an altogether different entity to that of Roman times, or indeed to *Lundenwic*. It had a whole new street plan, which is the basis of the one still visible in the City today. The same is true of its administrative organs: these include the earliest incarnations of some elements of the City of London's idiosyncratic government, which have persisted for a thousand years. Anglo-Saxon London is a much more direct ancestor of the modern metropolis than its Roman predecessor, and by the dawn of the eleventh century was fast securing a position as the leading city in England.

Looking back from the twenty-first century, Anglo-Saxon London thus comes across as a place of new beginnings. Central aspects of its profile which emerged in the pre-Conquest period have persisted ever since – above all its status as the principal city of England, and its close and unique relationship with the monarchy and national government. In a very real sense, the early medieval centuries were, as previous scholars have sometimes put it, 'the shaping of the city'.[1] They constitute the deepest roots of the modern community. This is one of the main reasons we might be drawn to look at Anglo-Saxon London, although there is a great deal more to its early past than a hunt for the first glimmers of manifest destiny. Early medieval London can only be understood as a city of its own time, and this book will show that Anglo-Saxon London holds an interest all of its own, like Pepys' or Dickens'. It was a place of living, breathing people who sought to get by as comfortably and productively as possible, often under difficult circumstances. Their homes, rubbish and bodies provide vivid insights into what life in London was like a millennium ago. Some inhabitants come alive through other sources: a treasure that was probably assembled in London and buried in Rome; or an account of a woman who was drowned for witchcraft at 'London Bridge', probably near Peterborough. London was a place that also featured prominently in the machinations of kings, warlords and bishops, attracting armies and major meetings aplenty. It was a place where trade was done with merchants and merchandise from all over Europe, and even beyond. It is, moreover, a city that only flourished because of its place within the landscape of England and Europe; it can therefore be set alongside towns and other communities of the period to get a better understanding of what made London distinct. By pursuing these aspects of its history, the Anglo-Saxon city starts to emerge out of a thousand years of hazy darkness as a real and relatable place.

Back to the Sources

Knowledge of Anglo-Saxon London depends on a potpourri of sources, mixed together in eclectic fashion. As if on some sort of vast carousel, different forms of material come round again and again for different phases in its history, rising and falling in significance. This inevitably means that some parts of the story are better served than others. Although the early Middle Ages as a whole are no longer called the 'Dark Ages', some times and places within them are still deeply obscure. London in the two centuries immediately after the end of Roman rule is poorly known on virtually all fronts, with hardly any relevant texts surviving and precious little archaeological material from within the city itself. From about the seventh century, the pickings generally become richer.

Particular attention is paid in this book to the issue of where information about Anglo-Saxon London comes from. Different kinds of source have their own strengths and limitations. Broadly speaking, they can be categorised into written and material remains. The former consist of histories, literary texts, laws and documents of many types. Even if quoted here in English translation, they can be traced back to originals in Latin or Old English (the language of the Anglo-Saxons) which survive because they were written by hand into books or onto loose sheets of carefully prepared animal skin. Many questions need to be asked of these texts. In the first place, is what we have preserved a reliable witness to what was written or done in the Anglo-Saxon period? Even before the Norman Conquest, enterprising monks and clerics were augmenting and fabricating earlier records to support current disputes. In the twelfth century the monks of Westminster Abbey became particular masters of this craft. They carefully imitated the script of authentic Anglo-Saxon documents to make their new ones look more authoritative.[2] All of this means that a great many documents supposedly relating to the Anglo-Saxon past of Westminster need to be taken with a severe health warning.

If one can be fairly confident of a text's authenticity, a further question is how it should be understood. Why might one version of the collection of Old English year-on-year records known as the *Anglo-Saxon Chronicle* mention an event, and another not? What would an Anglo-Saxon have understood by certain key words, such as when Alfred the Great *gesette* London in 886?[3] To approach an answer, one must try – as far as possible – to get behind the scenes of a text. Doing so brings us some way towards explaining why our sources have such a strong focus on religious affairs and kings, and why references to trade and the humble bulk of the population are rare. Anglo-Saxon texts were largely written by monks and priests, and hence are as much a product of how these writers viewed their world and society as the reality of the events that they describe. Finally, the body of writing we have now from the Anglo-Saxon era is just a tiny sliver of what once was, its survival determined in large part by the turbulent events of later times. Preservation of books and documents from this period depended on diligent curatorship and careful copying, and the destruction associated with periods of upheaval (such as the Reformation in the sixteenth century) put paid to untold quantities of medieval books and records. It is unfortunate that London's early records have fared poorly compared to those of some other places, such as Canterbury and Worcester. Indeed, a lot of information about London only survives in sources from other parts of England and Europe. The upshot is that the extant corpus of written material bearing on London is often small, and not necessarily representative of what once existed.

A historian once wrote that 'it has been said that the spade cannot lie, but it owes this merit in part to the fact that it cannot speak'.[4] This was never really the case: material remains can speak loudly and clearly when interrogated in the right way. There are many aspects of medieval life and society that can only be understood on the basis of archaeology and artefacts. The rich current understanding of *Lundenwic*, the seventh- and eighth-century trading town on the Strand, is essentially the achievement of archaeologists working since the 1980s.[5] Excavation of houses, workshops, potsherds and diverse other remains has completely transformed views of London's development, in a way that readings of the written sources alone could never have done.

Of course, archaeological material will speak only when spoken to, and is therefore as open to interpretation as texts. Are the scattered, disturbed signs of activity in late Roman London evidence of decadence and desertion, or of tenacious continuity muddied by damage to the relevant archaeological layers?[6] Is a deposit of viking-style weaponry found in the Thames the product of a shipwreck, a failed attack or a deliberate ceremonial placement?[7] The archaeologist brings her or his own perspective to such assemblages, informed by comparisons and background knowledge, including knowledge of historical sources. It is often the case that looking at the written and physical remains side by side brings both into sharper focus. For instance, coins minted in the later tenth and eleventh centuries all carry the names of the mint-place where they were made, and the name of the craftsman-official who made them (known as the 'moneyer'). Details about where these coins were found are also often known. Analysis of the coinage reveals the jaw-dropping scale on which London's moneyers operated, and the city's centrality in the making and distributing of minting stamps (dies): these observations complement references to its role in paying tributes and managing the currency found in the *Anglo-Saxon Chronicle* and in Domesday Book, the great survey undertaken in the 1080s.[8] Making connections like this is the ideal approach, taken wherever possible in the coming chapters of this book. Otherwise, individual sources, archaeological and written, are presented on their own merits.

Location, Location, Location

All of these sources are only useful if they are put together in the right way, and doing so requires us to take a step back so that London's profile as a location and a community can be set in context. These two parts of its identity are inseparable.

Situated on the banks of the Thames, London occupied the lowest point where the great river could be forded or bridged in pre-modern times.[9] Although now thought of as a place where most of the moisture descends from above as fog or rain, historically it came up from below in just as undesirable a quantity. The ancient and medieval London area was a very watery place: the Thames was significantly wider and slower than it is now, and the south bank in particular – what would become Southwark – was a string of islands interspersed with boggy tidal channels. Thoroughfares and patches of habitation were built on whatever land was not marshy or liable to flooding. Even on the north bank there was a lot more water and dampness than is apparent today. Westminster contained *Bulunga* fen, and 'London Fen' sat on the banks of the Thames outside the western edge of the Roman walls. Within the walls, too, there were marshes (the area of the former amphitheatre at what is now Guildhall Yard, for instance), and there was a large area of marsh just north of the city, at Moorfields. When this froze over in winter it could be used as a vast skating rink, according to one twelfth-century source.[10]

Nowadays, the Thames seems to meander through the city alone, but in the early Middle Ages there were several tributaries. These smaller rivers still exist, though they now flow below ground among tunnels and sewers, and eventually empty discreetly into the larger river.[11] A few are memorialised in the names of streets, such as Fleet Street, which once crossed over the river Fleet, the lower part of whose course roughly coincides with Farringdon Street, which dips down noticeably relative to Fleet Street and Ludgate Hill. In Anglo-Saxon times, the Fleet lay close to the western edge of the city, and ran into 'London Fen' as it neared the Thames. Another tributary known as the Walbrook bisected the City, flowing from Moorfields through the valley between Ludgate Hill in the west and Cornhill in the east. In the Roman era this was a significant watercourse, used for boats and mills. Further west, a small tributary known as the Tyburn (meaning something like 'the boundary stream' in Old English) cut through Westminster. The Lea joined the Thames in what is now the Docklands, while across the Thames were the Effra, Peck and Neckinger. Many of these little rivers, as well as the Thames itself, were extensively used for fishing by the Londoners.

The inhabitants of the city also exploited the drier land that they found either side of the river, and the resources it produced. London sat in the middle of the large and roughly triangular Thames basin, with marshes and eventually the sea to the east, and two ranges of hills pressing in from the north and south: the Chilterns and the North Downs respectively. Both were heavily wooded, as was much of the Thames basin itself. Indeed, according to Domesday Book, the region around London was one of the most thickly wooded in the country in 1086.[12] These were not simply trackless wastes: woodland in the eleventh century and before was actively farmed – most notably for the rearing of pigs – and provided London with good access to fuel and building material.[13] There was also extensive farmland, mixing arable and pasture, including on land within the walls and on the edges of *Lundenwic*. In 895, King Alfred and his army took up quarters in London to protect the citizens from viking attack while they collected their harvest, presumably from outside the protection of the city walls.[14] Of course, even at this date the Londoners could not have been growing and gathering all their own food from the immediate vicinity. The city was at the centre of a web of commerce and redistribution that pumped supplies in from the countryside; a web which must have realigned itself several times during the early Middle Ages, and gained in complexity as London expanded in size. London was necessarily always physically and economically close to its rural surroundings.

Urban Lifestyles: Forms of Town in the Early Middle Ages

Thanks to its location in this landscape London was relatively well placed with respect to many important resources: grain, meat, fish, wood and much else besides could be found locally, and its advantageous position on the Thames meant that other goods could be brought in comparatively easily, if need be. It was this accessibility that made the city so successful as a trading place. However, the physical scale of the city needs to be kept in perspective. It was minute compared to the agglomeration that constitutes modern London. Leaving aside the suburbs and surrounding settlements like Southwark and Westminster, Anglo-Saxon London at its greatest extent still fitted comfortably within the Roman walls. In Antiquity, these had been among the most ambitious city defences erected in northern Europe, running for a total of about 3 miles and enclosing 1.1 square miles. The walls would more or less define the territory of the City of London proper right down to the eighteenth century,[15] and even thereafter it did not extend its boundaries far beyond them – which is why the City is still known today as the 'Square Mile'. *Lundenwic* was even smaller, covering about 60 ha (just under a quarter of a square mile).

There is no way to determine the population of Anglo-Saxon London exactly, but estimates of about 7,000 in *Lundenwic* at its peak and up to 20,000 around 1066 are plausible.[16] This is of course small fry in modern terms, comparable to picturesque cities and towns like Ely, Melton Mowbray or Oban in the twenty-first century, not generally celebrated for their metropolitan hustle and bustle. But relative importance carries more weight than raw numbers. A town consists of more than just a mass of people: it depends on its economic and administrative role, a sense of community, and potentially other physical and institutional criteria. During the Anglo-Saxon period, London combined the tight-knit familiarity that comes from a small absolute size with the self-importance that comes with the consciousness of being a major city – which by early medieval standards it was. This counter-intuitive combination of small-town scale and big-city attitude reflects the nature of early medieval urbanisation. London formed part of a hierarchy in which notions of status depended on much more than size and economic function.

At a millennium's distance, this hierarchy is difficult to discern. Modern scholars' understanding of Anglo-Saxon towns is founded on two sets of criteria that might or might not coincide: commercial pressures on the one hand, and administrative and military needs

on the other.[17] Broadly speaking, the former are thought to have
been key in the seventh to ninth centuries, with the latter at least
initially playing a larger role in the later ninth and tenth centuries.
Very few other places combined both roles in this way, before a more
widespread growth of urbanisation that began around the end of the
tenth century. Two of the prevailing labels in modern scholarship for
early medieval English towns mirror this division: *wic*, commonly
used during the earlier period, came to be applied to a new form
of trade-based settlement that sprang up between the seventh and
ninth centuries, while fortress-towns of the ninth century and after
have long been referred to as *byrg* (sing. *burh*). This Old English
word meant something like 'enclosure', and was a preferred term
for 'fortress' or 'fortified town' in later Anglo-Saxon England.[18] In
addition, as ancestor of the common place name 'borough', *burh*
has persisted into modern usage. However, there is little sense that
contemporaries shared this classification, or indeed subscribed to a
single view of what a town, city, *burh* or *wic* actually was. Looking at
Anglo-Saxon definitions of urbanisation is a valuable reminder that
such concepts lie entirely in the mind of the beholder. The great historian of the eighth century, the Venerable Bede (d.735), thought that
the key criteria of a city (*civitas*) were a Roman past and, to a lesser
extent, a Christian present: he reserved the term largely for Roman
cities, especially those that had subsequently become bishoprics or
monasteries.[19] Whether they actually housed numerous people or
markets was by the by.

The new trading towns such as *Lundenwic* and its counterparts
around the North Sea were not, on this basis, 'proper' towns at all,
and contemporaries classified them as such: they called them *vici*
(substantial but informal settlements) or *emporia* (markets) in Latin,
and *wic* (specialised settlement) in Old English.[20] These settlements
were more like continuous marketplaces than towns, heavily geared
towards production and exchange. They tended not to be home to
kings, lords or major churches – though all of these agencies had
strong interests in trading towns, including property. The *byrg* or
boroughs have traditionally been measured against a quite different
yardstick. In practice, most of the *byrg* remained more fortresses
than towns until the latter part of the tenth century or after,[21] being

defended enclaves for key administrative functions rather than a permanent home to a concentrated population of specialised traders and craftsmen. Many never assumed an urban role at all.

London was exceptional for its long-lasting prominence. From about AD 600 onwards it had always been a significant place, and for this reason its history has played a part in shaping the larger narrative of Anglo-Saxon urbanisation. In the seventh and eighth centuries, it fulfilled the roles of both trading settlement and Romanised ecclesiastical centre: the Roman city, even if depopulated, had walls and a bishop, while the Strand settlement had throngs of people and commerce. In the course of the ninth century its population had shifted back into the city, at which point it was known sometimes as *Lundenceaster* – Old English *ceaster* was a common term for Roman sites – or, more commonly, *Lundenburh*.[22] There is no doubt that it operated as a town from this time onwards, and is one of only a few *burh* sites in the tenth century to show good evidence of a relatively dense and active population.[23] But it was also a fortress, often on the front line against the vikings. Its inhabitants had an enviable reputation for military prowess right down to 1066, and beyond. In this later Anglo-Saxon period, a martial role dovetailed with administrative and economic functions, and London ranked highly in all three.

London in Context: England and Europe

At least within England, London has always been a special case. It has tended to define urban criteria rather than be defined by them. That is not to say, however, that London was always prototypical; nor was it the only place of consequence in the kingdom, or even always the leading city in every respect. There was as yet no real capital city, in that the seat of kingly authority had always been wherever the king happened to be, and bureaucracy (such as it was) for the most part travelled with him.[24] In the eleventh century this started to change, in particular as London became a more regular venue for royal visits and even hosted some nationwide administrative functions; but in earlier times, the king would more often hold court at one of the many royal estates in rural Mercia or Wessex, rather than in or near a town. Other urban settlements besides London were sometimes also preferred by the king. Winchester in particular was a perennial favourite. It had a long-standing link to the dynasty of Alfred the Great, which originated in Wessex, and found renewed popularity under Cnut (1016–35). The king held extensive property in and around the city, including several estates often used as meeting- or stopping-places, and in the eleventh century Winchester probably already housed the royal treasury that would remain there until the 1180s.[25] There is no evidence that London housed a permanent royal treasury. Canterbury was of course the pre-eminent ecclesiastical centre, for reasons reaching back to the political circumstances of southern England around AD 600, when the Roman missionaries first arrived in Kent.[26] Meanwhile, in economic terms London was also by no means a clear front-runner until the end of the tenth century. It is difficult to asses its comparative status in the seventh and eighth centuries, but we know that while London was larger than the other major English *emporia*,[27] Ipswich had a much more developed local industry in its ceramic production.[28] What distinguished London at this time is a higher profile in the written record, and a wider and more diverse trading network within England, embracing abbots from Kent as well as pottery from Oxfordshire and kings and bishops from the west midlands.[29] The new trading town was not necessarily an autonomous entity, but kings were probably not the leading agents in *Lundenwic*'s creation or flourishing, and their main impact was to cream off profits rather than dictate patterns of trade.[30] In the later ninth and tenth centuries, coins give some impression of how London measured up against other towns, and what emerges is that London was one of several leading centres of roughly comparable significance. In the south, these included Winchester and Canterbury; further north, Chester, Lincoln, Norwich and York.[31] The coins may of course not be representative of the whole story.[32] Chester was a hub of Irish Sea trade, while Lincoln and York formed part of a network that looked more to Scandinavia than mainland Europe.[33] By about the year 1000, however, archaeological and numismatic criteria show London starting to pull away from other English towns, setting it on a trajectory that would continue well beyond 1066.

Casting around, even in this cursory way, helps clarify some of the ways in which London was distinct. What stands out is that the city combined ecclesiastical and royal associations with an economic role, and it was the growing ambition and articulation of royal governance alongside commercial growth that led to its most rapid and impressive expansion in the late tenth and eleventh centuries. This was not always a happy or willing union. London's massive production of coin in the decades either side of the millennium was as much a result of high-pressure fiscal demands as burgeoning trade, and Cnut imposed costly punitive measures on the city. Prominence and wealth came at a price, and the sometimes tense interplay between urban and regnal interests, which became a leitmotif of London's later medieval history, can already be detected as the city's role was amplified in the eleventh century. The other main ingredient in London's success was its being well placed for access to mainland Europe – especially the economic powerhouses found in Flanders, the rest of the Low Countries and along the Rhine. London's parallels are found as much among the major towns in these regions as in England: Cologne, Huy and Utrecht, among others, combined a Roman past with a mercantile present in the early Middle Ages.[34] Most of these places rose to prominence, at least in terms of trade and commerce, in the ninth century or after. London was different, in that it had hosted a major trading port as early as the seventh and eighth centuries, while the dominant ports at that time in Flanders and the Rhine mouth area were the newly established Dorestad and Quentovic, which, respectively, declined in the ninth and tenth centuries.[35]

These brief sketches of the wider context will be picked up in the chapters that follow; for now, the central point is that London was part of a very exclusive selection of places that persevered as important urban centres from the seventh century onwards, on the basis of several stages of reinvention that maintained both institutional and commercial significance.

London's early medieval history can be broken down into four phases. The first is the darkest, and consists of the period after the bright light that was Roman London had gone out. Chapter 1 sets the scene by briefly surveying the Roman past. The city's early history (in the first and second centuries A D) saw a peak in size and economic dynamism that would not be reached again for almost a millennium, but more attention is devoted here to the later stages of Roman London, which segue into the murky world of post-Roman Britain. What little we can tell of the two centuries from about A D 400 to 600 is surveyed in Chapter 2, which puts the collapse of the city in the context of a transforming society.

The second part of the story is that of *Lundenwic*. Founded on the Strand as a small-scale settlement in the decades around A D 600, it flourished and later morphed into one of the largest new trading towns in the North Sea area. The reasons for London's success at this time show some similarities with those of the first century:[36] it lay in the orbit of several rich neighbouring polities, in a geographically opportune spot with good access to the sea as well as river and overland travel. Chapters 3 and 4 look (respectively) at the political and economic aspects of London in the age of *Lundenwic*. Chapter 3 looks at how London related to the major powers of the era. What emerges is that many Anglo-Saxon kingdoms, including some with their main power base a long way from the Thames basin, were eager to muscle in and stake a claim to the town and its environs. But they tended to do so at arm's length, and the focal point of royal activity remained far from London. Chapter 4, meanwhile, turns to the rise of the new town and its heyday: what people made, bought and sold there, and its international context.

In the later eighth and ninth centuries, *Lundenwic* seems to have started to break up, and lost much of its momentum. The third portion of London's early medieval history thus begins with the move back into the walled Roman city in the latter part of the ninth century. It is not possible to pinpoint the moment when *Lundenwic* ended and the 'new' town began – not least because there had most likely never been a sense of *Lundenwic* as a distinct entity at all. But the process probably started in the mid-800s, and was seemingly complete by the middle of the reign of Alfred the Great, who famously visited London in 886 and refurbished it. The city, already a target for and battleground with the vikings, now became a front-line stronghold in the fight against them. Chapter 5 looks at these dramatic events, the martial legacy of which would influence the city's subsequent history, and Chapter 6 follows the story of the Alfredian city into the tenth century. At this point, it was one of several important centres in the growing kingdom of the English, home to bishops who figured prominently in the royal court, but as yet far from a regular fixture on the king's itinerary or an administrative hub for the kingdom as a whole.

The fourth and final portion of the tale is the one in which the pieces fell into place for London, and transformed its status for good. The makings of this process had been in position for some time. One was the growth of the kingdom of the English and the increasing assertiveness of royal government in the later tenth century, above all under Edgar (959–75) and his son Æthelred II 'the Unready' (978–1016). As these kings sought to weld the kingdom together in a more meaningful way, it became expedient to centralise aspects of its governance, and London – as a large town distinguished by its connectivity – was ideally placed to take on a larger role. Far away from the traditional heartlands of Wessex and western Mercia, it had been only sporadically associated with the king before, but late tenth- and eleventh-century London became one of England's principal royal cities. The importance of this change can hardly be overstated. It was a new kind of centre for a new kind of kingdom; one that was actively broadening its horizons geographically, administratively and symbolically. There were economic as well as institutional factors at work, bound up with the acceleration of the city's trade, which brought with it increased wealth, traffic and settlement. Other cities and even small towns benefited from the same acceleration in trade, but in London's case the twin factors of royal interest and economic growth compounded one another in symbiotic fashion, and had truly remarkable results. Chapter 7, therefore, looks at what might be called the real making of London as a national centre, in the 80 or so years leading up to 1066, while Chapter 8 concludes the volume by examining London's role in the historic events of that year. It was Harold Godwineson's base of operations against William, and the final objective of William's campaign following his victory at the Battle of Hastings. In 1066, winning London meant winning England.

CHAPTER I

Roman London and Its End

First to Fifth Centuries AD

One of the star exhibits in the British Museum's Roman Britain gallery is a bust of the Emperor Hadrian (117–38) (Figure 1.1). Cast in bronze and somewhat larger than life-size, it would once have topped an imposing full-body statue. Its serene countenance has gazed down on visitors to the museum since 1848. This particular bust of Hadrian holds special significance for Londoners, as it was found in the city, dredged up from the Thames in 1834. It evokes one of the most glorious points in the city's history when, in the year 122, Britain hosted a visit from Hadrian himself – the first reigning emperor since Claudius (41–54) to travel to the province. Where Hadrian actually went in Britain is not known for sure, but there is a very good chance that he at least passed through London, the greatest city of Britain and the principal conduit between it and the rest of the empire. He would have seen a city which, while still retaining a frisson of the 'wild north' in the eyes

Figure 1.1. Bust of Hadrian (117–38), British Museum.

of a well-travelled Mediterranean emperor, represented many of the great strengths of the Roman Empire at its height: grand public buildings; vigorous exertion of imperial authority; and a diverse, prosperous populace.

London had arrived at this point after less than a century of Roman rule. Another century after Hadrian's visit to Britain, its position would be rather less rosy, and go downhill during the fourth century. In the course of the fifth century, the city became a ghost town. Nevertheless, two of the cornerstones of medieval London's foundations had been laid. One of these was its physical form: its location and its walls exercised a powerful influence on the city's development in subsequent centuries. Indeed, the bounds of the City of London proper still roughly follow the lines of the Roman wall, which was its effective edge for more than a millennium after the walls were built. The other cornerstone was London's status. It held a symbolic eminence unique among Britain's cities in the early Middle Ages, and this magnetic quality was founded in part on awareness of its ancient past. As a bishop who travelled to London for consecration in the 830s proclaimed, it was 'that famous place built by the skill of the ancient Romans'.[1]

The survey of Roman London presented here is brief and selective. Many more expansive accounts have been written, which should be consulted for a broader and deeper picture.[2] What follows is above all intended as a sketch of the precursor of Anglo-Saxon London, the better to draw contrasts with developments from the fifth century onwards. It also establishes the approach that must be taken to London's history throughout the first millennium, which depends heavily on archaeological remains. Although the physical footprint of Roman London is known from a large number of small digs, collectively these myriad pinpricks have helped form one of the most thorough archaeological profiles of any city in the former Roman Empire. These excavated remains and artefacts – alas, there are hardly any standing monuments from this period – must be combined with the testimony of chronicles, letters, laws and the like. Diversity is the name of the game in the city's early history, and the historian must become a sort of magpie, picking from many sources and disciplines: no one form of evidence can tell the entire story.

Origins

The site of London – or, rather, the river that winds through its midst – had been important long before the Romans ever set foot in Britain. Rich offerings were deposited in the Thames, and dredged up in the course of building work in the nineteenth century. The beautiful Battersea Shield (also in the British Museum), for instance, was found during the construction of Chelsea Bridge in 1857. The sacred river is also thought to have lent a name to London: from its earliest appearance in the 60s or 70s, when its name appears for the first time on a recently discovered writing tablet, the settlement was known as *Londinium* or similar,[3] which probably derives from an early Celtic word *Plowonidā*, a word composed of two elements related to ships, swimming and water – so perhaps meaning 'place at Boat River' or 'overflowing river'.[4] It is assumed that, by the time the Romans appeared in A D 43, this had evolved into something like *Lōndonjon*, 'place at the overflowing river'. No large-scale permanent settlement developed at the place of the overflowing river, however: the concentrations of wealth and power in the south-east of Iron-Age Britain were situated elsewhere.[5]

Within just a few years of the Roman invasion of Britain, a new town had sprung into being on the northern bank of the Thames. It grew rapidly. A drain found at 1 Poultry, beneath the main east–west road of the fledgling city, was made from timbers felled in A D 47/8, probably as part of the initial land clearance and construction phase.[6] In its earliest years, London served as a civilian mercantile centre, supported and overseen by the Roman state authorities but probably driven by trading interests from outside Britain.[7] These incomers capitalised on the city's favourable geographical position, which served multiple surrounding kingdoms and their capitals via the developing road system, and allowed easy and rapid transit by both river and sea. The Roman writer Tacitus described London as 'undistinguished by the status of *colonia* [i.e. an outpost of Roman citizens], but widely known for its wealth of merchants and travellers',[8] suggesting that in its earliest days London drew its vigour from trade and easy, frequent connections with mainland Europe. Its rapid growth as part of the new regime in southern Britain made London

(along with *Camulodunum*/Colchester and *Verulamium*/St Albans) a
target of the famous revolt led by the Icenian queen Boudicca in 60 or
61. Although Roman forces did reach the city before it was set upon
by the Britons, the governor judged his men to be too few to resist
effectively, and so chose to make a tactical retreat and sacrifice London
in order to save the province.[9] Those who were left had to take their
chances, and the archaeological record suggests that their prospects
were not good: at least 56 excavations across London have produced
signs of burning thought to be associated with Boudicca's sack of
London.[10] The city that her army destroyed was already something
of a boom town. Almost 120 sites have now produced archaeological
evidence of activity from the earliest stages of Roman London, before
the burnt layers associated with the events of 60/1.[11] It had an open
area that may have served as a forum, and a timber bridge across the
Thames; the main focus of habitation was east of the Walbrook on
Cornhill, with subsidiary areas of build-up situated on Ludgate Hill
and across the river in what is now Southwark. As the inhabitants
of the city must have lamented when Boudicca's army marched into
view, there were no walls or other major defences around the city at
this time.[12]

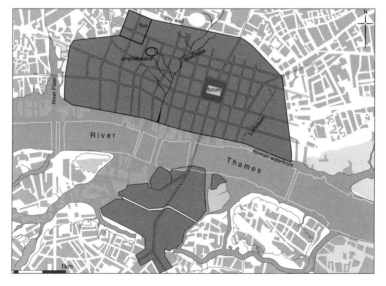

Map 1. Roman London, including principal streets
and selected major features of the city.

Reconstruction after the Boudiccan revolt was swift: a writing tablet from the city reveals provisions being brought to London under apparently normal conditions in October 62,[13] and a fort was erected to protect the recovering settlement.[14] Soon it started to gain a wider range of monumental architecture, and to come alive as a community with one foot in Britain and another in the provinces of the empire that tessellated Western Europe.[15] The century or so that followed saw Roman London reach its zenith in extent and population. In the words of the archaeologist Gustav Milne, 'this was not gradual growth but a sudden explosion'.[16] The city's population probably peaked at about 25–30,000, spread out over some 130 ha (Map 1).[17]

Living in Roman London

London at this time – and probably for most of the Roman period – was the largest city in Britain, a showcase for the imperial establishment. Although London's complement of monumental buildings and tombstones was fairly modest compared to that of cities in other provinces, it had a high concentration of them by British standards. Probably most impressive of all was the basilica: a place to conduct business and legal procedures, and a base for various city functions. It was a building of central importance in Roman cities. London's basilica (best known from a portion that has been excavated beneath what is now Leadenhall Court) grew to be exceptionally large: the biggest recorded one north of the Alps. Situated adjacent to the forum – an open space dedicated to public gatherings and business – the basilica was eventually 170 m in length and enclosed 2 ha of land (making it larger than Sir Christopher Wren's rebuilt St Paul's Cathedral). It stood three storeys in height, with walls up to 3 m thick. Overall, it was a formidable embodiment of the power of Rome and the significance of London. This basilica-forum complex was the second on the site, and took several decades in the second century to build.[18] Fire damage meant that it had to be repaired at least twice between the mid-second and third centuries. An earlier forum building had been erected in the aftermath of the Boudiccan destruction of the city, and before that there had been a still earlier proto-forum complex nearby.[19] Another aspect of the administrative machinery based in the city was housed further south, on the hillside rising up from the Thames, in what is thought to have been the *praetorium*, or governor's palace. Situated partly underneath Cannon Street station, it was a complex series of large buildings extending east to west, apparently begun in the late first century but with many later additions and modifications.[20] Interestingly, although arguments have been made for London's military origins,[21] it looks like the first major military presence was only established early in the second century, once the city was already thriving, in the form of a substantial fort north-west of the main area of habitation, on and south of later Cripplegate.[22]

Another essentially Roman expression of civic life, paralleled hundreds of times in cities from Spain to Syria, was the amphitheatre: a place for public spectacles such as gladiator fights, staged hunts and dramatic forms of execution. London gained its first amphitheatre (one of several in Britain) in about 70, situated beneath the later Guildhall.[23] At first a simple wooden structure, it was much expanded in the early second century, and eventually could seat up to 7,000 people – a significant portion of the population.[24]

Any visitor to Pompeii, Herculaneum or the well-preserved Roman cities of north Africa will have been struck by the number of bath houses. These were a standard amenity of Roman urban life. Public bath houses (of which Pompeii had four) could be used by anyone for a fee, while larger private homes might also feature their own bathing facilities. London seems relatively undersupplied with baths: just one probable public bath house has been found at Huggin Hill, with another at Shadwell about a mile to the east. None is nearly as grand as the bath house uncovered at Caerleon in Wales, while the relatively small but well-preserved city of Timgad in present-day Algeria had 14. In other words, London very probably had additional bath houses that are still to be uncovered.[25]

One of the other iconic features of classical cityscapes was a series of temples, dedicated to various deities. As with baths, London was relatively poorly furnished with them, at least as far as we know today.[26] Best known is the Mithraeum: a temple associated with one of the mystery cults, based on an adapted form of worship of the

Persian god Mithras. Replete with secret rituals and structured by grades of initiation, temples of Mithras proved particularly popular among the Roman military, and London's Mithraeum seems to have been patronised by a number of soldiers. The London Mithraeum was uncovered during the building of Bucklersbury House in 1954 (though some artefacts associated with it had been found in the nineteenth century). Post-war London was lit up by the blaze of publicity that surrounded its excavation, and the discovery within the temple of a series of impressive sculptural fragments from cult objects. Some of these related to the worship of Mithras (including a famous bust of Mithras himself), others to gods including Serapis, Minerva and Mercury. Structurally it was like other temples to Mithras, with a below-ground level used for rituals. However, being situated alongside the Walbrook proved a liability: the upper floor was repeatedly raised, probably in an attempt to escape the creeping damp. Erected for the first time in the mid-third century, the temple was apparently rededicated to Bacchus in the last phase of its history, early on in the fourth century. Eventually, the waters of the nearby stream won the long battle against the Roman builders, and the temple collapsed.[27] These circumstances, combined with a dash of good fortune, made the Mithraeum an especially fruitful archaeological find.

Although still the best-known temple from Roman London, it was undoubtedly not the only one, though few others are known in any detail. A large religious complex including two temples has been found on the edge of Roman London at Tabard Square in Southwark,[28] while a ceramic vessel (dating to the late first century) found at Tooley Street in Southwark carries an inscription referring to a shrine to Isis, and the same temple is referred to in an inscription on a third-century altar later reused in the river wall, which mentioned that the governor of the province had restored the temple of Isis from its dilapidated state.[29]

London was thus distinguished by an impressive range of public buildings. In terms of their quantity it was far from outstanding on an imperial scale, and even in the other western provinces many other cities had more; but London was uncommonly large in its extent, and some individual public buildings – above all the forum and basilica – were formidable in size and quality, as befitted the hub of a heavily militarised frontier province.[30] In the wide spaces between these public buildings were a variety of other buildings in which the city's population lived, died and did business of many kinds. These, too, have benefited from the patient attention of generations of archaeologists. A varied and vibrant society has emerged, at least during the most active phases of Roman London's history. Some of the most revealing remains came to light in 2010 and after, during the large-scale redevelopment of a three-acre site in the heart of the City (including the spot where the Mithraeum was uncovered in the 1950s). This large site was acquired for the future headquarters of Bloomberg, and the deep foundations needed for the high-rise that would eventually tower over the core of the City meant that archaeologists could penetrate 40 ft below modern ground level, to the very earliest layers of the Roman city. What they found has been hailed as 'the Pompeii of the north'.[31] The streets unearthed at this location, dating to the later first and early second centuries, belong to a more rough-and-tumble world than the basilicas, temples and baths that have historically grabbed most attention. If the latter represent a Roman version of Whitehall, the Bloomberg site unveils something more akin to Brick Lane, sunk into the damp earth on the east bank of the Walbrook. Even though the Walbrook itself is now virtually gone, the moist conditions it generated have preserved a wealth of wood and other organic material. These show how the site changed character over the period of its activity. Several small, simple wooden buildings were built first, followed by two round ones. Then, early in the second century, all were swept away by a very large complex that may have been a watermill engaged in processing great quantities of grain. This was destroyed by a terrible fire which swept across the city in the 120s. Development later in the second century took the form of more upmarket housing, though traces of the mosaics, porticos and flagstones of these layers have been badly damaged by later building. The floor levels of subsequent periods are completely lost, although post-holes and wells which projected below show that the area did continue to be used into the later Roman period. A vast range of artefacts has been plucked from this watery morass, over 14,000 in total. Pride of place goes to more than 400 writing tablets: one of the largest hauls of such material ever found, and already divulging vital information about early Roman London.[32] These show a child learning their alphabet and numbers; accounts and missives from assorted soldiers and businessmen; and the first known written reference to London itself. A tiny amber pendant shaped like a gladiator's helmet (evidently much worn, as evidenced by the wear and tear to its hoop) was another star find. Yet perhaps the most fascinating items were those that breathe life into the everyday existence of first- and second-century Londoners. These included 250 leather shoes, a straw basket, horses' harnesses, and even a large piece of leather decorated with gladiators fighting mythical creatures. The original use of this last item is a mystery: it may even have been a piece of upholstery. Traces of local manufacturing include the detritus of copper-working for assorted metal goods, as well as the moulds used to make ceramic lamps.

The Bloomberg site has produced one of the most important and diverse sets of material from anywhere in Roman London, and is especially crucial for the insight it gives us into the beating heart of the city's economy at a dynamic point in its development. There are smaller parallels elsewhere. At 1 Poultry, a series of houses on one of the city's main streets have been brought to light. From the first century alone, they include an inn, a carpenter's workshop, a pottery shop or warehouse, and a bakery; at a later date houses were erected for wealthier citizens, one of them enclosed with a box hedge to provide privacy.[33]

London supported a great many small-scale trades and manu-facturing enterprises of the sort seen at the Bloomberg site and 1 Poultry. To provide the population with more space, the northern bank of the Thames was painstakingly reclaimed from the river. At the beginning of the Roman period, the shoreline was some 100 m north of its present location, around Pudding Lane; but between the first and mid-third centuries, it was pushed back about 50 m in several stages, and the whole area from the Walbrook to the eastern edge of the city, beyond London Bridge, was built up with a complex series of quays backed up by closely packed buildings that served as both residences and warehouses.[34] Several shipwrecks have been found embedded in the mud and silt of the Thames.[35] South of the river, a beautifully preserved warehouse basement was found near the

Courage Brewery; appropriately enough, the Roman warehouse even had its own ramp, suggesting it may have held barrels of drink.[36] The settlement that grew up on the southern approach road to London Bridge in the vicinity of what is now Borough High Street attracted all sorts of crafts and trades, including work with metal, bone and antler. A metal pot of face cream was found in a drain on the Tabard Square temple site. After being opened for the first time in 2000 years, it was found to be a sort of foundation and moisturiser based on animal fat, tin oxide and starch, still in good condition, and even preserving the fingerprints of its last user.[37] This remarkable find encapsulates several of the distinctive aspects of Roman London: a wealth of archaeological material that combines the richness of day-to-day life at every level with the structured framework of temples and public buildings.

A City of the Empire

Although usually described as the capital city of the province of Britain, no such designation was formally used for London in the Roman period. In practice, 'capital' functions were vested more in individuals and offices than a specific location, and so could move between cities or fortresses. A governor's remit was even then quite restricted. He took charge of military, religious and judicial affairs that touched on the province as a whole; in the case of some smaller provinces, such as Britain, he was also responsible for financial affairs, which is to say the gathering of tax due to the emperor.[38] However, most day-to-day government in the Roman Empire was handled on a more local level, by a vast federation of largely self-governing city-states. Almost a thousand city-territories have been identified in total across the empire, from Portugal to the frontiers of Persia.[39] In provinces such as Britain, which had not traditionally contained Mediterranean-style cities, these had to be created from scratch, mostly on the basis of the tribes or kingdoms into which pre-Roman Britain was divided. Each bore the name *civitas*, which signified both the main urban centre and the surrounding dependent territory, regarded as a natural and organic pair. About 20 such units can be identified in Britain, at least a dozen of which had an identifiable urban centre.[40]

London did not fit comfortably into the patchwork of *civitates* into which Britain was divided, especially early in its history. Its status was anomalous, in that it was neither the centre of a *civitas*, nor one of the other two main categories of Roman town: a chartered *municipium*, or a more prestigious *colonia* which housed an enclave of Roman citizens, usually military veterans and their descendants.[41] London's earliest status may have been what scholars refer to as a *conventus civium Romanorum*, 'a gathering of Roman citizens', a less formal base of operations formed by citizens of the conquering power as they set about taking advantage of newly won provinces.[42] At the same time, it was evidently a key node in the web of roads that quickly started to criss-cross southern Britain, reinforcing the importance of accessibility and transport – by sea, river and land – in London's development, all backed up by the sudden and dramatic intervention of a major outside power.[43] Provincial élites from elsewhere in Britain looked to London for the latest fashions in, for example, architecture.[44] In one sense it was the key to Britain, while in another it was a somewhat artificial entity; what Richard Reece has described as a 'satellite [...], a foreign growth in the body of Britain, without visible means of [economic] support, a parasite'.[45] Certainly it was distinguished by a highly cosmopolitan population: there were many Romans and other Italians (often including the governor as well as senior officials and officers), and others from elsewhere in the empire. Inscribed tombstones include one for a man named Aulus Alfidius Olussa who had been born at Athens; another records Tullia Numidia, whose name suggests that she came from what is now Algeria.[46] A child from somewhere in the Greek-speaking eastern Mediterranean had his name, Hector, written (in Greek letters) on his leather shoe – as children have done for centuries since.[47] There would have been many more residents and visitors from provinces closer to home, such as Tiberinius Celerianus, a man from Beauvais in France, commemorated on a tombstone found in Southwark in 2002;[48] or a slave-girl who originally came from the Diablintes (a people just south of modern Normandy). She is known from a wooden bill of sale found at 1 Poultry, which paints an unexpectedly vivid picture of the life of slaves in Roman London. The girl is known by the rather ironic name of Fortunata ('lucky girl'), but the bill leaves open the possibility that this name was a new imposition, or might be changed by a new owner in future ('the girl known as Fortunata, or by whatever name she is known'). We are told that Fortunata is in sound health and, apparently, not 'liable to wander or run away'. She was sold for 600 denarii: a large sum of money (between two and three times what a legionary made per year), but by no means unusual for a female slave. What is more unusual is who her buyer was: Vegetus himself was under-slave to one Montanus, a slave to the emperor. Although still very much slavery, Montanus' status put him in a powerful position in the imperial administration.[49]

In the earliest phase of its development, prior to the Boudiccan revolt, London was overshadowed by Colchester. Thereafter, it was the closest thing to a capital in Britain, in that it seems to have become the preferred seat for the governor and his administration. As early as 65, it was the burial site of Julius Classicianus, *procurator* (governor) of Britain, a segment of whose tomb was discovered reused as part of late Roman repairs to the city wall.[50] Bricks and tiles were made for use at several sites – including the basilica, the probable governor's palace, the fort and one of the bath houses – stamped with P P B R L O N: probably *procurator(es) provinciae Britanniae Londinienses*.[51] The presence of the governor and the scale of the forum-basilica complex are enough to suggest that London's status had risen to a more formal level (i.e. *municipium* or *colonia*) in the later first or second century, though this step is never mentioned in any surviving source.[52] It is also significant that London boasted a strong military presence, despite its distance from any active frontiers – a reflection of its special role and of the presence of a major military-cum-administrative authority. The city had a fort in its north-west corner, about 11 acres in size and capable of housing some 1,500 men; it was erected early in the second century, and numerous inscriptions from London and elsewhere shed light on the nature of its military role. The soldiers stationed in London included special units such as *speculatores*, scouts who also served as guards and functionaries for high-ranking officials such as the governor. A tombstone from Blackfriars commemorated one *speculator*, and was erected by several of his counterparts serving the same role.[53] One of the numerous wooden writing tablets unearthed at Vindolanda, a fort on Hadrian's Wall west of modern Newcastle, mentions a soldier who had been detached from the main part of his unit (the men of which hailed from what is now Belgium) in the chilly north to serve at London.[54]

At some point in the late first or second century, a Roman soldier named Chrauttius, also stationed on the northern frontier of Britain at Vindolanda, wrote to his old friend Veldeius. The tone was warm and friendly: Chrauttius sent not just best wishes but 'warmest greetings' (*plurimam salutem*), and called Veldeius 'brother' and 'dear old barracks-mate' (*contubernali antiquo*). Evidently there was a long history between them; the two might even have been actual brothers.[55] But there are other undertones here, which suggest that Chrauttius was writing out of a combination of frustration and loneliness. He gave Veldeius a list of mutual acquaintances to look up and pass on his best wishes to. He also asked his correspondent – a groom to the governor (*equisioni consularis*) – to track down a veterinarian named Virilis, who had taken money from Chrauttius in return for a set of shears, but never actually delivered them. After all this, Chrauttius signed off by wishing his correspondent the best of luck (*felicissimus*) in fulfilling this shopping list of requests (he would probably need it), and wrote on the reverse the address where Veldeius could be found along with, it is likely, Chrauttius' old buddies and the vet who owed him: 'at London' (*Londini*).[56] This short letter brings home the magnetism London exerted in the Roman era. It was the place a soldier as far afield as Hadrian's Wall pictured as the place where his friend and, probably, the hub of his social life could be found. More broadly, London served as a switch-point for imperial state machinery in the province. It was distinguished by its unusual status and nodal position in Britain, and by a combination of impressive size and – by British standards – a magnificent concentration of major buildings serving and symbolising the Roman state. On an empire-wide level London was still in many ways quite provincial: the fine Mediterranean sculptures found in the Mithraeum sat side by side with distinctly more homespun local counterparts, for example. But for a visitor like Hadrian, or indeed Veldeius and Chrauttius, it was one of the most secure and refined cities to be found in the remote north of the empire.

Later Roman London

By the middle and later part of the second century, the character of Roman London had begun to change. Messages from different parts of the city are mixed. One of London's many foreign inhabitants, named Demetrios, left a long metrical inscription in Greek, full of magic words and pleas to 'Phoebus of the unshorn hair' to ward off plague, scratched onto a rolled-up sheet of pewter buried on the Thames foreshore. Whether it did any good is unclear, but there is certainly evidence of plague sweeping the empire in the 160s, when this invocation was probably written.[57] At the Bloomberg site, some streets went out of use in the later second century, and the large mill ceased to operate. Thereafter, houses of wealthier citizens occupied the site, perhaps hinting at 'suburbanisation' or even what would now be called 'gentrification', as trade and manufacturing receded in this part of the city.[58] Similar impressions are left by certain other changes: the large public bath house at Huggin Hill went out of use,[59] and in the later second century substantial military activity ceased at the Cripplegate fort.[60] After a last surge under Septimius Severus and his dynasty (193–235), of erection of new temples and other public buildings – one of them even with a grand stone arch at least 8 ft high and 23 ft wide – there was a strong turn against such magnificence in the later third and early fourth centuries.[61] The beginning of this iconoclastic phase coincides with the so-called Gallic Empire, which attempted to break away from central Roman rule between 260 and 274. Its emperors cultivated new power bases such as Cologne and Trier at the expense of existing ones, and hence deliberately set out to whitewash the legacy of the old regime in London and elsewhere by removing existing public edifices.[62] Part at least of the massive basilica and forum complex was also subsequently demolished between the late third and early fourth centuries.[63] By the fourth century, most of the great monuments erected in earlier times had been destroyed, transforming the city's landscape. Even London Bridge may have been gone by the middle of the fourth century.[64]

Other kinds of signal indicate important shifts in the lifestyle of London's population. From the later second century, many parts of the city start to produce what archaeologists refer to as 'dark earth':

richer, darker layers of soil suggestive of the decay of organic matter. This somewhat enigmatic description is deliberate, for 'dark earth' can result from a multitude of developments. Abandonment (followed by build-up of detritus) is one possibility, but so is a change in how rubbish was disposed of, or in horticultural practices within the city.[65] Individual cases need to be examined closely, especially as there is also a good chance that late Roman archaeological layers have been truncated by medieval and modern houses, basements and cellars which pushed down into the ground. Earlier and deeper Roman remains tend to stand a higher chance of surviving, while later Roman remains are often limited to pits and wells which intruded into the better preserved layers.[66] This might explain the contrast between the few digs which have produced rich late Roman material, at first glance suggesting a dramatic retreat in activity, and the widespread occurrence throughout the walled city and Southwark of coins and pottery from as late as the second half of the fourth century, which may be the decontextualized echoes of more extensive but largely obliterated late Roman settlement.[67] At 1 Poultry, for instance, the bustling streetfront of the first and second centuries definitely continued to be used right down to the second half of the fourth century, though over time its function shifted more towards high-status habitation than craft and commerce.[68] The fine houses of the fourth century survive amid extensive truncated areas, hinting at what might have been lost, and how long activity might have continued, at least in the heart of the city, along one of its principal thoroughfares.

Later Roman London undoubtedly housed fewer people, but the questions are how many fewer, and how their lives and cityscape had materially changed. This general impression of cautious pessimism on the part of modern observers is strengthened by comparison with other towns in the western part of the empire. In Gaul, Spain, Germany and beyond, one finds a trend towards fewer, larger houses away from urban concentration of industrial activity, as well as abandonment of existing public buildings.[69] But there were two important exceptions: churches and city walls. As Christianity gained popularity and won greater official acceptance in the fourth century, many larger, more monumental churches started to spring up in major towns across the empire.[70] London certainly had a bishop by 314, and it may also have gained a large basilican cathedral church in the second half of the fourth century, located in the south-east of the city, though this is known only from limited remains; so limited that they could alternatively belong to a heavily defended form of tax-gathering barn.[71]

It was also in the later Roman era that London gained its first set of walls. These were a truly huge undertaking, even by the high standards of Roman construction. They are among the largest building projects known from Roman Britain. The walls rose to a height of up to 6 m and were between 2 and 3 m thick. Some of the walls of the existing fort were incorporated into the new defences, but had to be significantly strengthened in the process. London's walls eventually extended over about 3 miles, pierced by five gates, and enclosed a total area of about 130 ha. Their layout would (as noted above) go on to have a profound influence on the geography of the medieval and even modern city. The construction of these land walls can only be pinned down to between the 180s and 220s.[72] About 50 years later, in around 270, an equally formidable river wall was added, running immediately behind the shoreline. Although this completed the circuit of the city's robust defences, it must have significantly limited access and development on the banks of the Thames, and may reflect diminished activity on the waterfront.[73]

Throughout the later Roman period London remained the most imposing of Britain's towns, and probably one of its most populous, even if that population did decline from its second- to third-century peak. Administratively, it also continued to be important. Britain was split into two provinces in the early third century, with York becoming the seat of the new northern governor, while London continued to be the base for his southern counterpart.[74] There was a further revision made in the time of Emperor Diocletian (284–305). Early in his reign, Britain had temporarily seceded from central Roman rule under two breakaway emperors named Carausius (286/7–93) and Allectus (293–6). Diocletian's new ally as co-emperor, Constantius I (293–306), turned his energies to neutralising Allectus' allies in Gaul and restoring the lost province. The great British weather proved pivotal in Constantius' final campaign in 296 to regain the island. A sudden fog blinded the enemy fleet, stationed near the Isle of Wight, allowing one part of his forces to land nearby and defeat

Allectus' army. Another portion of Constantius' men, separated from
their companions by the fog, landed in London, and protected the
city from the unwelcome attentions of Allectus' Frankish soldiers,
who had allegedly been planning to loot it before fleeing.[75] In commemoration of Constantius' victory, a gold medallion was produced
at Trier (Figure 1.2).

Figure 1.2. A gold medallion of Constantius I (293–305), minted at
Trier in 297, commemorating the recovery of Britain; the kneeling
figure on the right of the reverse is a personification of London, with
the city itself behind, and a label below (electrotype made of the
original – now in the Musée des Beaux-Arts d'Arras – in the 1920s).

Its reverse (the 'tails' side) shows an outsize, mounted emperor gazing
magnanimously at a figure crouched before him; a ship laden with
soldiers can be seen bobbing in the waves beneath, while walls and
turrets rise up behind the supplicant who welcomes Constantius. A
label identifies this figure as LON[dinium]: a personification of the
city which was saved by the emperor's men, and which serves as a
metonym for the whole province of Britain.[76] This unique medallion formed part of a hoard of coins and metalwork uncovered at
Beaurains near Arras, France, in 1922: a find packed with important
material, thought to represent the accumulated treasure dished out by
a succession of grateful emperors to an officer who served for several
decades either side of the year 300.[77] The London medallion would
have been a presentation piece for someone who had served in the
successful campaign of 296.

   In the aftermath of this campaign, Britain was divided into no
fewer than four (later five) provinces.[78] London was probably the principal city in one of these, Maxima Caesariensis, the province with the

ROMAN LONDON AND ITS END

most highly ranked governor, and the only one to host a mint, which issued coins from the time of Carausius until the mid-320s. It was one of only about 20 mints across the empire at this time.[79] London was also one of three British cities (along with York and Lincoln) represented by bishops at the Council of Arles in AD 314, suggesting that they were the key centres of their respective provinces.[80] The city continued to be the heart of Roman power in Britain throughout the fourth century. The *Notitia Dignitatum*, a complex document from the fifth century (but based on earlier information) which records the locations of military units and government officials across the empire, states that the chief financial official (*praepositus thesaurarum*) for all the British provinces was stationed in London, which means that it probably served as the seat for officials responsible for all the British provinces, grouped together into what became known as a diocese.[81] One prominent general based in Gaul who went to Britain in 360 to contain incursions of Picts and Scots made straight for London, where he could 'take counsel on the nature of the problem and hasten to the front', strongly implying its role as the lynchpin of the Roman provinces of Britain.[82] Six holders of the post of *vicarius* (i.e. lieutenant to the emperor) for the diocese of Britain are known from the fourth century. One, Alypius, was a cultivated and suave man who corresponded with literati of the mid-fourth century, and was eventually put on trial at Antioch in 371/2 for alleged acts of sorcery. Two of the *vicarii* for Britain around the end of the fourth century are known by name: Chrysanthus and Victorinus. Both enjoyed prestigious careers with postings across the empire, much like earlier men of high rank in the Roman world, though it is apparent that by this stage the governorship of Britain was a turbulent and thankless task.[83]

The *Notitia Dignitatum* and other texts from the later fourth century and beyond sometimes refer to London by a new name or epithet: Augusta. This probably reflects an association with one of the emperors (*augusti*), although the circumstances behind London's acquisition of the name are unclear. It first surfaces in the writings of Ammianus Marcellinus (d. *c.*391–400), a soldier who spent his life in the thick of late Roman military life before retiring to Rome to pen a history that doubled as a memoir. Ammianus describes how, in 367,

Emperor Valentinian I (364–75) heard the troubling news that a 'barbarian conspiracy' had overwhelmed the defences of Britain and led to the collapse of an effective frontier. At once a force was sent, with reinforcements following soon after. Leading the latter was Count Theodosius, father of Emperor Theodosius I the Great (379–95). They arrived at the 'old town of London, since called Augusta', and delivered the city from roving bands of marauders.[84] In the few later sources that refer to London, it is often coupled with – or simply referred to as – Augusta.[85]

Britain had been comparatively safe and wealthy in the first half of the fourth century. This was the era of some of the grandest villas and mosaics the province would produce.[86] But London, and indeed Britain as a whole, was entering into a rocky period at the time Count Theodosius and his men rode to the rescue in the later fourth century: one from which the province never really seems to have recovered. There were probably more systemic problems at work than a surge of barbarian aggression in Britain in the late 360s, for similar difficulties also afflicted the most complex, Romanised elements of society – towns, villas, large-scale industries – in northern Gaul and western Germany.[87] The entire Roman order in north-west Europe was coming under severe strain.

London at the Close of the Fourth Century

The last decades of the fourth century were hard ones in London. At 1 Poultry, the houses on one of the main streets that had been used for some three centuries fell out of use, probably around 380. When it came, the end was sudden: their abandonment has been characterised as more the result of evacuation than decline.[88] In one house, a fine table and set of glassware was just left behind in an empty room. A decapitated corpse was placed in a drain.[89] Other deposits in the city from around the same time share this chilling air of finality. A well in what is now Drapers' Gardens contained a whole kitchen's worth of metal vessels, all thrown in at once sometime after AD 375 (based on a coin found in the well), together with an iron handle pulled from a bucket – such as might have been used to draw water from the well – and a deliberately bent bracelet. On top of these was part of the body of a young deer: an animal not often found in Roman excavations, save in ritual contexts. This bizarre set of finds conjures a macabre image of a person or group coming to the watery, possibly sacred area of the upper Walbrook valley, casting their pots, pans and other metal goods into a well, followed by a fawn (minus its head and spine – what those were kept for, one can only guess); an act which can only be interpreted as ceremonial, or even in some sense supernatural.[90]

Life as the Romans knew it in the city of London seems to have been drawing to a close. Burials had started to encroach within the walls of the city. This was taboo under Roman tradition but had begun to ease under the influence of Christianity; in the case of London, the increasingly open space within the city walls was doubtless also a factor.[91] One place where burials started to appear was in the amphitheatre, now abandoned and its stone plundered. Eventually the latter was covered over with 'dark earth'.[92] Southwark, too, was nearing abandonment by the close of the fourth century, with one of its main roads becoming disused.[93] Some of the only signs of substantive activity from within the late fourth-century city come from the walls themselves, which implies that the urban and provincial administration still had a strong interest in maintaining London as an administrative focal point, whatever the fate of its inhabitants. A series of projecting bastions was added to the eastern side of the walls in the mid-fourth century, sometime between the years 351 and 375. Stones taken from the old cemetery to the east of the city were extensively used in their construction. These new towers allowed London's defenders to target any potential attackers much more effectively, and added significantly to the city's defensive capabilities. Their placement suggests that whatever threat they were intended to counter was expected to come from the east – potentially from seaborne raiders.[94] At the south-east corner of *Londinium*, the last years of the fourth century saw a final and substantial modification to the city walls. A second layer of wall was added just north of the river in the vicinity of where the Tower of London now stands, which may have created a kind of citadel. Banks built on the inside of the wall contained coins deposited during construction, one of which was only minted in the period 389–92, indicating that this section of wall must have been added during or after those years.[95] In the eighteenth century, a small hoard was found in the vicinity, containing gold coins of emperors Arcadius (395–408) and Honorius (395–423), along with a stamped silver ingot: this assemblage must have been put together in the same era as the walls, with the ingot perhaps suggesting a link with the fiscal machinery of the diocese.[96] Both of these late additions to London's fortifications could conceivably have been associated with military expeditions to Britain: those of Count Theodosius in the 360s, and another despatched by the general Stilicho between 396 and 399.[97] These efforts leave an impression of late Roman London as a place that had firm walls and a determined military-political establishment guarding an increasingly hollow core. Only a few archaeological sites in the city seem to have held on into the fifth century. At a house in Billingsgate, another cache of bronze coins was hidden in the roof of the private baths sometime after 395, and was scattered across the floor when the roof collapsed at some point thereafter.[98]

As the lights were beginning to go out in Roman London, its weakening centre of gravity seems to have shifted outwards. Several of the few sites to show signs of activity into the years around AD 400 lie outside London's walls in its suburbs.[99] On the edge of modern Trafalgar Square, the elegant neoclassical church of St Martin-in-the-Fields sits on top of a precious witness to the final chapter of Roman London: burials from the beginning of the fifth century and even later, including one in a huge, luxurious stone sarcophagus.[100] A nearby tile kiln also continued to be used into the early fifth century.[101] There may once have been much more here to find: John Stow, the great collector of London history and lore in the age of Shakespeare, noted that the discovery of a hoard of gold at this church sparked a riot in 1299.[102] A mile to the east of London, at Shadwell on the northern bank of the Thames, evidence has emerged of a satellite settlement that may have acted on some level as a replacement for London's own port facilities.[103] In the later Roman period it boasted a bath house, which continued to be used until the very end of the fourth century; even after it went out of use, new timber buildings were erected in the vicinity.[104]

Conclusion: London and the End of Roman Britain

After the opening years of the fifth century, a fog descends on London for the better part of two centuries, though it is alleviated, as will be seen in the next chapter, by archaeological and linguistic evidence for the wider social transformations that took place in the region.

London's story is keyed closely into that of the final decades of Roman Britain itself. This is a sorry tale. Still a heavily militarised set of provinces, but a long way from the focal points of Roman imperial authority, in the later fourth century Britain gained a reputation as a breeding ground for well-armed malcontents. Already in 350, Britain's officers tied their colours to the cause of Magnentius, a military usurper in Gaul, who was eventually defeated and killed by the 'official' emperor Constantius II (337–61) three years later. Constantius then decided to clean house in the breakaway provinces, and sent to Britain a notary named Paul, known as 'the Chain' because of his uncanny ability to manipulate gossip into webs of misfortune. After dealing with the army officers involved in the insurrection, Paul went above and beyond the call of duty, launching accusations against many civilians who were innocent. Martin, the governor (*vicarius*) of the diocese of Britain, spoke up on behalf of the accused – and found himself and his staff also threatened with arrest. Eventually, Martin attempted to kill Paul, and turned his blade on himself after he failed to land a fatal blow.[105] Treatment like this may have stoked the anger of Britain's military establishment. An exile called Valentine from what is now Hungary conspired with both military and civilian elements against Count Theodosius in the late 360s, but was foiled just before his plot could be launched into action.[106] A more successful sedition was hatched by a Spanish general named Magnus Maximus in 383. Power was allegedly thrust upon him by the soldiers under his command, who were discontent with the favour the previous emperor Gratian had shown towards new barbarian troops. Maximus drew a force from Britain, marched into Gaul and slew Gratian in battle. After five years as emperor, he and his son Victor were defeated and killed by the eastern emperor Theodosius I during an invasion of Italy.

Another rash of usurpations erupted in the aftermath of a barbarian incursion across the Rhine near Mainz in 405/6, which left the British forces unsure of their future. A string of three would-be emperors arose and, in two cases (Gratian and Marcus), fell in short order; but the third – known to posterity as Constantine III – enjoyed greater success. Like Maximus before him, in 407 he took an army gathered from Britain to Gaul, launching a bid for power and acceptance. Things went well for Constantine at first. The western emperor at the time, Honorius (395–423), pressed by campaigns on several fronts and concerned for the welfare of hostages, even granted him formal recognition as emperor. But Constantine's position soon became precarious. The withdrawal of so many units from Britain and Gaul left the north prone once again to attack, and when a new invasion came in 408, the provincials of the north took matters into their own hands. In the words of the Greek historian Zosimus, the Britons 'revolt[ed against] Roman rule and live[d] on their own, no longer obedient to Roman laws. The Britons therefore took up arms, and braving danger for their own independence, freed the cities from the barbarians threatening them'.[107] Britain, that is to say, effectively seceded from Roman rule.[108] Constantine III was in his turn defeated and slain in 411. As an anonymous Latin historian of the fifth century put it, 'the Britains were lost to the Roman name forever'.[109]

By this stage Britain was rapidly descending into darkness. A surge in the hoarding of coins and metalwork poignantly illustrates the level of disruption in the diocese. People were hiding their money and other treasures in droves, most likely because they were no longer sure of law and order, or of what the future would hold. Well over 200 hoards of coins and other metalwork have been found in Britain, terminating with coins of the period 395–423. They come from all areas, from the vicinity of Hadrian's Wall to the south-west, but they are most heavily concentrated in the wealthiest, most Romanised and densely populated zones to the east and south, including London. Some of these treasures represent impressive concentrations of wealth. The largest of all, the Hoxne Hoard uncovered in Suffolk in 1992, consists of about 3.5 kg of gold and 24 of silver, contained in about 15,000 coins and 200 objects, packed carefully into small boxes within a larger chest.[110] This is far above the number of hoards that might normally be expected to occur in an area the size of Britain. In fact, Britain accounts for some 64 per cent of hoards from across the empire of this period.[111] Something was clearly very rotten in the diocese, and those with the greatest investment in the Roman regime had the most to lose.[112] An atmosphere of crisis gripped the richer, more Romanised elements of Britain's population and led them to squirrel away their wealth.

The surge of abandoned gold and silver probably stems from two things: more people having cause to conceal their moveable wealth, because of disruption and uncertainty; and, more gruesomely, fewer people being able to come back and retrieve those treasures, because they were dead or displaced. Some, like those who dropped a bundle of pots and pans down the well in Drapers' Gardens in London, may never have expected to come back to retrieve their goods and money at all; their actions might have been a religious sacrifice, or a way of denying any benefit to their enemies.[113] As a group, the hoards of Britain in the early fifth century speak volumes about the climax of a long-brewing disaster; one which left the former provinces in disarray, and set them on a new and tortuous path during the fifth and sixth centuries in which London would play only a spectral part.

CHAPTER 2

Among the Ruins

Post-Roman London

Marvellous is this masonry, though fate
Has ruined and destroyed the city buildings,
The works of giants crumble, and the roofs
Have fallen in, the towers have tumbled down,
The barred gate has been borne away as plunder,
Frost cracks the plaster, all the ceilings gape,
Collapsed and pierced with holes, consumed by age.
The ground holds in its grip, the hard embrace
Of earth, the dead departed master-builders.
A hundred generations now have passed.

'The Ruin'[1]

The desolation of ruins was a recurrent theme in Anglo-Saxon liter-ature, as hauntingly expressed here in an anonymous poem known as 'The Ruin'. Remains of this kind gave writers an invitation to ruminate on the passage of time. These once proud, princely edifices had been humbled, worn down by the weight of untold years. For the Anglo-Saxons, ruined buildings stood as a reminder that, com-pared to the transcendent heavenly kingdom, anything man might accomplish on earth was transient. Those who thought long on the subject would turn to the conclusion that in time even they would be dead, and their own homes turned to ruin; as another poem put it, 'the wise must know how awesome it will be when all the wealth of earth stands desolate'.[2]

Such sobering thoughts owed something to the landscape the Anglo-Saxons inhabited. Ruins (or, as they were often called, 'the ancient works of giants') surrounded them. In modern times, Roman ruins are few in number and lovingly preserved as historical monuments, but in the first millennium, the men and women of what had been the provinces of Britain would have seen the remnants of Roman buildings all around them. Many of their churches were built in large part from the cannibalised remains of earlier, fallen buildings. At one of the few early Anglo-Saxon churches which still stands, in the picturesque village of Escomb, County Durham, pieces of Roman stonework – some of them inscribed – can still be picked out. In London, reuse of Roman stone and tile continued into the twelfth century. But the reclamation of ruins, whether by man or nature, was a slow process. Across the Anglo-Saxon period, centres of religion, government and trade would often have been situated in or close to what we now would call ghost towns. The brooding presence of a richer, grander past was inescapable.

By the fifth century, in the wake of the collapse of Roman infrastructure in Britain, London would have been among the largest and most impressive ghost towns in the land. In ambience it perhaps had something of both post-industrial Detroit and serene Machu Picchu. London's walls still stood to an impressive height, as did many other stone buildings within, decaying though they may have been. But there is no evidence for any significant habitation. At this stage, it was the empty husk of a city.

London c.400–600

The scarcity of available evidence means that it is simply not possible to weave a detailed or coherent narrative of London itself in this period. Its name, together with its walls, undoubtedly survived to be remembered and used in the seventh century and after. There might once have been more to fire the historical imagination in relation to these times. Geoffrey of Monmouth (d. after 1152), a master purveyor of historical fiction, preserves a particularly bizarre and specific tale about the body of the seventh-century British king Cadwallon being embalmed, encased in bronze and then mounted on a bronze horse above London's western gate as a warning to the Anglo-Saxons. It is just possible that this reflects an equestrian statue – long since dismantled – that once did stand somewhere in western London.[3]

Geoffrey's bronze statue, a monument as intimidating in the mind's eye as it is dubious to the critical historian, is symptomatic of the city's history at this time: from about the early fifth century until the years around 600 precious little can be said for sure about the former Roman city, and what there is has one foot in the realm of legend. In 456, according to the *Anglo-Saxon Chronicle*, Hengist and his son Æsc vanquished an army of Britons at an unlocated place named *Crecganford* or *Creacanford* (manuscripts differ on the spelling). Having suffered 4,000 casualties, the Britons abandoned Kent to the invaders 'and fled with great fear to London'.[4] On the face of it, this portrays the city as part of a British polity that embraced Kent as well as London, and as a bulwark against enemy advances. But the information in the annal for 456 is highly dubious. It is not clear what prior authority (if any) the writer who set down this annal in the late ninth century relied on, and the rest of the fifth- and sixth-century material in the *Chronicle* is heavily laden with glorious but doubtful tales of Anglo-Saxon victory and British defeat. At best, it preserves an echo of traditions circulating in ninth-century England about the heady days of settlement and conquest. Any pieces of reliable information are so submerged in layers of legend as to be unrecognisable.

The lack of any reference to the actual takeover of London in the *Anglo-Saxon Chronicle* was one point which pioneering archaeologists of the nineteenth and early twentieth centuries used to construct a case for an enclave of Romano-British rule centred on London, which resisted the rising tide of Anglo-Saxon conquest across the fifth and sixth centuries. They also pointed to the rarity of any early Anglo-Saxon remains from the area around London.[5] A century of further excavation and research has eroded the argument for the Romano-British enclave of London to nothing,[6] although the city itself remains almost devoid of evidence for fifth- or sixth-century habitation, Anglo-Saxon or otherwise. A brooch of early Anglo-Saxon style, found among the collapsed roof tiles of the very late Roman house at Billingsgate discussed in the last chapter, is still almost the only securely contextualised find of this period from within the Roman city.[7] Other fifth- and sixth-century items of less certain background include buckles from the Barbican, Guildhall and Custom House, together with part of a bracteate (impressed gold disc) from Queenhithe and a spear-head from Poultry.[8]

Large areas of what had been Roman London were clearly in a state of decay during the fifth and sixth centuries. Low-lying districts were subject to floods and erosion; land along the river wall, on the banks of the Walbrook and in the vicinity of the former amphitheatre turned into uninhabitable marshland.[9] Even the road layout was probably lost over time, and when the city was eventually resettled on a substantial scale from the later ninth century onwards a mostly new set of roads had to be imposed. One should picture a site still surrounded by sturdy walls (which would be brought back into use later in the Anglo-Saxon period) but containing a deserted, overgrown and at times boggy expanse punctuated by crumbling ruins. Modern excavations have, however, created a much rosier impression of early Anglo-Saxon settlement in the area around London. Probably the most important discovery lies beneath St Martin-in-the-Fields, at the edge of Trafalgar Square. A very late Roman cemetery and industrial site gave way to an early Anglo-Saxon burial ground: at least two Anglo-Saxon burials were uncovered there in the 1720s, with more coming to light in 2006.[10] Here, a mile and a half west of the walls of Roman London, there may have been continuity from around 400 into the seventh century.[11] At Clerkenwell, about half a mile north of the Roman walls, a series of pits and potsherds have revealed a settlement of c.450–550.[12] Many early Anglo-Saxon cemeteries and settlements have now come to light in the area of Greater London.[13] It would be wrong to call these villages: the coagulation of farms which led to the classic English village landscape lay several centuries in the future. Settlements of the fifth and sixth centuries were closer to scattered farmsteads.

As well as a physical footprint in the form of burials and settlements, the whispers of the post-Roman era have left long echoes in the landscape on which the city and its surroundings are built. The large majority of place names in the vicinity of London are thoroughly Anglo-Saxon. When these were first coined is known only loosely; all that can be said is that when the first references to locations in the area appear in the seventh and eighth centuries, they show overwhelmingly

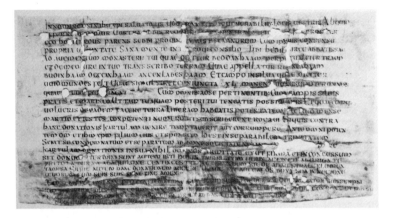

Figure 2.1. The earliest surviving Anglo-Saxon document relating
to the London area: a charter for *Beddanhaam*/Barking issued by
the East Saxon aristocrat Æthelred 685×693, though the date of
this copy is debatable, and it could have been written a century later
(S 1171) (London, British Library, Cotton Augustus II.29).

that Old English names were being used. One of the earliest surviving
documents from the area, issued between 685 and 693 (Figure 2.1),
records how an aristocrat named Æthelred gave land at five locations
in Essex to the monastery at *Beddanhaam*, known to Bede and in later
times as *in Berecingum* ('among the Berecingas') or Barking; one of
those five locations was *Deccanhaam* or Dagenham.[14]

Barking is one of many names in southern and eastern England
which refer to a people associated with a supposed founder, in this
case apparently *Berica*,[15] or (more rarely) a feature in the landscape.
Others in the London area include Ealing (*Gilla*'s people), Tooting
(*Tota*'s people) and Wapping (people of the *wapol*, 'marsh'). Other
place names refer to physical features, without connection to an individual or group. Islington was first recorded as *Gislandun*, meaning
'Gisla's hill (*dun*)'; Wimbledon as *Wunemannedune*, 'Winebeald's hill';
Holborn as *Holeburne*, 'the stream in the hollow'; and so on. The men
and (occasionally) women who created or featured in place names
can only rarely be identified, and for the most part the origins of the
names by which we know London and its environs are lost in the
murk of the early medieval period. Some may well have been created
well after the fifth and sixth centuries – and others stemming from

this period will have been lost, like those of the four other locations given to *Beddanhaam*/Barking in the years around 690. Most are only known from records dating to long after the period covered here: a significant proportion occur for the first time in Domesday Book from the 1080s, or later still. Place names in the early Middle Ages were constantly evolving to suit the needs of people around them.

But although the abiding impression imprinted on the landscape in and around London was made by the Anglo-Saxons, other groups have also left a mark. The London area is full of interest as a window onto how different communities may have interacted during the fifth and sixth centuries as the map of Britain was being redrawn. The most prominent survivor from earlier times is of course the name of London itself. Its modern form descends from Old English *Lunden(burg)*, *Lundene* and similar, which in turn probably derives from how the city was known in the ancestor of Welsh current in the late Roman and early medieval period – something like *Lūndein* or *Lūndyn*.[16] Even the city's preferred Latin name underwent an important change in the period between about 400 and 700, the preferred Roman form *Londinium* (a neuter word) metamorphosing into the Anglo-Latin *Lundonia* (feminine).[17] Other bastions of older cultures and languages persisted as the cultural and linguistic landscape changed. Some settlements were named (presumably by the English) as being characterised by clusters of *wealas* (sing. *wealh*), meaning 'slave' or 'foreigner', particularly with reference to the Britons or Welsh: instances near London include Wallington, Waleport/Wallpits, Walehulle and Walworth in Surrey.[18] Other place names actually retain elements of Brittonic language (i.e. the linguistic ancestor of Welsh, Cornish and Breton), suggesting interaction between speakers of Brittonic and Germanic languages at a grass-roots level in London's early medieval history. Rivers all over England also include a significant number of pre-Anglo-Saxon names, for these formed axial features in the landscape and were least likely of all to be relabelled; examples near London with a certain or likely pre-Anglo-Saxon origin are the Thames,[19] along with the Brent, which gives its name to Brentford (where it joins the Thames), and the Lea, which empties into the Thames near the Blackwall Tunnel.[20] Beyond London and its rivers, place names from before the time of the Anglo-Saxons are few. Penge (now in Kent, historically in Surrey) is one such case: it goes back to primitive Welsh words for a hill (*penn*) and a forest (*cet/ coed*) – precisely the same root as the town of Pencoed in south-east Wales.[21] There are in addition a few hybrid names: products of close contact between different languages in which names and people intermingled. Chertsey, for instance, first appears in one of the richest and most cherished Anglo-Saxon texts, Bede's *Ecclesiastical History of the English People* (completed around 731), as *Cerotaesei*, a monastery founded in the late seventh century by Eorcenwald, the bishop of London (675–93).[22] Its name combines Celtic and Anglo-Saxon features: *Cerotaes-* derives from the personal name Cerotus, Ceretic or Caratacus, as in the famous opponent of Claudius' legions – though there is no telling which specific bearer of that name was immortalised by the Surrey place name. Whoever he was, the second part of the name (*-ei* in Bede) is a widespread Old English word meaning island,[23] seen in Battersea (*Batriceseg*, 'Beaduric's island') and many other watery places around London. These few Celtic names of rivers, physical features and settlements reflect the survivors of what must have been a rich haul of Romano-British toponyms. The fact that some continued to be used speaks volumes about the capacity of early medieval men and women to incorporate diverse peoples and languages – but the scarcity of those survivals points just as strongly to a profound shake-up of most aspects of society in post-Roman London.

There is no denying that even in an age of meagre source material, the fifth and sixth centuries stick out as especially thin in a great many respects.[24] Some of this must be down to the level of disruption in Britain – above all south-east Britain – as described in the next section. But a great deal must of course have been going on behind this dark curtain. London was abandoned as an urban settlement, probably by the middle of the fifth century, and does not seem to have held much attraction for those who dwelt near the soaring ruins. In the land immediately around it, fresh settlements and cemeteries sprouted, inhabited by people who dressed and spoke quite differently from their Romano-British predecessors, and who in some cases had come from afar to settle here. None of these developments was unique to London. In order, therefore, to gain a fuller grasp of what lay behind these changes, it is necessary to cast a wider net.

'A Province Fertile of Tyrants':
London in its Post-Roman Setting

London sat in the midst of a rapidly mutating landscape in the fifth and sixth centuries. The political centre of gravity shifted rapidly downwards to a collection of relatively small kingdoms. Some, such as Kent and Essex in south-east England or Gwent and Powys in Wales, were the descendants of Roman-period city territories (*civitates*).[25] Others appear to have sprung into being as the old infrastructure of the province, and the loyalties it had fostered, broke down. Whether they had earlier precedents or not, many of these new territories traced their origins to the generations following the effective end of Roman rule in the early fifth century, even though the first reliable information about them often only emerges much later, in Bede's *Ecclesiastical History* and other sources from the same era or after. Bede claimed, for instance, that Kent had been established by two war-leaders named Hengist and Horsa, whose arrival he dated to 449, and the *Anglo-Saxon Chronicle* includes in its condensed, year-on-year record references to the foundation legends of Wessex and several other kingdoms. In Wales, a ninth-century assemblage of historical miscellanea known as the *Historia Brittonum* situated the dynastic origins of local kingdoms such as Powys and Gwynedd in these years as well. By the time Bede and the writer of the *Historia Brittonum* were at work, the political structure of Britain was a twisting kaleidoscope: smaller entities might forge their own path or be brought more or less firmly into the orbit of another power.[26] These patterns may have started to emerge already in the immediate aftermath of Roman rule. Force of personality and arms had, in Bede's view, been central to the formation of larger, albeit transitory, over-kingdoms since the fifth century. Whether on the level of local units of power or in terms of a more open horizon for asserting dominance, these writers remembered the fifth and sixth centuries as a time when old identities dissolved and new ones were brought into being, forged by legendary heroes. This was the foundational age for the Anglo-Saxons and the Welsh.

By the time of Bede, the *Historia Brittonum* and the *Anglo-Saxon Chronicle* – that is, two to four centuries from the events in question – the roots of the early medieval political landscape were framed in starkly ethnic terms. The establishment of kingdoms was associated with larger identities such as Anglian, Jutish, Saxon or Brittonic. Language, descent, religion and ancient grudges had blended together to produce these allegiances. In practice, however, they tended to reflect conditions at the time of writing, projected back onto a more fluid earlier age. There undoubtedly were ethnic and other divisions in the fifth and sixth centuries; there is also no doubt that they sometimes did reflect significant movements of people. But the circumstances of the period lent themselves to a flexible and multi-layered conceptualisation of identity. 'Roman' or 'post-Roman' London did not simply give way to 'Anglo-Saxon' London overnight.

In this respect, the London region was one cog in a much larger machine. In the fifth century, Britain as a whole entered into a period of obscurity and tumult during which much of the infrastructure of the province collapsed. Networks of distribution that had brought food, coined money and manufactured goods into Britain from across the Channel, and then along thousands of miles of high-quality roads, fell apart. Communities in post-Roman Britain were left in a precarious material position.[27] Those whose wealth allowed them to live in villas could no longer maintain such a lifestyle, and even if they had the means, the uncertainty of the times must have made cultured civilian life difficult. Specialists such as professional potters who depended on the Roman army or government, or on stable constituencies of wealthy patrons, found that they could no longer make a living. In contrast, those who worked on the land – and who constituted the bulk of the population – may have found themselves less burdened with the need to produce surplus for the landlord or tax collector. This might explain a broad move in the early Anglo-Saxon period away from arable (i.e. crop) towards pastoral (i.e. animal) farming, which was less demanding in terms of labour.[28]

Towns were one of the most conspicuous casualties of the end of Roman Britain. They depended closely on the demands of Roman culture and government, serving as a base for local administration, and for the gathering of taxes in cash and kind.[29] As such, the whole range of Roman towns in Britain, from major *civitas* towns and provincial capitals downwards – with just a few exceptions – experienced near or total collapse. London was in no way exceptional for ceasing to operate as a town in the fifth and sixth centuries. Some places may have continued to serve as a focal point of local power structures: Canterbury, for instance, although essentially abandoned in terms of Roman-style occupation, hosted settlements of more characteristically Anglo-Saxon form from a very early stage, hinting at its ongoing significance in the local landscape.[30] More exceptional still are Wroxeter (known in the Roman period as *Viroconium*) and a few other locations which show potential evidence of hosting some sort of ongoing habitation deep into, or even beyond, the fifth century.[31] At Carlisle (*Luguvalium*), St Cuthbert in the late seventh century marvelled at a working fountain, which could only have existed if the Roman plumbing still functioned.[32] But by this stage, what had been routine in the second century was now a sort of tourist attraction: survival of urban life and amenities after the end of Roman Britain was highly unusual.

The best evidence for such survival in the London area relates to St Albans (*Verulamium*). Possible evidence that water pipes in the town had been maintained and replaced in the fifth century has recently been challenged,[33] though even if urban life as such did not continue there is a solid case for its continued importance as a monument and religious centre in the post-Roman era. A four- or five-mile bank and ditch which runs through north-west Middlesex, known as Grim's Dyke, is of uncertain but probably late or post-Roman date,[34] and suggests the boundary of a territory extending north to St Albans; its ditch is on the south side, implying the builders lay to the north.[35] The profile of the place can be judged from a text celebrating the Christian martyrdom of Alban, who was supposedly a soldier earlier on in the Roman period killed for giving shelter to a fugitive priest. This saint's life was written around the fifth century, possibly in the circle of a powerful bishop from Gaul named Germanus of Auxerre (d. *c*.448) who had paid a visit to *Verulamium* in 429 in the course of suppressing heretical beliefs in southern Britain.[36] The story of Alban was clearly popular already, and became even more so as this text gained traction. At some point in the fifth or sixth century – opinion varies widely – an author in western Britain named Gildas lamented the difficulty that inhabitants of western Britain now encountered in travelling to the shrine of Alban, because of the presence of Saxon invaders. Even Bede, writing in the far north of England in the early eighth century, knew the story of St Alban. As a bastion of Christian martyrs, standing firm against persecution and pagan hordes alike, St Albans offers a rare example of a place in the vicinity of London that retained its prominence across these centuries.[37]

Settlement and Society in the London Region

From an historical point of view, the period covering the fifth and sixth centuries is one of the most obscure of the British past. But for the archaeologist, it is comparatively rich. One of the distinguishing paradoxes of the era is that the 'Britons' – heirs in a general sense to such a dynamic material culture – have left relatively little physical trace, especially in the eastern part of the former Roman province, whereas the 'Anglo-Saxons' are associated with distinct and fairly well represented archaeological remains. Weapons, ornaments and other diverse goods are found in their graves, and new forms of building with few Romano-British precedents mark their settlements.

Readings of the story behind these remains have swung back and forth between conciliation and catastrophe. The Britons could have been the victims of what amounted to genocide,[38] or, decimated by plague and economic turbulence, left in apartheid-like subordination to Anglo-Saxon settlers who took their land and confined them to small enclaves.[39] Still other interpretations posit that there might have been almost no migration at all: most 'Anglo-Saxon' remains would represent those of Britons who had taken on a new identity.[40] This range of opinion gives some clue to why one must be so cautious in interpreting the remains surviving from this era, and why terms such as 'Briton', 'sub-Roman' and 'Anglo-Saxon' need to be assigned with care. In this book, I am using them with reference to predominant forms of material culture, without suggesting that they necessarily had any other particular attributes. Just as not all modern wearers of (for instance) Chanel clothes, drinkers of champagne and drivers of Renault cars are French, so one must be wary of interpreting

'Anglo-Saxon' goods as the trappings of warriors fresh off the boat from Germany. Furnished burials of this kind in fact appeared at more or less the same time in northern Gaul and Germany as well as Britain, and were by no means standard in the Saxons' homelands.[41] They imply a widespread concern to assert a new kind of identity. What exactly that identity was is far from clear: there is no firm evidence that contemporaries ascribed ethnic or political significance to 'Anglo-Saxon' burial practices and the goods associated with them, nor does the distribution of major styles of brooches and other artefacts reflect the east–west fault-line that might be expected from a sharp British–Saxon divide.[42] In the context of the fifth century, the connotations of those weapons and ornaments may in fact have been primarily military.[43] The late Roman army recruited heavily from the lands beyond the Rhine and Danube, and stationed units of barbarians across the western empire. These troops of allied barbarians were known as *foederati* ('those bound by treaty'), and they came gradually to make up a large proportion of the late Roman army. Even the crème de la crème – élite cavalry units known as *vexillationes* – consisted mostly of non-Romans.[44] The kinds of buckles and brooches worn by these men fed directly into 'Anglo-Saxon' and other western European 'barbarian' metalworking traditions.[45]

Eastern England, roughly east of a line from Gloucester to York, was the melting pot in which these diverse elements bubbled together. London lay at its heart. As at other Roman towns, the pattern seems to have been for late Roman military and associated early Anglo-Saxon remains to occur immediately outside the walls.[46] Traditionally, this had been the more civilian portion of the province; a land of villas and relatively large, cultured towns, while major military units had been stationed in the north, west and south-west. But in the later years of Roman Britain, either the provincial authorities or individual city governments brought in barbarian recruits who would in time constitute the foundation of the Anglo-Saxon settlement.[47] Gildas describes exactly this process: the invitation of Saxon warriors to serve as defenders against an invasion of Britain from the north and west. Those warriors later turned against their hosts, plunging the land once again into crisis. In the case of Kent, an increasingly elaborate version of this narrative involving Hengist and Horsa, the

British leader Vortigern and a whole series of betrayals and killings unfolded in the pages of Bede's *Ecclesiastical History* and the *Historia Brittonum*.

The appearance of Anglo-Saxon graves and settlements is as much a matter of adjustment in existing communities as the arrival of newcomers. Soldiers and barbarians (especially Germanic-speaking barbarians) were becoming difficult to distinguish from one another. In this context, the origins of individual men or small groups could quickly dissolve: across Europe, the period from the fourth century to the sixth saw allegiances form and reform in quick succession.[48] There is no single story about how society transformed in the fifth and sixth centuries. Parallels from better-recorded provinces elsewhere in contemporary Europe – which also saw rapid changes in this period – together with modern scientific analysis have revealed the wide spectrum of possibilities that can lie behind stark categorisations of archaeological remains along ethnic lines. What these indicate is that there must have been legions of different experiences in late Roman and early medieval Britain. Individual people, families and communities would have had very diverse fates as power dynamics shifted and new ideas, as much as new people, came into the province.[49] There was definitely some migration. On the other hand, at Wasperton in Warwickshire the same cemetery continued to be used from the fourth century to the seventh, moving from late Roman burial practices to 'Anglo-Saxon'. Analysis of bones from Wasperton suggests that it was mostly filled with locals, at least in its later, Anglo-Saxon-period phases.[50] The people of this part of Warwickshire seem to have adopted 'Anglo-Saxon' burial practices without any sign of mass replacement of the populace. They might well have also moved towards other new practices – dress, language, and possibly a more martial ethos[51] – associated with spreading Anglo-Saxon culture, though it is by no means clear that the whole package would be taken on at once: some may well have still spoken Brittonic and identified with British ancestors, but dressed and been buried as 'Anglo-Saxons'. Neither was there a single, homogeneous package to take on: the blend of new immigrants with established soldier-migrants and acculturated Britons must have been as disruptive to the identity of 'Anglo-Saxons' as to the 'native' Britons. Bede's picture of coherent peoples being transplanted into Britain presents a carefully tailored version of a messier past.

There are a few signs of this very mixed culture in the early stages of the history of some Anglo-Saxon kingdoms. Wessex, for instance, traced its origin back to a figure named Cerdic, which is an Anglicised form of the Brittonic name Ceretic (the same as the unknown individual whose name lies behind Chertsey).[52] Kent, one of the earliest Anglo-Saxon kingdoms to emerge, appears to have preserved the name, territory and capital of the Roman and pre-Roman *Cantii*. What happened around London must remain obscure, though the fact that the city's centrality faded for several generations may in itself be telling. The factors that had brought London into being and maintained it into the late Roman period, even if in attenuated form, no longer applied: contact with the rest of the Roman world became less frequent and direct, and those links that did survive passed through different channels. Moreover, the few towns that may have retained some kind of central function in the troubled fifth and sixth centuries, such as Canterbury and Wroxeter, tended to be former *civitas* capitals that fitted into the new, smaller-scale political landscape.[53] London's status as a pan-provincial centre did not favour its chances of survival as larger-scale infrastructure came apart at the seams.

Conclusion: The Return of the Romans, AD 604

The story of London and its region in the immediately post-Roman period conforms in many respects to that of Britain as a whole, especially the south-eastern 'civilian' segment of the province which underwent the most rapid and thorough Anglo-Saxonisation. London is distinguished by the magnitude of its collapse, going from a symbolic and administrative hub to effectively nothing in the course of (probably) a few decades. Its plummet from grace reflects the particular circumstances of upheaval in post-Roman Britain: the machinery of the Roman state was the element of society at most risk, and the one that evaporated most rapidly – all of which was likely to affect London.

But some two centuries after the effective end of Roman imperial authority in Britain, a Roman expedition of quite a different form did return to London. In the 590s, as later Anglo-Saxon tradition would have it, Pope Gregory the Great (590–604) hatched a scheme to convert the English to Christianity. It was allegedly the sight of Anglo-Saxon slaves in Rome's marketplace which sparked his idea – that, plus a whole series of puns. When Gregory asked what people the slaves came from, he was told they were Angles (*Anguli*), which made them 'angels of God' (*angeli Dei*) in his eyes; when he asked their king's name and was told *Aelli*, he bent it into a form of 'alleluia'; and when he heard they were of a people called *Deirae* (who dwelt in southern Yorkshire), he shoehorned it into 'they shall flee from the anger of God (*de ira Dei*) to the faith'.[54] Such was the dismal start to English comedic tradition. The passage that tells this story was the work of an anonymous writer at Whitby in the years around 700, who penned a life of Gregory based on woefully little information but boundless enthusiasm. By that stage Gregory's mission had achieved legendary stature, and the story of it features heavily in the Whitby life and also in Bede's *Ecclesiastical History*.

Regardless of any humorous encounters Gregory may have had, he despatched a mission led by St Augustine in 595 or 596. It reached England in 597. The political situation Augustine found made it expedient for him to establish his first bishopric in Canterbury, chief town in the kingdom of Kent. Æthelberht, the king of Kent (d.616), was at that point the pre-eminent ruler in southern England, closely enmeshed in cross-Channel networks of power which had brought him a Christian wife, Bertha, from the Frankish royal family. A base at Canterbury thus made sense to Augustine as he surveyed conditions on the ground in England in 597. The Kentish city offered proximity to the leading ruler of the day, plus a ready patron in the form of his wife, and its extensive Roman ruins already included several churches.[55] But this was not Gregory's plan. A letter written by him to Augustine shortly after the latter's arrival laid down what sort of episcopal hierarchy the Pope anticipated: there should be two metropolitan bishops based at London and York, each presiding over 12 others.[56] Indeed, Gregory even thought of Augustine as the bishop of London, although he must have been aware that by the time he was writing in 601 Augustine was firmly ensconced at Canterbury. The Pope may well have had in mind a set-up based on the geography of late Roman Britain, devised on the basis of documents available at Rome.

Gregory's plan was never to be fulfilled. But the new Romans – soldiers of God rather than the emperor – returned to London in 604, when one of Augustine's assistants, a man named Mellitus, was appointed first bishop of the East Saxons, with his seat in London. The earliest cathedral church of St Paul's was erected there for him by King Æthelberht. Bede described London as at this point the 'principal city' (*metropolis*) of the East Saxons and as 'an emporium for many nations who come to it by land and sea'.[57] The London he referred to as a bustling hub of trade was a new, thriving entity to the west of the Roman city, the setting and development of which we shall turn to in the next two chapters.

CHAPTER 3

London Between Kingdoms

c.600–800

In 704 or 705, Waldhere, bishop of London, sent a letter to his superior Berhtwald, the archbishop of Canterbury. It happens to be the oldest letter on parchment from anywhere in Europe that survives in its original form, written in long lines of tightly packed and spidery script on a small, loose piece of cured animal skin (Figure 3.1). One can even see traces of how it was once folded up and addressed (on the back) to the archbishop. The letter owes its survival to its diligent recipient in Canterbury: the cathedral there preserved the richest collection of original Anglo-Saxon documents of any ancient English institution.[1]

The content of Waldhere's letter is just as interesting as its physical form. London's bishop was clearly wringing his hands over the delicate political situation before him, and so asked Berhtwald for advice; advice that he seems to have at once craved and feared to request, for Waldhere was afraid to do anything without the say-so of his boss. Indeed, he reminds the archbishop that he had ended up missing a recent meeting convoked by the king of the Mercians to discuss an (otherwise unknown) woman named Ælfthryth, because the archbishop had never told him what to say.

The circumstances that prompted Waldhere to ask the archbishop again for his views reveal the political tug of war into the middle of which London was thrust during the seventh and eighth centuries. A meeting at Brentford had been proposed, between the king and bishops of Wessex and their counterparts from Waldhere's own people. By 'his own people' he meant either the Mercians, or the East Saxons who were by this stage subordinate to the kings of the Mercians. Waldhere's main concern was that he hadn't the faintest

Figure 3.1. Letter of Waldhere, bishop of London, to
Berhtwald, archbishop of Canterbury, written 704×705
(London, British Library, Cotton Augustus II.18).

idea how to resolve the conflicts between them – especially if he
was not actually allowed to talk to the West Saxons, which was the
upshot of a decision made at a meeting of bishops the year before, held
to investigate irregularities in episcopal appointments. The overall
impression the letter conveys is of a man stuck between a rock and
a hard place, turning to an even bigger rock in desperation; so much
so that the actual substance of the proposed meeting at Brentford is
left obscure. One of its concerns may have been Surrey's ecclesiastical
affiliation. It had up to about this time been subject to London, but
just a few years later would be subject to Winchester, a West Saxon
see.[2] Situated on a Roman road, and right on the boundary between
Middlesex and Surrey, Brentford would have been an appropriate
place to hold such a discussion.[3]

We know neither what actually happened at Brentford,[4] nor
whether Waldhere's pleading letter ever received a response from the
archbishop, well larded though it was with platitudes and flattery.
Nevertheless, this letter is a tantalising snapshot of the fast-changing
nature of the landscape surrounding early Anglo-Saxon London. The
city had become a highly desirable prize. But London and its neighbouring regions were generally passive throughout the process: the
political centres of gravity lay elsewhere, and the rise to prominence of
a new kind of settlement at London, rich and economically engaged,
took place in the midst of a veritable dogfight between rival kingdoms
across the Weald and the Chilterns (Map 2).

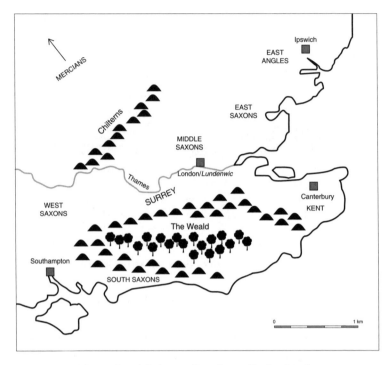

Map 2. Simplified map of south-east England in the seventh and eighth centuries (centred on London).

London and its Region in the Seventh Century

There was no single, overarching Anglo-Saxon kingdom of England before the tenth century, by which time the vikings had upended a patchwork of older kingdoms to leave only a few survivors standing. Traditionally, England before the convulsions of the Viking Age has been known as the heptarchy – that is, divided into seven kingdoms.[5] There is a certain amount of truth to this, but only some. In fact, it is incredibly difficult to say with confidence how many kingdoms there were at any one time: early Anglo-Saxon politics was a layer cake of larger and smaller kingdoms which combined, broke apart and realigned under the aegis of a few stronger players.

In the seventh century, London occupied an anomalous position as the icing on this layer-cake. It was not itself a major political power base; neither was it geographically central to the interests of any rulers who might have sought to claim it. Yet the fact that it lay at the intersection of so many different kingdoms, and had relatively good river and road connections, meant that it enjoyed a kind of pan-Anglo-Saxon centrality: it was everyone's border zone. This was undoubtedly one of the key reasons behind the success of *Lundenwic*, and also led to London and its diocese (including Surrey and Middlesex) being a preferred location for ecclesiastical meetings (synods), drawing bishops from across England south of the Humber to places like London itself, Brentford, Chelsea and Hertford.[6]

London was thus the fulcrum on which the cut and thrust of Anglo-Saxon politics pivoted. When Bede's *Ecclesiastical History* first sheds light on the political geography of southern England in about 600, London was the chief city and bishopric of the kingdom of the East Saxons. This was a small kingdom, though larger than its modern counterpart Essex. At this point, the territory of the East Saxons covered not only Essex but also Middlesex and probably parts of Surrey and Hertfordshire.[7] Three major powers from different sides of the Thames basin looked down onto this kingdom with greedy eyes: Kent from the south-east, Wessex from the south-west and Mercia from the north-west. Between them they carved up the kingdom of the East Saxons. By the end of the seventh century Middlesex had been detached from it and brought for good into the Mercian orbit, while Surrey was isolated and vulnerable to West Saxon encroachment. What remained of the East Saxon kingdom was under Mercian overlordship.[8]

Wessex was a large kingdom in south-west England, extending roughly from Hampshire to Devon, while the Mercians occupied a swathe of territory in the midlands, either side of the Trent valley. Their name meant 'boundary dwellers', though quite who that boundary was with (Britons? Northumbrians?) is unclear.[9] These larger kingdoms fought both hot and cold wars with each other, seeking to establish dominance by any means. The Mercians in particular were masters of ingratiating themselves into other parts of England: as well as in the London region, seventh-century Mercian kings advanced their interests among other midland peoples like the Hwicce in Worcestershire and the Magonsætan in Herefordshire, and also in Sussex and eventually Kent.[10] Force was only one weapon in their arsenal, though a very effective one; they also turned to religious conversion, ecclesiastical patronage, marriage brokering, support of exiled princes, and much else besides. Even when the Mercians did take on a more overtly superior role in relation to local groups, it was very much a two-way process: the Mercians needed support, and local rulers got as much out of the arrangement as they could. Sæbbi, a king of the East Saxons who recognised Mercian overlordship, was able to keep his throne for 30 years and secure the succession of his children before retiring to London shortly before his death in 694.[11]

An enigmatic document from sometime between the seventh and ninth centuries known as the 'Tribal Hidage' gives some flavour of just how messy things were on the ground.[12] It lists some 35 peoples along with their rating in 'hides', one hide being the amount of land notionally needed to support a family. Some of these groups are well known as major forces in the rough and tumble of Anglo-Saxon history, and possess large numbers of hides: the Mercians and East Angles have 30,000 each; the men of Kent 15,000; the South Saxons and East Saxons 7,000 each. The West Saxons are assigned a whopping 100,000: such a huge number that exaggeration is suspected, or alternatively that it incorporates subordinate peoples, consolidated by someone eager to magnify West Saxon power. But the main interest of the 'Tribal Hidage' lies in the plethora of other, smaller peoples who commanded much smaller numbers of hides – in some cases as few as 300. These peoples exude an air of obscure antiquity, of a lost and alien landscape dotted with little groups or kingdoms smaller than a modern county. Some of them are known solely from the 'Tribal Hidage', or from a smattering of place names: peoples such as the North and South Gyrwe, East and West Wixna, Cilternsæte ('people of the Chilterns'), Noxgaga and Ohtgaga.[13] It is thought that most of the bewildering undergrowth of smaller peoples in the 'Tribal Hidage' could be found in an area roughly between the Wash and the Thames, which formed part of a territory that the Mercian king Penda (d.655) delegated as a sub-kingdom for his son under the catch-all name of the 'Middle Angles'.[14] There were also even smaller peoples below and within those named in the 'Tribal Hidage', who can only be traced when they happen to be named in local documents. In the area of what would become Middlesex alone, Keith Bailey has identified about ten peoples, apparently accounting for between 30 and 100 hides each, among them the Gillingas, who gave their name to Ealing; the *Mimmas*, whose name survives in South Mimms; and the Gumeningas, whose pre-Christian shrine (*Gumeninga hearh*) is remembered in the place name Harrow.[15] It is not clear how integrated these ever were into either a coherent kingdom of their own, or the larger neighbouring kingdom, that of the East Saxons. By the time clearer evidence of them emerges around 700, they are already organised as the Middle Saxons. This name presupposes that they slotted into an already well-established landscape: there had to be other peoples (probably the East and West Saxons) for them to be in the middle of.[16] All this is to say that London and its surrounding territory was something of a frontier zone. Its contested nature prevented it from gaining an independent political identity,[17] while at the same time giving it prestige, accessibility and magnetism. This payoff makes the area's history in early Anglo-Saxon history very murky.

On a local level, small peoples like those of Middlesex were the backbone of early Anglo-Saxon infrastructure. Their lands formed cohesive, self-sustaining units larger than a modern parish but smaller than a shire, structured around a royal or aristocratic centre and, after the establishment of Christianity, a 'minster' or large church responsible for the spiritual needs of the community.[18] It was by welding together these smaller units, violently or otherwise, that larger patchwork kingdoms and overlordships came into being. These depended on personal subordination to kings and sub-kings, backed up by the promise of support in time of war, and tribute and recognition during peace. Within this relatively loose system, large-scale dominance could be both built up and demolished very rapidly. Bede listed a series of seven kings who had wielded supremacy over the kingdoms south of the Humber, and it is likely that the Mercian kings of the late seventh and eighth centuries exercised a similar level of hegemony.[19] The power of these kings was, however, essentially personal, and tended to collapse upon the death of each individual overlord. Rivals might then swoop in to seize the spoils, and local rulers had a chance to reassert their independence.

London's seventh century can be divided roughly into two segments: a long and obscure one thought to be marked by Kentish dominance (*c*.600–60/70), and a shorter one of complex and fissile interaction as Mercia and Wessex also muscled in (*c*.660/70–700). By the early years of the eighth century the political map of the south-east had been redrawn, and more secure Mercian dominance began an association with the midland kingdom that would persist into the tenth century.

The Scramble for Lundenwic c.660–700

London was, at the outset of the seventh century, the key city for the East Saxons, and its bishopric was set up specifically to minister to them in 604. It may be that the East Saxons had exercised significant power and independence before this, which is the first time that we begin to have a clearer picture of London after some two centuries of obscurity; but in 604 Æthelberht, king of Kent, was patron for the new church in London, suggesting that Kent was already exerting a very real superiority over the East Saxons. Æthelberht's reign seems to have been the high-water mark of Kentish power, although subsequent rulers could still make an impression in London and its vicinity. His son and heir Eadbald had coins minted at London, so presumably maintained something of Æthelberht's reach (Figure 4.5).

Yet the reach of the kings of Kent was by no means constant, especially after Eadbald's time as king. It is difficult to detect clear evidence of Kentish involvement in subsequent decades, and it may be that its power over Essex and London ebbed in the mid-seventh century, allowing the East Saxons to regain a firm foothold. But there was something of a resurgence in the 660s, as a new and more competitive era began to dawn.

In the tumult of the later seventh century, London itself seems to have been comparatively placid, like the proverbial eye of the storm. Although there was much interest in the area around London, including in lands abutting on the budding new trading centre, the town itself was treated like the goose that lays the golden eggs, and mainly discussed in matters pertaining to trade and tolls. The impression one gets of its position is mixed. Overlords from Mercia and elsewhere dealt with the town at arm's length, and mediated their influence through local élites. Until Middlesex was detached and effectively annexed by Mercia, the East Saxons may have remained de facto masters of London, even if they in turn were often answerable to other masters. But as East Saxon power waned, London may in practice have become a jurisdictional melting pot in which royal involvement had to be adjusted and reasserted on a constant basis.[20] The interests and assertions of Kentish, Mercian and West Saxon kings – plus the local East Saxons – overlapped in confusing fashion. It is no coincidence that they became noticeably more complex just as *Lundenwic*'s growth picked up speed, and the potential rewards of a controlling interest in the town multiplied.[21]

The decades after about 660 saw a complicated three-way (at times four-way) struggle over London and the surrounding region. The main destabilising factor was a new and assertive Mercian presence from the time of King Wulfhere (658–75) onwards.[22] By the mid-660s he was adopting the posture of an overlord with respect to Essex and the London region, which included a watch over religious affairs. Some of Wulfhere's earliest actions in the south-east included despatching a missionary to restore the lapsed Christian faith of the East Saxons in 664, and around the same time he allegedly sold the bishopric of London and gave land at London to the minster of Barking in Essex.[23] At this point his influence may only have extended to the Thames, for around the same time Ecgberht I (664–73), king of Kent, was still in a position to act as the principal patron of Chertsey, a new monastic foundation south of the Thames in west Surrey.[24] Before long, however, Mercian interests had pushed southwards and started to involve secular rulers too. Sometime between about 670 and 675, an enigmatic figure named Frithuwald, 'petty sub-king of Surrey' (*prouincie Surrianorum subregulus*), issued a charter for the benefit of Chertsey with the consent of Wulfhere. Frithuwald may have been a Mercian-supported invader from further north,[25] and at this date 'Surrey' (*Suðre ge*, which means 'the southern region')[26] need not have referred to the whole of the later county, but could have been just the western chunk, which had much in common with land north of the Thames and may once, as the name suggests, have been a southern portion of the East Saxon kingdom.[27] Central and eastern Surrey, in contrast, had more similarities with Kent, for instance in the long, thin shape of local administrative units, often with detached lowland and upland (Wealden) portions.[28] Whatever its history, from the time of its emergence into the light of historical sources Surrey was a 'leftover', a marginal yet strategically important area that never amounted to more than the sum of its parts, and hence its destiny was to be picked at and fought over by greater neighbours.[29]

Mercia was not the sole kingdom to pursue interests in the London region. As the foundation of Chertsey indicates, Kent was still a significant player, albeit not the force it once was. In the years around 690, part of it was even taken over by enterprising members of the East Saxon dynasty.[30] Prior to this, there may have been a resurgence of Kentish involvement in London, under rather different circumstances from the early seventh century: Kent and its representatives now had to navigate a more crowded political scene. One success may have come in about 675 with the appointment of Eorcenwald as bishop of London (d.693?). His name, along with the names of his family members, strongly suggests a connection to the royal house of Kent.[31] In practice, Eorcenwald proved himself to be a master of bending in whichever direction the wind blew, and over his long career he managed to schmooze and co-operate with kings from Essex, Kent, Mercia and Wessex.[32] His were exactly the skills needed to negotiate the dangerous straits of seventh-century south-east England.

Another dimension of Kentish involvement related to trade. Between 673 and 685, a pair of Kentish kings issued a law code which mentions the existence in London of a king's hall and a king's town-reeve. These presumably served the Kentish king and his subjects specifically. But the way in which these laws are phrased implies that the men of Kent were only one cohort among many: they for instance made provision for traders unable to track down their previous customers, which was unlikely to be as pressing a concern in the heart of Kentish territory, where the king might in principle expect more control over traders' movements.[33] The king of Kent may therefore not actually have ruled London, but rather operated a sort of commercial embassy there.[34] This provides a

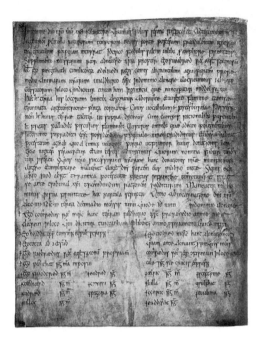

Figure 3.2. Charter containing the first reference to the Middle Saxons, issued by Swæfred, king of the East Saxons (*c.*694–704 or after) and *comes* Pæogthath, with the consent of Æthelred, king of the Mercians (674/5–704); this copy was probably written in the later eighth century (S 65) (London, British Library, Cotton Augustus II.82) (image: Bond, *Facsimiles*, I, no. 3).

valuable insight into the brisk business already going on in London at an early point in *Lundenwic*'s growth, and the special arrangements that were being made to facilitate trade from different quarters in the town.

Wessex was the other major new force to muscle in, which the warlike King Cædwealla (686–8) did with a vengeance during his short but vigorous reign. Supremacy suddenly tipped westwards. As well as laying waste the South Saxons and men of Kent, Cædwealla was clearly a force to be reckoned with in the area around London, and temporarily pushed back Mercian encroachment. Charters show him granting land in Surrey and possibly influencing the actions of East Saxon rulers.[35] Bishop Eorcenwald seems to have co-operated closely with Cædwealla, as one of his favoured bishops alongside St Wilfrid (d.710), a northerner with a knack for stirring up controversy and raising hackles.[36] Cædwalla's successor, the longer-lived King Ine (688–726), exercised more of a soft power over the south-east, though may have kept a grip on Surrey. He cited the help and advice he had received from 'my bishops' Hædde of Winchester and Eorcenwald of London in putting together a law code for his kingdom.[37] Ine also presided over the intrigue that prompted Waldhere's letter, including the transfer of jurisdiction over Surrey from the bishop of London to the bishop of Winchester.[38]

West Saxon machinations ran up against a recovery of Mercian interests under King Æthelred (675–704). He made or confirmed grants of land in Surrey and Middlesex.[39] It was in the last year of his reign that Middlesex was for the first time referred to as a separate people or territory (Figure 3.2).[40] Æthelred sometimes still acted there through the kings of the East Saxons, but at other times in his own right.[41] Middlesex, once part of the East Saxon realm, was moving more into a Mercian sphere of influence.[42]

Mercian London

The eighth century was for London, and indeed southern England as a whole, very much the Mercian century. This powerful midland kingdom had been a mighty force in Anglo-Saxon politics since the time of its assertive King Penda (d.655), crafting what modern historians have often called the 'Mercian supremacy'.[43]

By the opening years of the eighth century, this supremacy was nearing its height: Mercia dominated England south of the Humber. Its effectiveness rested on a large core area in the west midlands which Mercian rulers could call on for men and resources. The regime behind the Mercian supremacy was volatile and predatory. Like most other early Anglo-Saxon kingdoms, Mercia did not have an entrenched royal family, and on the death of each king power was contended by eligible members of an extended ruling clan.[44] Violence and competition were thus bred into the kingdom's élite. The first kings of the eighth century, Coenred (704–9) and Ceolred (709–16), were cousins, the sons of Wulfhere and Æthelred respectively,[45] but Æthelbald (716–57) and Offa (757–96), the two most successful and long-lived Mercian kings of the eighth century, were only distantly related to them and each other. Each had to build up his position afresh, and did so in a different way. Æthelbald essentially followed the pattern of exercising loose overlordship that had emerged in the seventh century, but considerably extended and amped up its scope.[46]

Bede described him explicitly as overlord of all the kings and king-doms south of the Humber,[47] and a charter from Worcester likewise touted Æthelbald as 'king not only of the Mercians but of all the kingdoms generally known by the name "south Angles/English"'; this was quite a mouthful, and was cut down to just 'king of Britain' in the shorter attestation given by the king later on in the document.[48]

Æthelbald's exercise of wide-ranging authority did not mean the demotion or removal of local kings. In East Anglia, Essex, Sussex and elsewhere, the same local dynasties persisted. Some even bought into the Mercian regime with gusto: a life of St Guthlac written in East Anglia and dedicated to the local King Ælfwald (713–49) included a chapter in which the hermit saint met Æthelbald as a wandering exile, and predicted his future greatness.[49] As might be expected, Æthelbald also won his share of enemies and critics. An excoriat-ing letter written to him by the missionary and spiritual watchdog St Boniface (d.754) – a West Saxon long resident in what is now Germany – called the king out among other things for taking his pleasure with nuns in their own monasteries.[50] To rebuild his repu-tation as a good patron of the Church, Æthelbald collaborated with the archbishop of Canterbury on a programme of land grants and reforms.[51] The end of Æthelbald's long reign – the longest securely attested one of any Anglo-Saxon king – came when he was slain by his own men at Seckington, Warwickshire, in the heart of Mercia, for reasons unknown.[52]

But while Æthelbald is primarily known for an extensive but loose form of rule, London in particular seems to have come defini-tively under Mercian authority during his reign. An extensive series of charters granting exemption from the tolls on trading ships in London vividly attests to his control over trade and officials in the town.[53] He also continued to wield authority over the East Saxons and in Middlesex (the situation in Surrey is less clear),[54] and the tightening of the Mercian grip on London has been read as a key change in southern England.[55]

Offa, the second great Mercian overlord of the eighth century, remade the supremacy Æthelbald had commanded on quite dif-ferent terms. Where Æthelbald spun a fine web, Offa wove a steel net, gradually imposing a more rigid and structured interpretation of Mercian authority across his kingdom.[56] This was done at a distance: Offa generally remained in the heartland of Mercia, and made petitioners and subordinates come to him. Local rulers ceased being kings and became 'petty sub-kings' (*subreguli*) – if they remained in power at all, for some were replaced with new men more amenable to the Mercian regime.[57] Offa also shook up the coinage of his kingdom. Silver pennies took on the broader, thinner format now popular in the Frankish kingdom across the Channel, and began to name a king explicitly. For part of his reign Offa was portrayed on his coins in guises that evoked Roman emperors (especially Constantine the Great, the celebrated patron of the Christian religion) and the biblical King David.[58] Yet the centres that produced these coins celebrating Offa's kingship were far from the heartland of Mercia: the coinage is thought to have been the exclusive product of mints in south-east England and East Anglia. London in fact is believed to have been especially innovative and engaged in minting Offa's coinage, being responsible for the most beautiful and sophisticated portraits; this was also the one and only point in the Middle Ages when a bishop of London temporarily possessed the right to mint coin in his own name, reflecting his importance in Offa's regime.[59] In his charters, Offa laid emphasis on his wife and son's participation in his rule, in an effort to foster a real dynasty and thereby break the dependency on individual kings that was characteristic of the Mercian supremacy.[60] He even had his son Ecgfrith anointed king in 787, while he could still rule jointly with his father and prepare for succession.

As the evidence of the coinage suggests most strongly, London played an important role in Offa's kingdom. Even the cessation of charters granting away tolls (save a few confirmations of grants made by Æthelbald) should be read as Offa trying to keep hold of a lucrative resource – one which was potentially in decline as *Lundenwic* and its business shrank.[61] Moves to reaffirm Mercian authority in the area surrounding London point in the same direction. Probably in the latter part of his reign, Offa came to Surrey in person and, at a place called *Freoricburna* (possibly Kingston upon Thames), dispensed land to a minster at Woking.[62] Chertsey may have come under his direct control, as one of several favoured monastic houses appropriated by the royal family; one document records how Offa, his queen, his son and four daughters were expected to benefit from giving land to the monastery.[63]

London seems to have been even more central to the regime of the last great Mercian overlord, Coenwulf (796–821), who spent the opening years of his reign reclaiming Kent and East Anglia from local rulers eager to detach themselves from Mercian overlordship. Coenwulf was the first Mercian king to visit London on a frequent basis: several of his charters record that they were issued during meetings held at what was described as a royal estate (*villa* or *vicus regalis*) in London, or nearby at Chelsea.[64] In the course of a long and acrimonious debate with the archbishop of Canterbury over rights to certain minsters, Coenwulf once summoned the archbishop to a gathering of his leading men in London, a location where the king was comfortable and the archbishop himself was willing to visit – perhaps because Wulfred (805–32), the archbishop in question, came (it is thought) from a Middlesex family.[65] These are exactly the sorts of occasions at which the famous Coenwulf *mancus* – a unique gold coin bearing inscription DE VICO LVNDONIAE ('from the estate of London/*Lundenwic*') – might have been minted, to be used by the king's entourage for his more prestigious expenses or gifts.[66]

It was also under Coenwulf that London was briefly touted as an alternative seat for the pre-eminent bishopric in Britain.[67] England's ecclesiastical hierarchy had been overturned in 787 when Offa secured the promotion of Lichfield to an archbishopric – an act probably tied to the consecration of his son as king that same year, and to Offa's well-known antipathy to the current archbishop of Canterbury.[68] The creation of the archbishopric of Lichfield reopened the question of where bishops' allegiances should lie. Lichfield took responsibility for bishops north of the Thames, Canterbury for those to the south which had traditionally been 'Saxon' and therefore also included London.[69] Coenwulf faced a fluid situation immediately after taking the throne in 796. For unknown reasons, the bishop of London had left the country in 796 along with the bishop of Lindsey (in what is now Lincolnshire),[70] while in Kent the city of Canterbury lay under the rule of a local challenger to Mercian power, Eadberht 'Præn', and its archbishop (a Mercian appointed under Offa in 792) lived in exile. England's ecclesiastical establishment seemed to be coming apart at the seams, and Coenwulf took the view that drastic action was needed. In 798, he wrote to Pope Leo III (795–816) in Rome to seek his views on the matter, and floated a radical proposition which would solve all his problems in one go: that Gregory the Great's original plan for an archbishopric in London be resurrected, and in effect Canterbury's primacy transferred. Coenwulf was cautious in how he presented the idea. While conceding that St Augustine had been based in Canterbury, he noted subtly that when Augustine had received the *pallium* – the mark of office of an archbishop, sent directly by the Pope – Pope Gregory the Great in fact considered him to be bishop of London.[71]

In the event, the scheme never got off the ground, for Pope Leo III decisively squelched it in his response to Coenwulf's letter: Canterbury was, in his view, the proper seat of supreme ecclesiastical authority in England.[72] So it has remained ever since; even the archbishopric of Lichfield was left to fizzle out in the next few years. But Coenwulf's plan perhaps made sense at that particular moment in 798: as a Mercian king fought to re-establish authority over Kent, an archbishopric closer to home and acceptable both north and south of the Thames as a compromise candidate would have seemed desirable. In any case, the attractions of a London archbishopric soon evaporated after Mercian victory in Kent led to the re-establishment of an amenable archbishop in Canterbury. London was never to attain the honour proposed for it at this time.

At the start of the ninth century London remained at the heart of the Mercian regime, as a bastion of royal tolls and officials, and (at least in the time of Coenwulf) the venue of royal visits. Where his base in the city might have been situated remains anybody's guess. Antiquarian reports of a palace near Cripplegate, on the site of the old fort in the Roman city, have as yet found no good support, either from archaeology or historical sources.[73] Unless all of *Lundenwic* was in some sense a royal estate, it may well have been situated somewhere in or near the Strand settlement (one possible location is a high-status settlement on the site of the Treasury building in Westminster) – at least until, in the course of the ninth century, the nature of the city started to change. It remained a Mercian city at this time, to the extent that when it was briefly taken over in 829 by the king of the

West Saxons, Ecgberht, it was used by him as a mint for producing coins as king of the Mercians (Figure 5.4).[74] Seizing London was a signal that Ecgberht had taken over the attached kingdom, not that London was changing hands. But its Mercian, indeed Anglo-Saxon, status was to come under new and more dire threat as the ninth century wore on and the vikings arrived on the scene in southern England. This story will be taken up in Chapter 5, after a closer look at the inner workings of the fascinating new city of the seventh and eighth centuries.

CHAPTER 4

Lundenwic

'An Emporium for Many Nations'

In 679, two of the superpowers of Anglo-Saxon England came to blows somewhere along the course of the river Trent. The Mercians under King Æthelred (675–704) triumphed over the Northumbrians under Ecgfrith (670–85), altering the balance of power in central England for good. One of the ill-fated northerners who fought in this battle was a man named Imma: a young warrior from the retinue of Ecgfrith's brother Ælfwine, who was himself killed in the battle. Imma barely escaped with his life, lying among the dead for a day and a night until he could muster the energy to slip away. He was soon caught and brought before one of the leading men among the victorious Mercians. Imma concealed his true identity, saying that he was a humble peasant who had not engaged in any fighting. As an honourable man, the Mercian tended to Imma's wounds, but out of caution ordered that he be kept bound at night. Much to everyone's amazement, Imma's bonds would simply not stay tied. The Venerable Bede, to whom we owe the account of this story, explained this as the result of prayers said by Imma's brother, a priest, who thought Imma had died in the battle; indeed, Imma's fetters had a habit of coming loose at exactly the times when services would be offered in church.

There were other odd things about Imma. His captors realised from his appearance, speech and bearing that he was not in fact a peasant, and eventually Imma came clean and told his host the truth, in return for a promise of safe conduct. The gracious Mercian agreed, although once Imma was healed it was time for him to move on, and his captors took him to London for sale as a slave to a Frisian trader. This merchant too was stymied by Imma's miraculous ability to shed all bonds (which severely limited his usefulness as a slave), and he allowed Imma to ransom himself with the financial help of the king of Kent. At last the warrior was able to return home, and share the wonderful story with his brother.[1]

London, called by Bede 'an emporium for many nations', was by the 670s *the* place to go for Mercians hoping to pass on a slave. It drew traders from across the North Sea, and was one of a series of new towns that popped up across Europe as both local and international trade recovered steam, from Kaupang in Norway to Venice at the head of the Adriatic.[2] This was a far cry from the largely abandoned city of the fifth century, although the Roman city itself was still relatively quiet at this time: London's nerve centre had relocated a mile or so to the west, across the Fleet, and lay between what is now Lincoln's Inn Fields and Trafalgar Square. Like early Roman London, the rekindled Anglo-Saxon city was driven by a strong pulse of trade. Visitors from far and wide came to make, buy and, as the Mercians did with Imma, sell. It is less clear what the settlement's formal status was; another point in common with early Roman London. The city's location continued to make it a lucrative and accessible prize for surrounding powers. Traditionally associated with the East Saxons, as we have seen London passed back and forth between the spheres of several more successful powers over the course of the seventh and eighth centuries, particularly Kent and Mercia. What drew these acquisitive rulers to London in the first place? How, and why, did the city start ticking anew in the seventh century, and what was life like in *Lundenwic* during its heyday and eventual decline in the eighth and early ninth centuries?

Rediscovering Lundenwic

Although not obvious at first glance, the imprint of Anglo-Saxon London can still be found in some of the streets along and immediately north of the Strand. Of course, the street plan of the area has been redrawn so many times in the intervening millennium that it bears only the slightest relationship to how the thoroughfares of the eighth century might have been laid out. What looks like the most prominent allusion to the area's early medieval significance,

Aldwych ('the old *wic*') – the crescent that arcs west from St Clement Danes – exists only for antiquarian reasons, and this old name in fact applies to one of the newest routes carved into this part of the city. Its reinstatement was the brainchild of Sir George Laurence Gomme (1853–1916), a scholar of English folklore and of London history (and founder of the blue plaques that mark sites of interest in the city), who happened to be serving as clerk to London County Council at the time the bold plans for this intervention in the cityscape were made at the end of the nineteenth century. He advocated strongly for resurrecting this antique-sounding name, which had been used for the road that ran from St Clement Danes to St Giles-in-the-Fields until the sixteenth century, when it took on its modern name, Drury Lane, after the eminent gentleman-lawyer Sir Robert Drury (1456–1535).[3]

There is good reason to believe that Drury Lane is an ancient street, perhaps going back to the time of *Lundenwic*. Christening the new street as 'Aldwych', meanwhile, fitted the Edwardian taste for solidly English-sounding names, and had the added attraction of memorialising nearby Wych Street, another possible reference to *Lundenwic*.

Wych Street was once a narrow and characterful road cluttered with houses from the seventeenth century and before (Figure 4.1); it was one of several venerable London streets obliterated by the building of Aldwych in the opening years of the twentieth century (Figure 4.2). This destruction formed part of an effort by the civic authorities to transform the environs of Holborn, and rid them of what were considered to be disorderly and undesirable elements. A report from 1904 invited Londoners to imagine 'the symmetry and order which will be evolved out of chaos'.[4] A century later, the decision to adopt the name 'Aldwych' turned out to have been highly fortuitous, for it did indeed lie in the middle of old *Lundenwic*. This was even recognised, in a more refined way, in 2015 when a new coffee shop opened on Aldwych. The brainchild of a pair of entrepreneurs who had made their name with the best Scotch eggs the capital had to offer, its selling point was homemade and high-quality fare of a traditional variety. As such, a name that reached back into London's past seemed appropriate, and given the location it was only natural that they should settle on 'Lundenwic'.

Figure 4.1. Engraving of Wych Street (by Robert Cutts, *London Illustrated News*, 1 January 1870).

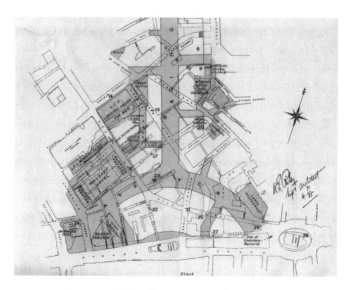

Figure 4.2. Plan of new streets in the area north of the Strand, superimposed on the earlier layout (from G. L. Gomme, *Opening of Kingsway*).

London's position between the fifth and ninth centuries remained an enigma until the 1980s. Mortimer Wheeler, one of the greatest names in British archaeology during the twentieth century, placed such weight on Bede's words about the burgeoning trade of seventh-century London that he firmly identified London as 'an urban anachronism', standing strong against the devolution of culture and town life in the post-Roman centuries.[5] In his view there must have been some sort of activity in the city throughout the early Middle Ages, even though when he was writing in the 1920s and 1930s the material evidence for this was thin. The conundrum he faced was a yawning gap between the relatively strong historical impression of London's status, and the absence of any signal for this in the archaeological record. Wheeler read the slim pickings optimistically, his best guess being that most of the evidence had been wiped out by subsequent development.[6] Others took different views. Francis Haverfield wrote London off as 'empty and untenanted' in the post-Roman period,[7] and in much the same vein Sir Frank Stenton condemned 'the starved and barbarized existence' that was all London's unfortunate inhabitants could hope for at that time.[8] In the 1960s another eminent archaeologist, William Francis Grimes, tried to reconcile the two conflicting impressions by proposing that early Anglo-Saxon London was simply a lot smaller than Wheeler and others had thought.[9]

The reason that early Anglo-Saxon London posed such a problem was that everyone was looking for it in the wrong place.[10] As later Anglo-Saxon London used the site of the Roman city, it was assumed that any intervening settlement must also have done so. Scattered 'groups of huts or houses' had long been noted in the land between the Fleet and Westminster,[11] and in the 1980s the penny dropped: early Anglo-Saxon London's main centre of activity had not been in the City at all, but along the Strand. Realisation came from the convergence of new archaeological finds with a fresh examination of topography and place names. One of the two scholars to first make this breakthrough, Martin Biddle, had his eureka moment while riding on a bus down the Strand (whose name denotes a shoreline road suitable for beach markets), which then turned onto the Aldwych – both names closely associated with sites of settlement and trade in the Anglo-Saxon era.[12] Further digging at Jubilee Hall in Covent Garden in 1985 confirmed what had at first seemed to be a bold and speculative proposition.[13] Extensive signs of seventh- and eighth-century activity emerged. Knowledge of the settlement's physical remains has advanced by leaps and bounds in subsequent decades, and about 70 sites excavated down to 2008 have produced evidence for *Lundenwic*, giving a fairly clear view of the town at its height.[14]

Defining Lundenwic

The espresso-drinkers and kale-eaters who now frequent *Lundenwic* the coffee shop sit in the midst of what was early medieval London. In modern scholarship this settlement is generally known as *Lundenwic*, and it is convenient to keep this label for the sake of clarity even though its significance in the Anglo-Saxon period is less clear. The name was certainly current at the time: it occurs in the laws of two Kentish kings produced around 680, and also in various charters, the latest of them dating to 857.[15] But as with other place names from this period, its meaning needs to be unpicked. The second element, *wic*, is one of two terms commonly used to describe early medieval trading towns, the other being *emporium*. Both attempt to get at the essentially commercial function of these settlements. *Wic* – which is declined like 'sheep', with the plural being the same as the singular – is often found in Old English place names, including those of some of the other main trading towns that sprang up at the same time as London: Ipswich, *Hamwic* (Southampton) and *Eoforwic* (York).[16] It is related to the Latin *vicus*, which carried rather loose connotations revolving around the idea of an informal settlement, such as those found outside Roman forts – places full of shops, prostitutes and the quasi-legitimate families of soldiers.[17] In the early medieval context, *wic* could apply to a wide range of specialised settlements. So trading places were *wic*, but not all *wic* were trading places.[18] *Emporium*, meanwhile, is a Latin label drawn ultimately from a Greek word meaning 'market' which enjoyed occasional use in the early Middle Ages,[19] but has gained wider modern currency thanks to the eminent anthropologist-historian Karl Polanyi, who used this word (as well as 'port of trade') to define places where people from different societies could come together for the purpose of exchange.[20]

All of this matters because, in the eyes of contemporaries, *emporia* sat rather awkwardly in the mental landscape, which categorised towns and cities according to institutional rather than economic criteria. As new creations without much of a monumental, religious or political footprint, the *wic* or *emporia* simply were not cities according to prevailing definitions. These stressed precisely what the *emporia* did *not* have: walls, churches and a formal, typically long-established identity.[21] One of the most celebrated scholars of the eighth century, Alcuin of York (d.804), praised these features in a poem honouring his home city of York, 'with its high walls and lofty towers [...] first built by Roman hands'.[22] A hubbub of people did not in itself put an *emporium* onto the map as an urban entity, even if it was much larger and more trade-oriented than many contemporary cities. These new settlements were more like permanent bases for production and trade. As some modern archaeologists have observed, the *emporia* or *wic* had something about them of today's 'non-places' such as prisons, airports and shopping centres: locations that might have attracted lots of people, and perhaps even been settled on a long-term basis, but which lacked the essential qualities needed to make them a real 'place'.[23] Consequently, scholars are often hesitant to describe *emporia* straightforwardly as towns or cities, for doing so conjures up unhelpful associations with the functions and features of modern urban settlements, as well as with the Roman and ecclesiastical centres that also formed the urban map of eighth-century western Europe. These quandaries are a good way to remind ourselves that early medieval urban settlements were different sorts of places from modern towns and cities, but they also involve exchanging one problem for another: if these were not towns as we understand them, it is also risky to apply another set of less familiar definitions that imply another kind of homogeneity. We therefore need to be prepared to take each case on its own merits.

London in particular was a special case among the *emporia*, in that *Lundenwic* lay adjacent to a Roman city that possessed the traditional qualifications of an urban centre. York was the main English parallel in this respect: its smaller *wic* or *emporium*-style settlement lay to the south-east of the Roman city on the Foss. Alcuin may have had this portion of the place in mind when he praised York for the 'divers peoples and kingdoms all over the world [who] come in hope of gain, seeking wealth from the rich land, a home, a fortune, and a hearth-stone for themselves'.[24] If Alcuin had ever thought to compose a similar poem about London, he could have found much to speak of, with the important caveat that the hustle and bustle of urban life would have mostly or entirely taken place outside the walls and away from the grand churches. At London, the urban functions were split across two nearby sites, neither part ticking all the boxes that Alcuin or others thought were important. In this sense, *Lundenwic* was akin to a permanent fair or market, where traders and craftspeople lived in or by their stalls, while the walls and churches of *Londinium* loomed in the distance.

These two dimensions of London – what we might characterise as *Lundenwic* and *Londinium* – were normally rolled into one by observers in the seventh, eighth and ninth centuries.[25] *Lundonia*, the most popular Latin name for the city at this time, could be applied without qualification to both the Roman city and the new western settlement. If more precision was needed, the word *civitas* could be used to denote the Roman city; this designation carried stronger associations with the Roman past and the church infrastructure of the early Middle Ages.[26] Bede normally used it when discussing St Paul's and the bishops of London. Tellingly, he did not describe London as a *civitas* in his story of Imma.[27] Similarly, the new settlement to the west could be specified with *portus* ('port') or possibly *vicus*.[28] Hence one finds *Lundonia* but also *civitas Lundoniae, portus Lundoniae* and so on. These niceties of usage matter, because early medieval Londoners did not necessarily think of *Lundenwic* as separate from the Roman city; on the contrary, the two were closely linked, and may have been considered parts of a single, larger entity, somewhat like how the modern City and 32 boroughs together form one agglomeration divided into separate parts – though a better comparison may be twentieth-century Lima, with an historic core surrounded by a much larger but less formal growth of new settlement.

Life in Lundenwic

Lundenwic's eastern fringes began about half a mile west of the Roman walls, on the far side of the Fleet (Map 3). The attractions of this area were augmented by the challenges of resettling the Roman city. The Roman river wall would have still been intact in the seventh century, at least for much of its course, limiting access to the water,[29] while the preponderance of stone remains hampered building in wood in some parts of the walled area, and *Londinium's* vast fortifications would have been too much for the meagre local population to man.[30] The critical factor, however, was the priorities of the new settlers who laid the foundations of *Lundenwic*. Their need was for an open place accessible by water. Hence London's centre of gravity shifted beyond Roman London's western limits, and across the marshy mouth of the Fleet immediately outside its western gates, to the drier shores that curved gently round towards Westminster.[31] One side of *Lundenwic* ran along the edge of the Thames, the shoreline of which lay about 50 m further north than it does now – which is to say, close to the Strand. *Lundenwic's* eastern

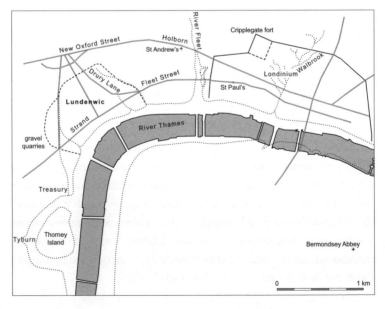

Map 3. London in the age of *Lundenwic.*

edge lay approximately at the end of the crescent that constitutes the modern Aldwych.[32] Covent Garden, where rebuilding of the Royal Opera House and London Transport Museum allowed some of the largest excavations of *Lundenwic* to take place in the 1990s and 2000s, was at its core.[33] The northern limits were around what is now Kingsway and Shorts Gardens, while to the west they lay around Trafalgar Square. Altogether, *Lundenwic* took up about 60 ha. Its population is more difficult to estimate, but probably peaked at around 7,000. This is of course small fry in modern terms, barely more than a village. *Lundenwic* was also about half the size of Roman London in terms of area, and a quarter in terms of population.[34] But in the much reduced economic circumstances of early medieval Europe, London was a veritable hive of activity. It was probably one of the largest of the *emporia* or *wic* around the North Sea.[35]

By the standards of the day, *Lundenwic* was quite a diverse, cosmopolitan place. Aside from the Frisian slaver who bought Imma, two other Franks owned property at *Lundenwic* in the late eighth century and gave it to an abbey near Paris (discussed later in this chapter). Pots and other goods excavated at Covent Garden and elsewhere suggest regular interaction with the Rhineland and other areas around the rim of the North Sea and English Channel, as does a hoard of brass ingots from (probably) Germany.[36] A hoard of ninth-century Northumbrian coins probably indicates the presence of a northerner.[37] There may well have been others from more distant lands, like the prominent churchmen Theodore and Hadrian who organised and attended church councils in the vicinity of late seventh-century London. They had arrived in England in 669 as (respectively) archbishop of Canterbury and abbot of St Augustine's, Canterbury. Sent from Italy by the Pope in the first instance, Theodore originally hailed from Tarsus (now south-east Turkey) and Hadrian from somewhere in North Africa (probably what is now Libya).[38] Learned Greek-speaking ecclesiastics like Theodore and Hadrian were exceptional in seventh-century England, but a wide range of languages would have been heard, and products of diverse lands seen, by anyone taking a walk through the streets of *Lundenwic*.

Our putative walking tour of *Lundenwic* would have been confronted with a mass of small buildings which contained the homes

and businesses of the town's inhabitants. These were mostly single-
-floored rectangular constructions about 12 m by 6 m in size, made
out of wood, with walls of wattle and daub: that is to say, a weave
of thin branches coated in a mix of sand, soil, clay and dung, which
would then harden in place.[39] In *Lundenwic*, this seems generally to
have been left plain – not whitewashed or decorated. Floors were
usually made of dirt. Roofs were pitched and with gable ends, either
thatched or shingled. The whole result would probably have resem-
bled cabins made up to look like cottages. Its atmosphere might have
been described as both bustling and austere.

At first there was room for relatively generous space around and
between the buildings of *Lundenwic*, but as the town ballooned in
the late seventh and early eighth centuries those gaps were quickly
filled up.[40] Although the buildings were (at least for the most part)
single-storey and small, there were a great many of them and they
were tightly packed together in central parts of the town, thinning out
towards its edge. The Anglo-Saxons were well aware of the practical
obstacles and risks to which unfettered building in this way might
lead. At Canterbury in the ninth century, there was a mandatory
width of 2 ft required between buildings for eavesdrip.[41] In London,
what ensued was a mesh of small alleyways weaving outwards from
a few main roads. The Covent Garden site passed over one such
arterial road: it was well maintained, frequently resurfaced, and with
wood-lined drains along its sides. This road does not match the line
of any surviving street, but ran north–south. The Strand and Drury
Lane may be survivors of other main thoroughfares of *Lundenwic*.[42]

The buildings that lined these roads included many houses as
well as workshops; the two would often have been synonymous,
with different parts of the same building dedicated to different uses.
Families or trades along the lines of 'Tatberht & Sons Blacksmiths, of
Lundenwic' sometimes kept up business in the same premises across
generations. The range of those trades was highly diverse. In the core
part of the city there were signs of glassworking, tanning, bone-,
horn- and leather-working and carpentry, as well as the manufacture
of iron and other metal objects.[43] Further out, there are signs of less
dense building and more emphasis on farming and, in the south-
west of the town, quarrying.[44] Across the river in Bermondsey, iron

was being brought from some distance into the city to be worked.[45] Weaving was ubiquitous (and represented in the archaeological record mostly by loom weights), as it was widely practised in the home by women. Butchers were situated at several places across the city, furnishing early Londoners with their meat. They probably combined commercially driven operations with work for landowners who siphoned meat from rural to urban properties, to feed dependants who had no alternative.[46] For most, however, meat would have been a luxury: the bulk of the day-to-day diet was based on cereals such as wheat, barley, oats and rye. Bread, gruel and beer were common. When times were hard people could turn to eating bread or gruel made from acorns or hazelnuts. Better days might bring delicacies like grapes and figs. There is even a rare find from James Street of a group of eighth-century honeybees killed by fire, either in a house fire or as part of the destructive process used to harvest honey in the early Middle Ages.[47]

Such a dense concentration of people presented a sanitary and logistical challenge which Londoners of the eighth century were ill-equipped to cope with. *Lundenwic* was pockmarked with wells and cesspits for rubbish, sometimes dangerously close to each other. The first inhabitants of the town in the later seventh century had spread their rubbish on the open spaces between buildings, but fresh construction on top of these layers of waste put paid to that way of dealing with refuse. As the population rose and the need to dispose of human and industrial waste multiplied, the shortcomings of early medieval hygiene and construction would have become all too apparent. Early medieval London must have been a highly unhealthy place, filthy and squalid by modern standards. Its inhabitants would have suffered from the creeping presence of mice, rats and other vermin, as well as a contaminated water supply, resulting in widespread illness and parasitic infestations.[48]

Nonetheless, one of the most arresting objects found in *Lundenwic* brings its inhabitants to life through the detritus of their unsanitary living conditions. At one of the farms on the fringe of the settlement, discovered during excavations beneath the National Gallery, two men cut their names onto different sides of a sheep's vertebra. They used runes to do so: the alphabet created by Germanic-speaking peoples of northern Europe as an alternative to Roman script. One of the men, Tatberht, carved boldly and clearly, sometimes deliberately making two cuts per line (rather than the customary single cut) to leave his name standing out all the more prominently. The other's name is not quite so easy to divine, for it is probably abbreviated: all one can see is 'Dric', which, if we expand the first character to the full name of the runic letter (*daeg*), may be short for Dægric. Dægric was not quite as adept a runesmith as Tatberht: his work was rougher, 'as if made with a hunter blade', in the judgement of the runic scholar Ray Page. Why would these two men have scratched their names onto this piece of cooked bone? It certainly would not have been well suited to a functional or display role. Page's suggestion is that Dægric and Tatberht indulged in a bit of after-dinner fun, the latter showing off his more polished technique, the former his knowledge of the deeper meanings of individual runes.[49] It might equally have been done in an educational context: perhaps a father showing his son how to spell out his name, as a new community evolved on the banks of the Thames.

The Genesis of Lundenwic

In the Roman period, the site of *Lundenwic* had been open land beyond the marshes that lay outside the walls, not a major concentration of population. The settlement's origins remain shadowy. Scattered rural settlements of the sixth and earlier seventh centuries have been uncovered at Clerkenwell and Long Acre,[50] but there was also probably settlement on the riverbank heart of the later town, as yet only hinted at by a ring of cemeteries that date back to the late sixth century.[51] The earliest of these was found beneath the London Transport Museum, while another, larger burial ground has been identified at St Martin-in-the-Fields, on the same site as the very late Roman burials discussed in Chapter 1. The Transport Museum burials contained the remains of men and women whose corpses had been either cremated or buried, often with a range of grave goods that hint at unusually extensive long-distance contacts. Brooches, ornaments, pots and weapons have all been found; one of those from Covent Garden is a spectacular gold disc-brooch, dating to the mid-seventh

Figure 4.3. A treasure from the beginning of *Lundenwic*: a mid-seventh-century gold and garnet brooch, excavated in cemetery on the site of Covent Garden (Museum of London).

century (Figure 4.3). When they were disturbed in the 1720s, the burials at St Martin-in-the-Fields even produced a pair of beautiful glass goblets made in the Rhineland during the seventh century.[52]

The formation of a more substantial town, when it came, was swift, and left the earlier settlement submerged in its wake. In the 670s, the modest initial stages of development at London were overtaken. A larger, more elaborate settlement was laid out and grew quickly, while the shoreline was reinforced. Wood from revetments used to shore up the waterfront at what is now Buckingham Street was cut down in the year 672.[53] The cemetery at Covent Garden was forgotten and built over before the end of the seventh century, in the course of rapid expansion. A range of texts from about the same time shed light on the transforming town from a different direction, as surrounding kings and élites started to take a more direct interest in *Lundenwic*.[54] There are the laws of Hlothhere and Eadric mentioned in Chapter 3, and around the same time the charter of Frithuwald from Chertsey (dating to 672×675) gave the bishop a plot of land next to what the charter calls the 'port of London' (*portem Londonie*), 'where the boats land on that river, towards the southern side, beside the public road (*uiam publicam*)'. Although it sounds detailed, this description leaves a number of possibilities open for where the new *portem* actually was. The best guess now is that the bishop received a large estate in Lambeth, with the 'public road' being an old Roman road that ran from Westminster to Lambeth and thence to Southwark.[55] Another abbey founded by the same bishop at Barking also received land at Battersea and near the *wic* of London (*supra vicum Londoniae*), formerly owned by a queen, as part of a series of properties acquired in the 680s.[56]

This bustling new *emporium* has sometimes been seen as a product of the scramble for *Lundenwic* among major kingdoms of the later seventh century: the brainchild of a builder-king who recognised the potential of the existing settlement, put it on a sounder footing and brought in new settlers. Kings have often been identified as founder figures of England's major *emporia*;[57] Wulfhere, king of the Mercians, is the favourite candidate in the case of *Lundenwic*.[58] He and others stood to gain significantly from trading centres of this kind. In 808 Godofrid, king of the Danes, sacked an *emporium* on the shores of the Baltic named Reric, and brought its merchants to a comparable centre under his authority at Hedeby. He did this, according to the *Frankish Royal Annals*, 'because of the taxes it paid [which were] of great advantage to his kingdom'.[59] But there is one important difference between Wulfhere and his counterpart in Denmark more than a century later: Godofrid operated in a world where *emporia* and trading settlements were well established and integrated into the machinery of royal power; this was not the case in England in the 670s. It was much more of a challenge to will a large number of traders and craftsmen into being. While Godofrid transplanted a pre-existing mercantile community, the founder of *Lundenwic* would have had to build almost from scratch not just its houses and streets, but a large part of its population. This was a very different proposition – and in any case there were other players to take into account besides kings.

Early medieval traders are now thought of as relatively autonomous agents: savvy boatmen whose success stemmed from intimate knowledge of the coastal regions fringing the North Sea.[60] From about the year 600, the coastal regions of eastern England, northern France and the Low Countries gave rise to a vigorous seagoing society. London was at the forefront of this new brand of trading association. The Rhenish glasses and other exotic goods found at St Martin-in-the-Fields reflect a community of traders who had set down roots at an opportune spot in the landscape. The merchants of early *Lundenwic* and their partners around the shores of the North Sea had several things going for them. They typically occupied the periphery of contemporary kingdoms, resulting in limited demands being placed on them by their rulers. Access to major rivers and the sea also meant that they could establish connections in distant locations and enjoy relatively easy access to imported goods, and thus act as middlemen, selling on imported goods to local élites.[61] London and its counterparts acted as staging posts in this trading network, which was the creation of enterprising merchants rather than kings.[62]

Lundenwic therefore was, at the time of the first written references in the 670s, an organic growth established by canny settlers who sought to take advantage of a promising location and favourable economic conditions. The earliest stages of the *emporia* are thought to be the result of their initiative. Even the orderly layout of trading towns, sometimes seen as a hallmark of top-down organisation, could equally result from strong property rights or a robust communal infrastructure.[63] Instead of Reric in the Baltic, a better parallel to *Lundenwic* might be found in the Adriatic. Venice, *la Serenissima*, sails into the historical and archaeological spotlight in the eighth century. There is no indication that kings or emperors had played any direct part in its formation as a major settlement. It was the product of seagoing merchants, and had much in common with seventh-century London. Venice sat in an even more watery location, on a cluster of islands in a brackish lagoon. This gave it unfettered access to the sea, and to the goods that could be brought in by ship, but it was also well situated to take advantage of inland routes by road and especially the Po river. Also like London, it sat on a political fault-line. Venice traditionally moved in the Byzantine political orbit, but was close to the mainland that lay under Lombard and later Frankish dominion.[64] In the later seventh century, the twisting kaleidoscope of Anglo-Saxon politics combined with London's high degree of connectivity by sea, river and road to put the town in an even stronger position than Venice. A symbiotic relationship took shape between *Lundenwic* and the surrounding political entities.

Bede's famous description of London as an 'emporium of many nations' encapsulates one of the main reasons for its success. The town was far from a monopolistic royal enclave; rather, London flourished precisely because it lay at the intersection of so many spheres of interest. It profited from how important it *wasn't*, at least as a power base in its own right. As the East Saxons were politically overshadowed,[65] London found itself central to no major kingdom but on the periphery of many, which in trading terms was a positive boon, as was its accessibility from several directions. It was well situated on the Thames to serve both riverine traffic deep into southern England and international travellers heading in from or out to the North Sea. It additionally benefited from overland connections to various centres north and (after a ferry crossing over the Thames) south.[66] Bede himself was an indirect beneficiary of London's connectivity. One of his key sources, gratefully acknowledged in the preface to the *Ecclesiastical History*, was Nothhelm, 'a godly priest of the church of London'.[67] Nothhelm had put Bede in touch with various figures in the south, including Albinus, abbot of St Augustine's in Canterbury: a critical source for Bede's knowledge of Kent's place in the conversion story of England. Nothhelm went above and beyond the call of duty in travelling north to share with Bede a remarkable set of letters relating to the pioneer days of the English mission, which he had found in the papal archives at Rome. Bede's glowing endorsement of London's status may well have owed something to what he learned from Nothhelm, and the success the Londoner evidently enjoyed in gathering information. In an important sense, Nothhelm and his formidable range of contacts helped make Bede's history the gold mine that it is.[68]

Nothhelm's effectiveness in what would now be called networking was founded on the frequent comings and goings of a dynamic community of merchants and craftsmen, who were naturally drawn to places like London which offered a good outlook for sustained demand and limited interference.[69] From a base on the Strand, they could tap into multiple seams of élite demand: those of the East Saxons on their doorstep, Kent to the south-east, Wessex to the west and Mercia to the north-west. There may well have been a growing groundswell of smaller-scale custom as well, founded on lesser landowners and even peasants. It was a return to the nexus of polyfocal demand and strong overseas trade that had made *Londinium* so successful in the first century A D.[70]

Trading activity at London resulted in an increased flow of goods, which attracted the attention of kings, which in turn reinforced demand for further trade and craft. Having tasted the nectar, rulers sought to reap the fruit as the new *emporium* blossomed. As we know, the kings of both the Mercians and of Kent, as well as the local East Saxons, had some stake in London during the 670s and 680s. However, possession of overall supremacy probably did not mean cutting off the interests of other kingdoms. There is little doubt that Mercia was the leading power in the London area from about 670, but this did not preclude the king of Kent having a hall in which to protect his interests and those of his subjects. Keeping the city open, and trade flowing, was what swelled royal income and facilitated access to prestige goods: kings thus worked with, not against, existing trading interests.[71] Any input from Wulfhere or other kings would have been geared towards making *Lundenwic* welcoming to all comers, so as to be more lucrative for the dominant power that could cream off the profits.[72]

The Growth of Lundenwic

The heyday of *Lundenwic* came between the last decades of the seventh century and about 730 or 740, coinciding almost exactly with the adulthood of the Venerable Bede: a time of economic growth and cultural dynamism across England and beyond. If *Lundenwic*'s growth around the 670s benefited from a moment of political equilibrium, during which a new Mercian hegemony was becoming established in the south-east, its prosperity in subsequent decades was secured by an increasing measure of stability in southern England. Trading towns were always vulnerable to sudden jolts in supply and demand: they depended on fortuitous alignments of communication and élite wealth. Any adjustment to these could generate far-reaching economic shockwaves.[73] For *Lundenwic* to survive and prosper, stability, or at least a sequence of favourable economic configurations, was needed.

The crystallisation of Mercian authority and the detachment of Middlesex went some way towards providing a safety net for the sustained growth of the *emporium*. Thus it remained an open town, where Kentish abbots as well as Mercian bishops could still have trading interests in the eighth century.[74]

The town would not, however, have looked very familiar to modern eyes. Indeed, it would have left a lot to be desired, relative to either its modern descendant or even the Roman city further east. *Lundenwic* was a functional, no-nonsense kind of place. As far as can be seen from surviving texts and excavations, it had no monuments or public buildings, unless one counts the beach market and potentially other market sites elsewhere in the town, though even these have as yet proven elusive.[75] Neither were there any churches (or at least none definitively identified),[76] though that is not so surprising: the age of *Lundenwic* came long before the proliferation of small, local churches in either town or countryside. Responsibility for ministering to the religious needs of the Anglo-Saxons in the seventh and eighth centuries instead lay with a smaller number of minsters. St Paul's would have been one, possibly with others at Westminster and Bermondsey, and others could also have shared responsibility for *Lundenwic*.[77]

Evidence of London's economic importance in the later seventh and eighth centuries is abundant. It was in this period that *Lundenwic* diversified from its commercial roots to host craftsmen of many kinds.[78] In these terms, *Lundenwic* was not so dissimilar from later medieval towns as is sometimes thought: it combined craft and exchange functions, and was tied into local as well as long-distance trade. As the town became more established its trading horizons widened commensurately. More trades started to be practised, and output and circulation of coin attributable to London spiked. The point of departure is Bede's famous description of London, which hints at its in-betweenness: the 'many nations (*multorum populorum*)' who frequented it were probably not (or not just) different peoples of northern Europe, but the diverse peoples of England. Traces of how these contacts developed can, for example, be seen in the pottery uncovered at *Lundenwic* from this era. The thousands of pots and potsherds include many from south-east England: types tempered with small pieces of shell that could have been made in Essex or Kent.

At its peak in the early to mid-eighth century, *Lundenwic* also saw widespread use of what is known as Ipswich ware – a form of pottery made in Ipswich, and which is important in Anglo-Saxon England for being the first mass-produced ceramic in the country, with the most widespread distribution seen in England up to that time.[79] More local forms of pottery made a comeback in the later phases on *Lundenwic*'s history,[80] while just over an eighth of the ceramics from London came from outside England: from northern France, the Rhineland and the Meuse valley.[81] The Covent Garden site was also littered with chips from quernstones (millstones), used in grinding grain, which in the eighth century were made and distributed from the Eifel region of Germany, notable for unusual geology that made its stone especially well suited to this purpose.[82]

Lundenwic is usually, and rightly, thought of as a place primarily focused on exchange, but it was also a site of production – mostly of worked goods made from raw materials – and to some extent of consumption. Its people needed to eat, drink, build and spend. While the distance over which large-scale exchange was viable extended further and further, production and consumption depended on the infrastructure closer to home. London's hinterland within England possibly stretched in two directions: northwards to Cambridge and the fenland, and west up the Thames valley into Mercia.[83] From these areas food and raw material flowed into the town. What flowed back is less clear – the imported goods found in London are not generally seen at nearby rural sites, and on the basis of coin-finds it appears that *Lundenwic* was actively sucking up some of the business that had once gone on at smaller centres in the vicinity.[84] The town comes across as a taker of local resources, and a giver only for a more select clientele.

It is probably no coincidence that ways of handling production were also in a state of transformation in the late seventh and eighth centuries. *Lundenwic* developed at a time when settlements across the eastern English countryside entered what is known as the 'Middle Saxon Shuffle': a sort of dance in which rural habitations relocated to sites that were better from an agricultural point of view.[85] The point was to get more out of the surrounding land, in order to have more to give the landlord and perhaps to sell at markets. At London, food probably came from a mix of very local sources (*Lundenwic* thinned out to farms on its fringes) and some from further afield, including oysters from the Suffolk coast.[86]

It is thought that the same élites – churches and secular land-owners as well as kings – who benefited from the towns were also responsible for reorganising their lands for greater productivity. Some of the food consumed in London was probably sourced, via patterns of trade and tribute, from élite landholding;[87] these may have been associated with the properties held in the city by landowners. In other words, élites were involved with both ends of the process: enhancing production of food and animal goods, and patronising the town craftsmen and traders who could transform or exchange those goods.

Elites probably also had a strong part to play in the middle part of the story that brought rural goods and people into the sphere of commercial trade. There are dozens of rural sites – known to modern scholarship by the rather vague term 'productive sites' – which show evidence for heavy use of coin and sometimes other goods suggestive of trade. Some of these were adjacent to known minsters, like East Tilbury on the Thames east of London, while others were royal or aristocratic, such as Rendlesham in Suffolk, which Bede described as a 'royal estate' (vicus regius).[88] These places may have served as intermediate points of contact between the large trading towns and the mass of rural communities, churches and lords.[89] On both sides of the North Sea, there were in addition many coastal settlements that served as stopping-places en route to larger centres or as secondary points for redistribution. Although much more obscure, these con-tributed significantly to the brisk business of eighth-century trade. A good example is Sandtun, Kent: a landing-place near a Roman road which served as one of many small ports dotted around the Kentish coast.[90] It was through places like Sandtun that London was plumbed into southern England's agricultural richness.

Lundenwic *and Northern Europe*

As well as being a hub for trade within England, London served as one of the main intermediaries between the Anglo-Saxon kingdoms and the rest of northern Europe, resuming in new guise the role it had played under Roman rule. In the seventh and eighth centuries, however, the mighty Roman state was no more, and the driving force behind London's trade was a varied and fragile web spun across England. Kings and other élites from various kingdoms played a large part, but so too did a dense undergrowth of lesser patrons; collectively they were able to support bulk trade over long distances.[91] Some of these smaller trips are described in the life of St Boniface, a cleric from Devon originally named Wynfrith, who became a leading figure in the mission to Germany. This text tells of how in the early years of the eighth century Boniface journeyed from Wessex to 'a place where there was a market of merchandise' called 'Lundenwich', so that he could find a ship heading for Dorestad: another major trading port situated close to modern Utrecht. Soon after returning home Boniface resolved to go on another long journey, but again his route took him through *Lundenwic* and onto a small ship that conveyed him to Quentovic, another important link in the network of North Sea trade situated near what is now Boulogne in France on the river Canche.[92] Boniface's purpose on his first trip was to bring the good news of Christianity to the people of Frisia (though in the event his trip was frustrated by political upsets), while on his second the ultimate destination was Rome. In both cases he was able to take advantage of a ship that was evidently already planning to make for other ports as part of a brisk trade into and out of London.

The network of coastal trading towns that underpinned this trade has come sharply into focus since the 1980s, through the combined efforts of archaeologists and historians.[93] *Emporia* rimmed the North Sea and the English Channel between the seventh and ninth centuries, and it is also now recognised that similar ports were growing up in the Adriatic at Venice and Comacchio during the latter part of the same period.[94] These towns constituted a new kind of settlement in early medieval Europe. As we have seen with Venice, common characteristics include a coastal location (or on a river with good access to the sea) and a prominent role in the making and redistributing of goods, as well as the same lack of churches, monuments and public spaces noted in *Lundenwic*. Dorestad and Quentovic were two of the principal centres, the former being especially well known thanks to extensive archaeological excavations;[95] other important sites in mainland

Europe include Rouen in France, Domburg in the Netherlands and Ribe in Denmark. In England, the main examples besides London are Southampton, Ipswich and York.[96] While sharing points of contact, each of these towns had its own distinct flavour and history, and needs to be viewed as a locally specific development as well as part of a broader phenomenon. London was the biggest in England and may have experienced the largest, fastest leap in expansion, whereas Ipswich had the strongest – or at least most clearly identifiable – local industry in the form of Ipswich ware pottery. Across the Channel, Dorestad and Quentovic both flourished for longer than their English neighbours, though the latter was significantly smaller in the eighth and early ninth centuries.[97]

These towns need to be kept in perspective and did not exist in splendid isolation. During its growth spurts, *Lundenwic* would have attracted incomers from neighbouring parts of southern England and beyond. Reliable traffic in people bearing commodities constituted the lifeblood of the early medieval exchange economy, and it was on the strength of such connections that London formed part of the top rung of trading centres; it was one of the places one went for specialised goods, or perhaps to buy and sell in bulk when more local options were not sufficient. Application of cutting-edge network analysis techniques has shown how in Viking-Age Scandinavia exchange of this kind was at the same time both glaringly simple and blindingly sophisticated. Individual traders plying long-distance routes from (say) Hedeby in Denmark to the Norwegian town of Kaupang would rely on familiar paths and stopping-places, doubtless knowing every point along the way in intimate detail. This is why there are so many of the same commodities found only at widely separated but large ports. Similar but increasingly localised networks then helped goods to get from places like Kaupang out to the rural population. They would be taken from there to local centres of redistribution, and so on down to farms and settlements across Scandinavia.[98]

No similar study has been carried out on *Lundenwic* and the trading network of the seventh- and eighth-century North Sea, but a larger version of this same mechanism was probably at work. In the absence of formal structures for commerce that reached between kingdoms and over seas, movements of people were of critical importance.

Contacts built over handshakes and drinks were the bread and butter of successful trade, then as now, and the livelihood of merchants depended on them. Indeed, in the suspicious world of the early Middle Ages, acquaintances in key ports were a valuable commodity. Anyone who was not a friend or family member would have been treated with a certain amount of caution, verging on hostility. This was a society in which multiple kingdoms shared a law that travellers off the main roads needed to advertise their presence by shouting or sounding a horn, or else be treated as a thief.[99] The poem *Beowulf*, which some believe to have originated around this time, recounts how the eponymous hero had to introduce himself three times to progressively more important authorities after landing in a new kingdom.[100] Unfamiliar faces in London from Kent, Essex or further up the Thames valley would be treated with just as much wariness as those from further afield, but the corollary of this is that established friends from near or far played a central part in the new community as it took shape.

Of Ships and Coins

Lundenwic was, therefore, one link in a chain stretching across the Channel and the North Sea. It is illuminated by many sources, but two in particular stand out: a series of documents that records the exemption from toll of ships landing at the town; and coins made or found in London. Both these shed a special light on the nature of the town.

The ship charters are a group of ten records from eighth-century England, which convey to the recipient exemption from the tolls normally demanded by the king's representatives from each newly arrived ship.[101] What these documents contain can be illustrated by a grant made by Æthelbald, king of the Mercians (716–57), in the city of London itself to the abbess of Minster-in-Thanet in 748. The text, however, only survives in a copy made in the early 1400s at St Augustine's Abbey in Canterbury (which later absorbed the defunct Minster-in-Thanet's properties),[102] by a monk named Thomas Elmham. This is by no means unusual: just a small minority of

Anglo-Saxon charters survive in their original form as a loose piece of parchment. There is, therefore, an inevitable risk that the surviving text has been altered in the course of transmission, but there is more reason to be confident about this charter than many others. Elmham was an obsessive and passionate devotee of his monastery's history, and copied its records into his book with a remarkable degree of care. He even drew reproductions of some of the earliest Anglo-Saxon charters, as well as a map of the Isle of Thanet and a plan of the main altar. Alas, it was such an ambitious work that Elmham never completed it.[103]

The charter in question states that Æthelbald grants to the abbess, named Eadburh, exemption from half of the toll due on a ship that she had recently bought from a man named Leubucus (probably a Frank). Æthelbald then states that he has done so in hope of divine remuneration and for love of the patron saint of Eadburh's monastery, St Mildrith. He commands all his 'magnates, ealdormen, companions, tax gatherers, agents and other public officials' to respect his grant, and adds that the exemption may be passed on to another ship should the current one be lost to shipwreck or decay. This is significant, for it shows that the grant was vested in a specific ship, which was presumably marked out in some way.[104] Finally, the king stipulates that anyone who infringes on the charter in subsequent times will be subject to divine wrath. There follow details of the date and location of the grant, and a list of the key figures who witnessed it.[105]

It is never actually stated where the toll was supposed to apply, but because the charter was issued in London, that is the most likely place for a ship flying the colours of St Mildrith to have exercised this privilege. It would fit in well with the other documents of this kind. Five do say explicitly that the ships they cover were exempt from tolls in London, while two relate to the whole realm of the Mercians (which extended far beyond the west midland core of Mercia), and two confer exemption from tolls due at the Kentish ports of Fordwich and Sarre.

What is even more striking is the range of parties who had an interest in London.[106] As is common with Anglo-Saxon charters of this period, the ship charters are all in favour of bishops, abbots, abbesses and the church institutions they represented. Among those with a stake in London's trade are the abbess of Minster-in-Thanet, one of the many rich monastic houses in Kent, but apparently one of the most persistent and successful in securing exemptions for its ships: half of the surviving corpus of ship charters derives from Minster.[107] Also in Kent, the bishop of Rochester received a charter for one ship in London.[108] At London itself, the local Bishop Ingwald was the beneficiary of two ship charters.[109] Further afield, the bishop of Worcester also obtained a charter exempting two of his ships from toll in London.[110]

Evidently bishops and monasteries across England had active commercial interests in eighth-century London. Some also possessed plots of land in or close to *Lundenwic*: in addition to bishops of the more local Barking and Chertsey, the bishops of Hereford and Worcester are also known to have done so.[111] The former owned land at Fulham which was sold to the bishop of London in the 700s,[112] while the latter received an urban property in London from Æthelbald, situated between two streets named *Tiddbertistret* and *Sauinstret*.[113] More surprisingly, the abbey of St Denis just north of Paris (now home to the Stade de France) also possessed a charter laying claim to land 'in the port which is called *Lundenuuic*', bequeathed to it by two brothers named Agonawala and Sigrinus who had died in London. There are reasons to be cautious about accepting this document as genuine in every detail, but if broadly reliable it adds a fascinating international dimension to the story.[114] The charters documenting these interests on land and sea provide some of the best evidence for just how important London was in the movement of goods at this time. Its markets were called on by diverse authorities, including institutions as far away as Worcester. On the basis of the ship charters, London exercised impressively wide-ranging appeal. It comes across as the dominant trading centre for high-level business interests in the eighth century.

The evidence is of course open to other interpretations: it may simply be that King Æthelbald (by whom most of the ship charters were conceded) was open to negotiating a right that the rulers responsible for Ipswich and Southampton were not. His decision to grant exemption from toll in this way is in itself unusual. The ship charters represent a significant departure from the usual practice of Anglo-Saxon charters, which was for kings to grant rights over pieces of land. Kings did not give anything away lightly, and for exemption on toll to be bestowed in this way and written up in the same grand manner as charters conveying landed property, speaks volumes about the importance of trade to the recipient. The charters also indicate how desirable it was to escape the king's toll collectors. These officials must have been watching like hawks when any ships came to shore, ready to extract their due. The collectors' demands probably ran to 10 per cent, a common figure among the Anglo-Saxons' Frankish contemporaries; in addition, they sometimes reserved (for the king) the right to pre-emption, or first pick of whatever goods the traders had brought.[115]

Fortunately for the many other traders who hawked their wares on the beaches of *Lundenwic* only after paying a toll, the toll charters were a relatively short-lived phenomenon. Almost all date from between the 730s and 760s (most to the time of Æthelbald). A couple were renewed later, but on the basis of earlier grants. Their brief vogue may reflect a period in which Æthelbald chose to follow the lead of his Frankish counterparts, while his successors decided not to compromise this stream of income.[116] In this way, the ship charters illustrate the likelihood that kings were constantly adjusting their relationship with important, rich trading towns like *Lundenwic*.[117]

Something similar can be seen in the coinage of London in the age of *Lundenwic*. Coins seem to have been made at London from even before the boom years of the later seventh century. Some of the earliest pieces of coined money produced by the Anglo-Saxons in the first half of the seventh century include gold pieces inscribed with a more or less legible version of the word LONDVNIV (Figure 4.4).[118]

Figure 4.4. Gold shilling/*tremissis* minted in London in the early/mid-seventh century.

Some of these carry a striking image of a facing bust flanked by two crosses, which could represent one of the saints cultivated at St Paul's, or even one of the early bishops of London. Gold coins of this period were mostly very small, weighing less than a gram and a half. Nonetheless, they contained great value – something in the region of £200 or more in modern buying power each. Their probable Old English name, *scilling* (ancestor of the pre-decimal shilling), has etymological roots in the cutting up of precious metal; however, by the seventh century *scilling* probably denoted a gold coin modelled on the dominant denomination of Merovingian Gaul, the economic powerhouse of western Europe in the sixth and early seventh centuries. In turn, the Merovingians' main gold coin was derived from the *tremissis* of the later Roman Empire.

For London to be the source of such coins testifies to its concentration of wealth and power already at a very early stage. Even choosing to place the name of the mint on the coins points towards its prominent position: the only other place referred to explicitly on coins of this period was Canterbury. The two cities are both named on gold coins of Eadbald, king of Kent (616/17–40), who evidently held sway over London in the same way as his father Æthelberht, founder of St Paul's (Figure 4.5).[119]

Figure 4.5. Gold shilling/*tremissis* of Eadbald, king of Kent (616–40), minted in London.

London was again referred to directly in the inscription placed on a group of silver pennies made around the 720s, with the words DE LVNDONIA. These were probably issued under the authority of an ecclesiastical patron, for on the other side they carry the word S[*an*] C[*t*]ORVM, 'of the saints' (Figure 4.6).[120]

Figure 4.6. Early penny/*sceat* minted in London.

Other coins of approximately the same period carry a more man-gled form of the mint-name and may or may not actually come from London,[121] which was indeed the only mint ever named on the small, thick silver pennies produced in England between about the 670s and the 750s.[122] Subsequently, one of the bishops of London, Eadberht, active in the 770s and 780s, was named on coins that can safely be assigned to London (possibly minted near St Paul's, within the walled city), and in the 800s one of the most dramatic Anglo-Saxon coin-finds of recent times brings to life the later years of *Lundenwic*. In 2001 a gold coin was unearthed in Biggleswade, Bedfordshire, bearing the name of Coenwulf, king of the Mercians (796–821); finding any Anglo-Saxon coin is interesting, but this one is of exceptional rarity. It belongs to an era when the standard currency consisted of silver pennies, and indeed the gold coin is similar in appearance to pennies of Coenwulf from about 805–10. There is a subtle difference on the obverse, which omits a circle dividing the bust from the outer letter-ing – a minor change, but enough to make it obvious to anyone in the know that this coin was not made from run-of-the-mill equipment. On the reverse, the usual inscription naming the maker of the coin has been replaced by DE VICO LVNDONIAE: 'from the *wic*/*vicus* of London' (Figure 4.7).

Gold coins at this time were prestigious and valuable, likely to be made at the express command of kings or other wealthy figures for specific purposes. Coenwulf could have had this coin made during one of his visits to London recorded occasionally in contempo-rary charters. These speak of the 'royal town of London' (*oppidum Lundaniae vicus*), 'royal estate of London' (*vicus regis* or *villa regalis*

Figure 4.7. Gold *mancus* of Coenwulf, king of the Mercians (796–821), minted in London *c*.805–10 (British Museum).

Lundoniae).[123] *Lundenwic* as a whole might have been in some sense a royal property or even a royal estate, or else the coin and charters might have referred to a part of the town belonging to the king.[124]

Unfortunately, the vast majority of Anglo-Saxon coins made before the tenth century carry no direct reference to where they were made. It is therefore likely that London contributed far more to the pool of Anglo-Saxon currency in the seventh and eighth centuries than is evident just from the coins with actual mint-names. Around the same time that the town's growth took off and Ipswich ware started to circulate, the silver coinage also expanded rapidly to become a vast and complicated currency. Each one of the thousands now found, usually by metal-detector users, reflects a frustrated Anglo-Saxon who lost a valuable silver penny, probably in the course of handing his or her money over to someone else. Enough finds of this kind are now known that they offer a clue to the shape of the monetary economy as a whole.[125] The period of greatest growth and activity at *Lundenwic* in the first decades of the eighth century coincides with the peak in circulation of coin, as judged by the number of modern finds. The two developments are closely intertwined, as part of a circle of demand and supply centred increasingly on the *emporia*.[126] There is little doubt that London was a major contributor to this deluge of silver coin. Some of the largest coin issues of this period have been tentatively attributed to *Lundenwic*;[127] in fact, one of the more substantial buildings excavated in Covent Garden may have been an early eighth-century mint.[128] It was probably not, however, *the* mint. *Lundenwic* could easily have supported the simultaneous production of several different kinds of penny: early Anglo-Saxon coinage was enormously diverse – with over 600 identifiable issues during a period of about 75 years – and it is likely that minting was open to all kinds of individuals and institutions.[129]

It is also believed that London was a major contributor to the coinage of Offa and his Mercian successors into the ninth century. Assigning coins to a London origin is again difficult without mint-names, and rests on fine judgements of style and political background. The earliest coins of Coenwulf, for example, were made at a time when Kent and East Anglia were both outside his effective control, and so have traditionally been attributed to London as the main known town and mint-place still open to him. It follows that coins of a similar style made by moneyers who did not work for the Kentish or East Anglian rulers are also likely to have originated in London.[130] This process is far from watertight, and there may have been additional minor mints at work elsewhere in Mercia – though there is no question that London was one of the leading contributors to the currency throughout the seventh, eighth and ninth centuries.

Finds of coins in modern London reinforce the impression of a city awash with silver and gold. Those from before the ninth century are strongly clustered in the area of *Lundenwic*, rather than the City,[131] and when compared to other *emporia* the finds from London and its vicinity demonstrate how effective *Lundenwic* was at swallowing up some of the trade that had gone on in nearby areas during the eighth century.[132] Later in the eighth and ninth centuries, London remained a significant focal point in the circulation and production of coins, even though its star was no longer in the ascendant.

The Waning of Lundenwic

A series of sources report that London suffered from fires in 764, 798 and 801. Given its cramped, dirty houses, with fires often roaring in many of them for domestic or business purposes, it is a wonder that more are not recorded earlier. But the spate of conflagrations, and especially the pair that occurred in quick succession around 800, may have been one factor that contributed to London's rockier position in the later eighth and ninth centuries. From about this time it became a much smaller producer of coins for the Mercian kings, being significantly overshadowed by Canterbury.[133]

Other symptoms of difficulty can be seen in the archaeological record. The Covent Garden site seems to have remained vibrant for longer than many other parts of *Lundenwic*, perhaps because it was so central: it prospered until about 770, and was used into the ninth century.[134] Elsewhere, there are signs that from the mid-eighth century fewer new buildings were being erected, at least outside the core of the settlement, and peripheral sites started to be abandoned.[135] At some point in the ninth century, a large ditch cut through the now more thinly settled Covent Garden site. Elements of the same or another ditch have been uncovered at other nearby excavations. It could have been either a boundary or a defensive structure, or indeed both; either way, it appears to have enclosed a much reduced area.[136]

Overall there is little doubt that late eighth- and ninth-century *Lundenwic* was very different to the city of a century earlier. But it is more helpful to think in terms of change than decline. There is plentiful evidence that *Lundenwic* remained a going concern well into the ninth century. Later archaeological layers belonging to this period are more prone to obliteration by later activity, so may be under-represented, and the increasingly scattered traces of late eighth- and ninth-century habitation could hint at a more dispersed, polyfocal settlement.[137] Metalworking continued apace at James Street,[138] and a high-status site dating to the later eighth and ninth centuries was found underneath the Treasury building on Downing Street in Westminster during the 1960s, with an ornate sword of similar date coming to light beneath the House of Lords in 1948.[139] Nonetheless, the lights seem to have effectively gone out in the former area of *Lundenwic* after the mid-ninth century. A bishop of Worcester who acquired property *in vico Lundonie* in 857 apparently took possession of a piece of land immediately outside one of the western gates of the Roman city, well away from the nucleus of *Lundenwic*.[140] The first archaeological signals of renewed activity in the City begin in the mid-ninth century and pick up steam during the reign of Alfred the Great, setting London on a new trajectory.[141]

There was probably no one factor behind *Lundenwic's* slow demise after about 750. It coincides with a contraction in monetisation, hinting at London's dependence on relatively sophisticated, fluid aspects of the economy. In an important sense it may genuinely have been a boom town, with the remarkable period of activity in the generation either side of about 700 being the aberration in need of explanation. The onset of a more liquid economy, perhaps galvanised by the firmer establishment of the ecclesiastical infrastructure in the late seventh century, would have been an essential ingredient in the process that gave birth to *Lundenwic* and the other *emporia*.[142] Contraction in this sector of the economy in the mid-eighth century seems to have been largely restricted to England. Dorestad remained buoyant until after about 830, as vividly reflected in coin-finds.[143] These divergent fates perhaps stem from the setting of each town. London may have been more vulnerable to fluctuations in long-distance trade than some of its English or continental counterparts; as such, it was hit harder by a downturn in the flow of silver coin and associated goods, and left out for the count once viking raids destabilised North Sea and Channel trade.[144]

CHAPTER 5

Alfred the Great and the Vikings

The Royal Exchange, close to the Bank of England in the City of London, contains a wealth of cafés, restaurants and boutiques. This grand Victorian building has a rich heritage founded on wealth management on a larger scale. A commercial exchange (the first purpose-built one in England) has operated on the site since the time of Elizabeth I, and the current building housed Lloyd's insurance market for more than 150 years. As one of the premier locations in the Square Mile, the Royal Exchange was chosen in the 1890s as the venue for a set of murals celebrating the glorious past of the City of London. This enterprise began at a sensitive moment, when the ancient Corporation of London felt threatened by the new and energetic London County Council, which encircled it on all sides. Hence, artists working on the murals were encouraged to give prominence to officials of the urban administration, and to national heroes associated with the City. It was in this spirit that the artist Frank Salisbury (1874–1962) was commissioned by Viscount Wakefield (1859–1941), the colourful city father who had

Figure 5.1. Mural of Alfred the Great in the Royal Exchange, City of London, painted by Frank Salisbury.

made his fortune with the Wakefield Oil Company, now known as Castrol, to paint one of the murals.[1] The subject of Salisbury's mural, completed in 1912, was Alfred the Great supervising the restoration of London in 886 (Figure 5.1).

The king himself perches atop a great black horse, resplendent in a red cloak and white boots, both trimmed in gold. He has everything a red-blooded medieval warlord could hope for within arm's reach: shaggy-coated and heavily bearded warriors, hunting dogs, and a colourful assortment of banners. He is expounding boldly to a similarly well-attired man, Ealdorman Æthelred (imagined here as a predecessor to the City aldermen), who is in turn instructing an architect. The scroll the ealdorman holds, prominently inscribed LUNDEN, leaves the viewer in no doubt of what is going on or where, even if it gives the Anglo-Saxon architect relatively little to go on.

Everyone in England was seeking to claim Alfred for their own at this time, for all sorts of feats,[2] and it was his supposed refoundation of the city in 886 that struck the most resonant chord in London itself. Yet despite the vivid grandeur of Frank Salisbury's mural, the nature of the event it depicts is far from clear. By 886, Alfred – who had started out as king of the West Saxons in 871 – was claiming a larger role as 'ruler of all the Christians of the island of Britain, king of the Angles and Saxons'.[3] This acclamation comes from the opening of a remarkable text on a remarkable king: a biography of Alfred, written during his lifetime (early in the 890s) by a Welsh bishop named Asser (d.908/9). Asser was one of several foreign scholars assembled by Alfred to support a revival of scholarship and literacy in England. From a ninth-century outlook, this was a logical corollary to Alfred's efforts in fortification and warfare. It was not enough to have the earthly tools to win: one also needed to secure divine favour.[4] Consciousness of Alfred's new political position fed directly into this intellectual enterprise too, for great prominence was assigned to literature in the vernacular or, as Alfred himself put it in the preface to one translation of a Latin text, 'the language that we can all understand'.[5] Angelcynn, 'English-kind' or 'the English people', became a veritable buzzword in Old English writings from this time, one which tapped into a maturing, if still fuzzy, wider English identity – that is, embracing both Mercians and West Saxons – which was being solidified by confrontation with the vikings.[6]

According to both Asser and another historical record put together in Alfred's reign, the *Anglo-Saxon Chronicle*, the events at London in 886 constituted a turning point in the construction of this larger allegiance. What Alfred actually did for the City of London at this point is open to interpretation. As the *Chronicle* puts it, 'that same year King Alfred occupied (*gesette*) London; and all the English people that were not under subjection to the Danes submitted to him.'[7] The Old English word *gesette* permits several meanings, ranging from 'occupied' or even 'besieged' to 'restored', and if he did 'restore' the city, it is not clear whether this refers to walls, streets, buildings or jurisdiction.[8] Asser, using the *Chronicle* within a few years of these events, evidently understood it as 'restored' (*restauravit*), and added that Alfred 'made [the city] habitable again' (*habitabilem fecit*).[9] There is much less ambiguity about the events that immediately ensued. As Asser put it, 'all the Angles and Saxons – those who had formerly been scattered everywhere and were not in captivity with the vikings – turned willingly to Alfred and submitted themselves to his lordship'. One imagines a solemn oath, marked by all the fanfare and pomp a weary kingdom could muster.

Ceremonies of this kind, carefully choreographed to make a statement in terms of action, place and language, were popular in the ninth and tenth centuries. In 842 the brother-kings Charles the Bald and Louis the German, together with their armies, met at Strasbourg and swore oaths of mutual support, each king using the vernacular of his ally's soldiers – the forerunners of French and German respectively – to make his point as widely understood as possible.[10] In England, Alfred's grandson King Æthelstan (924–39) had a series of kings from Wales and north Britain submit to him in 927, at Eamont Bridge in Cumbria on the frontier of his expanding domain, while Alfred's great-grandson, Edgar (959–75), undertook a second coronation at Bath in 973 and subsequently had a coterie of seven or eight other kings row him down the Dee at the Roman city of Chester, while he himself guided the rudder.[11] Alfred's selection of London as the setting for formal recognition of his status reflects the same sensitivity to geography – location, location, location, as the mantra goes. London was a city with monumental Roman walls at the convergence of Britain's road network; it was also, historically, a frontier city between Mercia and the southern territories beholden to Wessex. Restoring it and hosting a deeply symbolic meeting there are both acts which underscore its high status in an enlarged kingdom.[12]

The ceremony and restoration that took place in 886 were the high points in a turbulent and critical phase in London's history. From an unprotected mass of craftsmen and traders in the eighth century, one of just a few of its kind, it had turned into a hotly contested and highly militarised fortress-city at the close of the ninth, a time when the urban landscape was becoming more crowded and complex. Now, the crucial change was a shift from *Lundenwic* back into the relative safety of the Roman walls. London was by no means the only town that underwent a transformation in Alfred's reign. Winchester in particular was also laid out afresh,[13] and Asser alluded to other towns and cities that were rebuilt or founded by Alfred.[14] These boroughs (Old English *burh, byrg*) were above all nodes in a larger military framework which had the capacity to shelter key administrative functions and the local populace;[15] just a few of them had a significant economic role at this stage.[16] In the preferred Old English terminology of the period, London went from being *Lunden, Lundenwic* or *Lundenceaster* to *Lundenburh*.[17] It inherited especially large and formidable defences, and even if it was no longer the economic powerhouse of the early eighth century, it remained significant throughout the ninth – and was vibrant enough that an impressively wide range of agencies wanted a stake in its prosperity during the time of Alfred. Those with interests in London extended from the king to Ealdorman Æthelred, the archbishop of Canterbury and the bishop of Worcester. They capitalised on the city's wide-ranging economic interests, as others had done a century earlier by means of ship charters for *Lundenwic*. A rich suite of texts, coins and archaeological excavations can be marshalled to illustrate this process of recovery. The city was set in a new direction by the events of Alfred's reign, and came out of them as the core of a great metropolis. All of this was accomplished in the teeth of raids, sieges and temporary takeover by Scandinavian raider-merchants: the vikings.

The City Before Alfred

As we have seen, from the mid-seventh century onwards London's centre of gravity had been situated west of the Roman city, in *Lundenwic*, and hardly anything is known about what was going on within the city walls. It seems to have been lightly settled, with most activity, or even tentative evidence for activity, concentrated in its western portion. Much of the area within the walls was probably given over to open land, pockmarked here and there with Roman ruins. Even these would have been relatively few, as most of the buildings of Roman London were made from perishable materials, so would have been long gone already by the seventh century. Yet, between the walls and other stone ruins, there was enough to make an impression. A profession of orthodoxy made by Helmstan, the bishop-elect of Winchester, to the archbishop of Canterbury at London in 838 or 839 resonates with the impact the city's Roman remains could leave on a visitor: it says that the profession was carried out 'in that famous place built by the skill of the ancient Romans and known commonly throughout all the spaces of the earth as the city of London'.[18] The city's population at this time has left only few and enigmatic traces, pointing to the walled city (or at least its edges) as a liminal zone where misfits and outcasts might sometimes be disposed of. A probably seventh- to ninth-century burial from Rangoon Street near the eastern wall contained two bodies in one grave, one on top of the other, the upper one hunched up to fit into the lap of the lower.[19] Just as arrestingly odd are a pair of interments that took place right on the waterfront at Bull Wharf at some point in (probably) the eighth century. The two bodies were treated in quite extraordinary ways. One – a small, middle-aged woman – was simply laid into a hole in the ground with no evidence of any artefacts or other furnishings at all: just a corpse in the damp earth. Nearby, and probably at the same time, another woman aged between about 28 and 40 who had been killed by a grievous blow to the head was laid out for death in a much more elaborate way. She was placed directly onto the shore, not into a grave, and wrapped in some kind of sheet or shroud, separated from the ground by a bed of reeds. Immediately above and beneath her were sheets of bark, which formed a kind of simple coffin, while bundles of moss were laid on her face, pelvis and knees. There may have been a mound and some posts marking the burial, later washed away. A cartwheel-shaped lead spindle or amulet lay nearby. What exactly these strange burials on the fringes of the city brought to mind for eighth-century Londoners can only be guessed at: one tempting possibility is that they represent the mortal remains of criminals or outcasts of some kind, buried in unusual fashion on the edge of the community.[20]

These bizarre and macabre remains hint at the marginal nature of the city in the eighth and earlier ninth centuries. It was a domain of antique power and, as a defended and still symbolically important edifice, what activity it did attract tended to be high-status. St Paul's had been founded in 604 on Ludgate Hill, and it was probably there that Helmstan pledged obedience to the archbishop. Indeed, the area around and especially to the immediate south of St Paul's has produced most of the (still fairly meagre) haul of archaeological material of pre-viking date in the City, which beyond casual and unstratified finds consists of potsherds and a few burials.[21] The hulking presence of Wren's cathedral, plus that of several later medieval incarnations of St Paul's, has obscured the earliest layers of the cathedral's archaeology. If any remains of Anglo-Saxon St Paul's do survive, they must lie buried underneath the current cathedral. The same goes for a series of nearby parish churches with dedications to saints that are characteristic of the early Anglo-Saxon period, and which have sometimes been assigned to the first centuries of the cathedral's existence.[22]

A case has sometimes been made for a royal palace in the northwest corner of the pre-viking city, in the neighbourhood of the former Roman fort. But no palace or other high-status settlement has ever been located archaeologically in this vicinity, and although it is tempting to think of the walls and watchtowers of the legionaries' fort as a base for later rulers, the fort would probably have been invisible above ground after the fifth century.[23] The existence of the Cripplegate palace thus depends entirely on later medieval and early modern assertions, and should be treated with caution.[24] The royal properties held by seventh-century Kentish kings and their eighth- and ninth-century Mercian counterparts were most likely situated elsewhere, quite probably in *Lundenwic*.[25] Wherever they lay, the upheaval that began in earnest in the ninth century with the advent of the vikings shook things up for good.

The Viking Threat

The vikings were seafaring raiders who preyed on England and the rest of northern Europe from the end of the eighth century onward. They came originally from Scandinavia, and travelled along routes established in earlier times through more peaceful contacts. What exactly prompted this surge of far-flung violence remains a matter of intense debate.[26] One possible explanation is that as more (and more desirable) forms of moveable wealth became available – gold, silver, slaves and more – a sort of economic arms race started within Scandinavia, which prompted those who felt that they could not keep up by means of the drip-feed of luxury goods back home to take them by force from others.[27] This ties in well with an important second dimension to the viking expansion: it was not solely a matter of 'smash and grab'. The raids themselves were carefully co-ordinated, and as time went on the Scandinavians abroad also created new communities and (peaceful) economic ties.[28] The very word 'viking', rarely used in the ninth century itself, probably designates an activity or profession (raider-trader) rather than an ethnicity, for which reason it is more accurate to think in terms of lower-case, often part-time vikings than dyed-in-the-wool Vikings who defined themselves through rampage and slaughter.[29] In northern England, these vikings settled down, mingled with the locals and left a lasting stamp on the place names and spoken language of the region, some of which has been transmitted into Modern English.[30]

In the ninth century, however, the violent face of the vikings was the most familiar one. It is quite possible that their depredations on ships and the commodities they carried had indirectly contributed to the contraction of *Lundenwic*, and there may well have been unrecorded raids in the early years of the ninth century.[31] But the first securely recorded viking presence in London was a 'great slaughter' inflicted on the city in 842.[32] Nine years later, in 851, the city was again laid waste by raiders who had passed the previous winter on the isle of Thanet.[33] But the most severe impact came with the appearance of what the *Anglo-Saxon Chronicle* calls the 'great army' which arrived in East Anglia in 865. This force would in time wipe out two Anglo-Saxon kingdoms altogether (East Anglia and Northumbria) and cripple a third (Mercia). As a mutual enemy, it also helped reinforce the alliance between Mercia and Wessex that had been budding since the 840s.[34] These kingdoms needed all the help they could get, for unlike other viking forces which had attacked in fairly short, sharp strikes, the 'great army' had longer-term ambitions and would remain active for decades, ranging far and wide across Britain. It was probably quite a heterogeneous entity, made up of numerous smaller bands who would come and go as circumstances dictated, and would have included warriors with years of campaigning experience on both sides of the Channel.[35] Wives, children and other hangers-on would have been part of the army while it was on the march.[36] In many respects it was far from what a modern observer would recognise as an army, and the word used for it in Old English (*here*) could also mean something like 'throng' or 'horde'.[37]

The 'great army' was nonetheless a lean and fast-moving entity. After spending time in East Anglia, Northumbria and eastern Mercia, it invaded Wessex in 871 and fought King Æthelred I (865–71) and his brother Alfred to a stalemate. Then, towards the end of the year, the force moved from Reading down the Thames to London, where it set up quarters for the winter and stayed until 872. The exact location of the viking camp at London has never been identified. A flavour of what it might have involved can be gained from Torksey in Lincolnshire, where the *Chronicle* says the army spent the winter of 873/4. Profuse finds have come to light in a group of fields beside the river Trent. Investigation by archaeologists has revealed that this was once an island in the river: a natural stronghold. The range of finds discovered here (of which many thousands are known in total) reflect a diverse range of activities. Coins from northern and southern England, together with hack-metal (cut-up pieces of silver objects) and silver dirhams (also usually cut up), imported all the way from the Muslim world through Russia and Scandinavia, reflect vibrant economic exchange. Metals were being melted down and remade. Hundreds of thimble-like lead objects tentatively identified as game pieces might indicate a victorious and well-supplied viking force spending its spare time playing or gambling.[38] At London, there is no clue to exactly where the vikings went. They may have stayed within or near the Roman walled city itself. One possible product of this visit is a hoard of coins and silver objects uncovered while building a railway line at Croydon in 1862. This parcel included some English coins of the form the locals might have been using in the early 870s, but it also contained continental European silver pieces, plus a few dirhams, ingots and pieces of hack-silver (Figure 5.2). On this basis, it has been convincingly identified as a viking hoard, put together by a member of the 'great army'. Its coins are compatible with a date in 871/2 when the vikings were encamped nearby at London.[39]

To defeat the vikings in the field and expel them by force of arms was no easy matter. Discretion often proved the better part of valour, and in 872 the Mercians adopted the time-honoured tactic of paying off the vikings. In the *Anglo-Saxon Chronicle* this is expressed somewhat elliptically, with the euphemism 'made peace with',[40] but a charter from Worcester may provide a glimpse behind the scenes of the carefully worded version of events in the *Chronicle*: it shows the bishop of Worcester leasing one of his estates to a layman in return for 20 gold pieces because of the 'very pressing affliction and immense tribute of the barbarians, in that same year when the pagans

Figure 5.2. Photograph of the Croydon Hoard, showing it on display in the window of a jeweller's shop shortly after its discovery in 1862.

stayed in London'.[41] It is possible that the detail about London is an embellishment added by an historically minded scribe as he copied this charter into the later manuscript in which it survives. But there is little reason to doubt the general impression it and other sources convey, that the pressure exerted by the vikings was driving the kingdom of the Mercians to desperate measures.

Kings and Coins in the 870s

The situation went from bad to worse in 874, when the vikings drove the ruler of the Mercians, Burgred, completely out of his kingdom. He was replaced with a man named Ceolwulf, decried in the *Anglo-Saxon Chronicle* as a 'foolish king's thegn [i.e. servant]',[42] although there is every indication that in the immediate context of the 870s he was (at least initially) a perfectly respectable king, who issued charters and coins in the same way as his predecessors and maintained the traditional alliance with Wessex.[43] Coins of these Mercian kings and of Alfred, including many probably minted at London, throw critical light on the rapidly shifting balance of power in the mid-870s. A decade earlier, Mercia and Wessex had formed a kind of Anglo-Saxon Eurozone, in which the same coinage was used by both kingdoms and their currencies were mutually interchangeable. The pennies known as the 'Lunettes' type, made between 871 and about 875 – Alfred's earliest years and Burgred's last – exemplify the dire straits the English found themselves in by that stage: their silver content was drastically cut and productivity cranked up, most likely in order to support action against the vikings and, possibly, for tribute (though the vikings themselves, who reckoned silver by purity and weight, would not have been impressed with the English coinage of the early 870s).[44] Coins of this era typically only carry two short inscriptions, one naming the king under whose authority the coin was issued, and the other naming the moneyer (or craftsman-official) responsible for production. Details such as where they were made, and when within a king's reign, depend on fine judgements of numismatic minutiae. London is generally thought to have been the primary mint-town for Mercia – at times possibly the only one – for much of the ninth century: after a dip in productivity during the early decades, London revived thanks to technical assistance from West Saxon-controlled Rochester in 845–50, and, during a much larger burst of minting in the 860s and 870s, it may have been the most active mint-place in southern Britain.[45] Productivity does not necessarily always mean prosperity, however; in the context of the mid-ninth century, it perhaps also meant desperation and pressure resulting from the viking presence.

From around the time of Burgred's departure there are signs in the coinage that something unusual was afoot in London. Already on a small scale in the time of Æthelred I, and then more commonly under Alfred, pennies of the 'Lunettes' type in a style normally associated with Burgred and London began to carry the name of the West Saxon king.[46] These reflect the marginal position London found itself in by the 860s and 870s. It was still nominally a Mercian city, but in practice had strong ties south of the Thames in West Saxon-controlled territory as well: the bishops of London had attended meetings of the West Saxon king (and not his Mercian counterpart) since at least 860.[47] Therefore, when Burgred abdicated in 874 the moneyers of London looked to Alfred as the most trustworthy authority on the scene. They produced multiple short-lived coinages in the mid-870s, as Alfred and Ceolwulf sought to restore higher standards of purity.[48] These new coins were experimental in several respects. One (made at London in the name of Alfred) departed from the traditional weight standard of Mercia and Wessex to adopt that of the Carolingian Empire, which covered much of western and central Europe. Another, issued for both kings, carried an elegant, Roman-inspired bust on one face, and on the other a representation of two emperors sitting side by side, again based on Roman precedents. An image of rulers working together in this way perhaps called to mind the position of Alfred and Ceolwulf, at this stage still very much collaborating,[49] although some specimens of the 'Two Emperors' coinage go a step further for Alfred and entitle him REX ANGLO[rum], king of the Angles/English, implying dominance over Mercia as well as Wessex. Another coin of the so-called 'Cross and Lozenge' type entitled Alfred REX S[axonum et] M[erciorum].[50] 'Cross and Lozenge' was the largest coinage of the period c.875–80. It includes numerous specimens of both Alfred and Ceolwulf, and was produced at multiple places including London, Canterbury and other locations in Mercia and Wessex. The changing balance of production at London is especially important. Alfred dominated the coinage in the early years of this issue, with the proportion minted in the name of Ceolwulf starting small but increasing during the issue's later stages.[51] All of these coins – previously very rare – have been thrown into the spotlight by the discovery of the Watlington Hoard of 2015. Part of the attraction of numismatic evidence is the way in which it continues to multiply and evolve, changing our perspective as new finds come to light. Most probably that perspective will change even further as the ramifications of this new hoard are worked out.[52]

This is one of the times when it pays to mind the pennies. The coins, more than any other available source, reveal the unique conditions that prevailed in London during the 870s. It was a city where regimes intermeshed in the shadow of the viking threat. In principle, though, it remained a Mercian city. London's moneyers continued to issue coins for Burgred and then Ceolwulf, although Alfred was by this stage the senior partner in the alliance and also had a stake in the city founded on long-standing West Saxon interests. On the ground, both kings must have had a measure of recognition and authority which played out in ways that can be traced only faintly through the coinage. Of course, some of the initiative may have been taken at a more local level, by powerful figures in or near London and by the moneyers themselves. The quick progression of the coinage might be more of a reaction than an imposition – a way for authorities in the city to frame their relationship with major powers of the day during uncertain times.

Between a Rock and a Hard Place: London, Alfred and the Vikings from c.880

Collectively, the coins build a strong case for London being a place at the heart of Mercian and West Saxon – as well as, increasingly, viking – interests during the 870s. The city had been occupied, probably temporarily, by the raiders in 871/2, and after the vikings appropriated the eastern part of Mercia in 877 and then retreated to East Anglia following their failed campaign in Wessex in 878, the Londoners would have found themselves dangerously close to a new frontier.[53] A treaty made between Alfred and Guthrum (d.890), one of the viking leaders, marked the boundary between their lands along the Thames and then up the Lea, which departed from the Thames at Bow Creek in what is now the Docklands: in other words, London was left within about three miles of viking territory.[54] Surviving copies of the treaty may stem from St Paul's – an institution with a strong vested interest in knowing how its diocese had been divided.[55]

This treaty probably only represents one stage of the rapidly shifting frontier between the Anglo-Saxons and vikings, but even if London was only temporarily in a front-line position, it was a key stronghold in the fight against the vikings, and possession of it was contested several times.[56] In addition to being taken in 871/2, London was the setting for a confrontation between the English and the vikings in 883.[57] The background to this action is obscure: even by the laconic standards of the *Anglo-Saxon Chronicle*, the 883 annal is terse and allusive – 'they [the English] opposed the [viking] army at London, and there, by the grace of God, their prayers were well answered after that promise'. Nothing is said here about where the vikings had come from, who led either side or what the outcome of the fighting was. It has often been interpreted as an attempt by the English to dislodge the vikings from London, after an occupation that could have begun in 872, or with the viking takeover of eastern Mercia in 877.[58] Other scholars have taken the fact that some manuscripts of the *Chronicle* lack the 883 annal as a signal that it has been miscopied (perhaps from 885 or 886) and assigned to the wrong year.[59] But there are equally good reasons to take it as a genuine account of events in 883, culminating in English victory.[60] Whether the English had to wrest it back from viking control following a long or short occupation, or (more probably) the vikings assaulted an English army, is not clear. The most likely reading is that the English had to fend off a viking assault on the city that they had held for most of the preceding decade. The real question is how London fitted into the large, conglomerate kingdom Alfred was putting together.

Numismatic evidence is again key in showing London's importance to Alfred at this time. A new and extremely elegant coinage was issued at London from around the year 880,[61] which unusually did away with the moneyer's name in favour of a newly conceived monogram for LVNDONIA. This occupied the reverse of each coin, while the obverse carried a new and attractive representation of Alfred in the likeness of a late Roman emperor, surrounded by his name and title (Figure 5.3).

Figure 5.3. Penny of Alfred the Great (871–99), minted in London *c.*880 (Fitzwilliam Museum, Cambridge).

These arrestingly attractive pennies are among the first of a new wave of currency in Alfred's last two decades which used a different, heavier weight standard. The London monogram issue is well known, thanks in large part to several hoards from London itself and the surrounding area, deposited in the 880s or soon after. Along with the Alfred Jewel – an inscribed gold and crystal object, tentatively identified as a pointer to help with the reading of manuscripts – the 'London Monogram' silver pennies are among the most iconic relics of the Alfredian era.

The events of 886 have been discussed already, but it should be emphasised that interest in London by no means came out of the blue. For generations London had been a meeting point for Mercian and West Saxon interests, and was most certainly central to Alfred's regime before 886. The upshot of that year, in political terms, was a realignment of its position that preserved the city's status as a point of crossover between Mercia and Wessex: London was entrusted to Ealdorman Æthelred, but under Alfred's overall suzerainty. This arrangement was only for Æthelred's lifetime. After his death in 911,

London (together with Oxford) was taken into the direct control of Edward the Elder (899–924), Alfred's son and heir as king. This shift does not seem to have left much of a mark on London, not least because already in the 890s the reorganisation and (possible) rebuilding had had a marked effect on the Londoners. The relative passivity of the 880s and before gave way to belligerence, a characteristic that would define London and its inhabitants for the rest of the Anglo-Saxon period. The Londoners were numerous and confident enough to be a significant force in Alfred's later campaigns against the vikings. In 893 the city served as a gathering-place for goods and captives taken from a viking fortress at Benfleet, stormed successfully by the English.[62] The Londoners had worse luck when they failed to take a fortress somewhere on the river Lea in 895, but later returned to seize or destroy the viking ships once the army itself had moved off.[63] As it was remade and tested in the closing decades of the ninth century, London gained a strong collective identity: something which had been distinctly lacking in dealings between *Lundenwic* and earlier rulers. The city had become an integral part of the new kingdom and its struggle against the enemy, all while 'restoration' within its walls continued.

Alfred's Restoration in Context

The well-known accounts of London's apparent restoration in 886 give the impression of a one-time event. In practice, Alfred's involvement with the city's revival seems to have been a much more prolonged process, rooted in developments that had begun long before he became king, and continuing well after 886.[64] Indeed, it is likely that some aspects of administration and government such as minting had either always been housed within the walls, or had started to move back inside them during the first half of the ninth century. One of the few mint-signed coins of the early ninth century was a penny produced during Ecgberht of Wessex's brief tenure as king of the Mercians (829–30); it carries the words LVNDONIA CIVIT[as], 'city of London', implying a location within the Roman walls (Figure 5.4).[65]

Figure 5.4. Silver penny of Ecgberht as king of the Mercians, minted in London 829–30 (British Museum).

Later, in the 870s, a lead weight stamped carefully with 'Cross and Lozenge' dies of Alfred, was lost in the vicinity of St Paul's, and found there in 1841. It might have been part of the equipment of a moneyer, trader or silversmith working near the cathedral (Figure 5.5).[66]

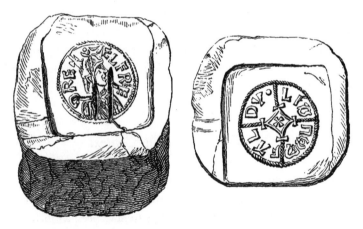

Figure 5.5. Lead weight (163.6 g) impressed with obverse and reverse dies of Alfred's 'Cross and Lozenge' coinage in the 870s (British Museum); the weight has deteriorated since it was found in the mid-nineteenth century, and is shown from an early drawing.

Reorientation of London's population away from *Lundenwic* and towards the walled city seems to have been ongoing in the mid-ninth century.[67] In 857, the bishop of Worcester was granted an urban estate – known locally as *Ceolmundingchaga*, 'the estate of the descendants of Ceolmund' – at London. The charter that records this gift appears to specify that the land was in *Lundenwic* (*in vico Lundonie*), but adds that it was 'not far from the west gate[s]'.[68] *Lundenwic* did not have a wall of its own, and its archaeologically attested remains would not fit very well with a description of being close to the Roman defences: *Lundenwic* seems to have extended no closer to the Roman wall than Lincoln's Inn Fields, about half a mile away. Hence *Ceolmundingchaga* probably lay close to the west gates of the Roman city (modern Ludgate Hill and Newgate), most likely immediately outside them.[69] Wherever it was, this property was apparently thriving, with active business going on around it: the charter presumes that trading profits were part and parcel of the deal, and assigns control over relevant weights and measures to the bishop.

The first physical traces of substantive settlement within the walled area also belong to the mid-ninth century. A set of fairly modest remains of waterfront building south-east of St Paul's at Bull Wharf (on the very site where the two women had been buried under such unusual circumstances half a century or more earlier) have been tentatively dated to the mid-ninth century on the strength of two Northumbrian coins of that date.[70] These finds point to the establishment of a beach market in the western part of the city, geared to meet river traffic coming down the Thames from inland, rather than foreign sea-traders coming up it.[71] The site remained in use under Alfred, producing no fewer than three coins of his reign.[72]

How development proceeded from this starting point is not easy to follow. The famous description in Asser and the *Anglo-Saxon Chronicle* of Alfred 'restoring' London in 886 probably overplays his role somewhat; there must have been a budding settlement in the city by that time, where coins of Alfred had been minted for many years already. Neither did Alfred's efforts result in the former Roman walls being filled with fresh urban sprawl. His restoration was probably intended first and foremost to nurture a node in regional trade and defence, not to revive *Lundenwic*'s long-distance exchange network.[73] The scale of the new settlement hence needs to be kept in perspective, and comes across as patchy to say the least. Its core was a rectangular block of about 300 m by 1000 m, roughly bounded by St Paul's, Cheapside and Old Billingsgate.[74] Even within this part of the City, only a few sites have produced archaeological evidence of

Alfredian-period activity. The genesis of a rough grid of streets can be detected, formed of short north–south routes extending down to the river from a few longer east–west roads (such as Cheapside). Two clusters of remains datable to the late ninth or early tenth century have been found: one in the west (including Bow Lane, Great Trinity Lane, 1 Poultry and Bull Wharf), and another in the east (Botolph Lane, Fish Street Hill and St Mary-at-Hill).[75] The latter could reflect an early effort to develop the bridgehead area, and possibly even London Bridge itself, although current evidence indicates that this was only rebuilt much later, around the year 1000.[76]

By Alfred's death in 899, London was evidently important and thriving compared to the other towns of England, but was still a long way from the economic and political supremacy it would enjoy in the late tenth and eleventh centuries. Two charters from Alfred's later years give a glimpse into how the town's revival was maintained.[77] These texts each record the grant of a *curtis* or *haga* (urban estate) to the bishop of Worcester and the archbishop of Canterbury, respectively. Dating from 889 and 898/9 respectively, they reveal how much work was still under way in the late 880s and 890s. The 898/9 document in particular speaks volumes. It states that it was drawn up as a result of a meeting concerning 'the restoration of the city of London' (*de instauratione urbis Lundonie*) held at Chelsea in either 898 or 899 between Alfred, Ealdorman Æthelred, the latter's wife Æthelflæd (Alfred's daughter) and the bishops of Canterbury and Worcester.[78] The bishops were of course major players in the city, and their holdings are early representatives of a pattern of large estates held in London by the élite, several more of which can be identified between the ninth and eleventh centuries.[79] The bishop of Worcester might have used such estates as an outlet for salt and other products made on his lands in the west midlands;[80] they could also have provided a place to stay when visiting the city, or produced income from being rented out.

The two charters describing the bishops' properties in London contain precise-seeming descriptions of their size and layout.[81] They were essentially city blocks, each described (perhaps loosely) as an acre in size. The 898/9 document situates both estates with reference to the Thames and a 'public street' (*uia publica*) which ran north–south between them, while the city walls bisected them east–west. It describes the location of these estates as Ætheredeshythe – Æthelred's hythe or landing-place – which later medieval sources in turn equate with Queenhythe:[82] the very area where waterfront excavations have found traces of Alfredian-period building. It is not clear whether the bishop of Worcester's land in this text was the same as that in the earlier charter of 889. The estate in the latter was situated around what the charter describes as an 'old stone building' (*antiquum petrosum ædificium*) – presumably a Roman ruin – named *Hwætmundes stane*, and extended up to a public road (*strata publica*) and the walls.[83] The river must have been adjacent too, as the bishop had rights to tolls on sales executed both in the street and on the 'mercantile rivershore' (*ripa emtorali*).

A picture of much more gradual change emerges from the charters and excavations of ninth-century London. There is no sign of a sudden burst of growth in the latter part of Alfred's reign, as might be expected had 886 brought a total rebirth. Clearly it was already by that date a significant community living in a key stronghold. It is possible that 886 was the occasion when Alfred laid out a new street plan.[84] He might also have repaired the walls and put in place new arrangements for mustering armies.[85] But the difficulty in pinning down the material impact of Alfred's 'restoration' probably stems from its being just one episode in a longer story.

Conclusion: London's Alfred[86]

Alfred has long held a special place in conceptions of the history of London. His restoration of the city in 886 has fascinated historians ever since the ninth century, and is tied closely to Alfred's role as the unifier of the English. For some observers it was essentially the city that made Alfred. As Roger of Wendover (d.1236) put it, London underpinned Alfred's claim to kingship of England, for it was by gaining the recognised capital of the English that Alfred affirmed his status.[87] This is anachronistic: London would not become anything approaching a capital until at least a century after Alfred's death, and although the meeting held there in 886 was important in framing Alfred's growing power, it was not conceived in the terms Roger thought.[88] Alfred's part in binding the stories of London and England together was nonetheless a snowball that would grow in size and momentum as it rolled through time. As Alfred's reputation flourished, and London became more central in the national life of England and (later) Britain, he was cast as a major contributor to the city's rising place in the national consciousness. Already at the end of the thirteenth century Alfred was thought to have held parliament in London twice a year, as effective founder of a key medieval English organ of government.[89] The king's decision to settle in London formed the climax of a massive 'epick' 1723 poem on Alfred by the physician Richard Blackmore (1654–1729), dedicated to Prince Frederick, eldest son of George II:

> And now attended with a noble Train
> The *British* Monarch from *Cunetio*'s Plain
> Did to the Banks of spreading *Thames* retreat,
> And made *Augusta* his imperial Seat.[90]

London's Alfred was a builder, both of cities and kingdoms. Other interpretations of him, rooted in other themes and locations (not least Winchester), have stressed different aspects of his legacy. Stripping away the layers of mythology still leaves an impressive core of achievements: halting the vikings and establishing a series of countermeasures against them, including fortresses, military reorganisation and spiritual renewal; and overseeing London's accommodation into this scheme, making it one of the central pillars of the new kingdom that took shape during his reign.

CHAPTER 6

London in the Tenth Century

c.900–75

At some point in the years around 940, a holy man named Cathróe from what is now Scotland set out on a long journey. Like many charismatic Irish (or, in this case, Irish-trained) wanderers, Cathróe won admiration on his travels and, after crossing over from Britain to mainland Europe, he eventually ended his days in or after 971 as abbot of the monastery of St Felix and St Clement near Metz, nestled in the rich lands where France, Germany and Luxembourg now meet. One of the monks of Metz wrote an account of the life of his abbot soon after his death. He revelled in the exotic and eventful story of Cathróe's epic journey from Scotland through Britain. The saint had been fêted along the way: by Constantine/Constantín (d.952), the wily and long-lived ruler Alba, ancestor of medieval Scotland; by the more enigmatic Donald/Dyfnwal, king of Strathclyde/Cumbria; and, after crossing the boundary between Cumbrian and viking territory at Leeds, by a viking ruler in York named Erik. At length he passed into the kingdom of the English, and travelled to London, where he was entertained by a local man named Ecgfrith. But disaster struck during Cathróe's brief stay by the banks of the Thames when a fire broke out and threatened to consume the city. After Cathróe's host begged him to help, the saint leapt into action. Placing himself between the flames and what remained of the town, he prayed to God to halt the conflagration. And the flames, this being a life written to celebrate the saint's holiness and power, duly stopped. London was saved, if only for the moment (another fire in 962 would reduce St Paul's to ashes).[1]

The sequel to these events illustrates something of how London fitted into the power politics of tenth-century England. Although London was an important city – as indicated by the fact that it was

where Cathróe had ended up, presumably intending to leave Britain –
there were others which figured just as prominently. Winchester, for
instance, was a more regular fixture in the perambulations of the king
and his entourage, and it was there that word reached King Edmund
(939–46) of Cathróe's wondrous deeds in London. The saint was
summoned thence to meet with the king, and was subsequently
conducted by Oda, archbishop of Canterbury (941–58), to Lympne
in Kent so that he could depart from England by ship.[2]

London around the time of Cathróe's visit was thus significant,
if not yet clearly surpassing other towns of England in economic
vitality, governmental importance or general standing. This period
of equilibrium in the first three quarters of the tenth century is
nonetheless important for the range of insights into life in the city
which have survived. These stem from a blend of textual and archaeological remains that will by now be familiar. However, our impression of London takes on a more personalised flavour, as individuals
like Bishop Theodred and an unnamed witch emerge more clearly;
they are complemented by institutions like the ominously named
'peace-gild' and the restored monastery of Westminster, and artefacts
including the remnants of a glorious, ornate wooden building and a
cache of buried treasure from Rome that may have been assembled
in London.

Town and Country in Tenth-Century London

London in the time of King Edgar (959–75) had probably expanded
somewhat since Alfred's reign, but pinning the extent of its progress
down is problematic. This can in part be ascribed to difficulties with
the material record: much of the relevant pottery, on which archaeological chronology often relies, can only be dated quite broadly, and so
assigning a chronology even within the tenth century is difficult.[3] But
among the relatively plentiful and more precisely datable continental
pottery, London finds only start to mount up from c.970.[4] It is likely
that the city simply did not quickly outgrow the basic framework
laid down in the late ninth century, and remained largely confined
to the area between Cheapside and the Thames. Only a few sites

can be positively identified as having been established in the earlier
part of the tenth century: examples that have been found include a
pit on Milk Street (slightly north of Cheapside), a well and building
on Cheapside itself, and timber from Botolph Lane further to the
east.[5] At the Bull Wharf site which began to be used again in the
late ninth century, occupation continued.[6] Pudding Lane and Lovat
Lane may have emerged in the tenth century, though the frontage
itself was not yet extensively built up.[7] In short, the city largely kept
to the template laid down in the late ninth century, and expanded
only slowly before the end of the tenth to reach Gresham Street in
the west and Leadenhall Street in the east. At this stage its footprint
and population were probably smaller than those of *Lundenwic* two
centuries earlier.[8]

Across the river, however, this period emerges as more important.
London was unique in England for having a distinct and jurisdiction-
ally separate town only a few hundred yards away across the Thames.
Historical and archaeological evidence of Southwark starts to emerge,
if still through a glass darkly, in these decades. The name itself can
probably be seen in the list of fortress-towns known as the *Burghal
Hidage*: *Suþringageweorc*, 'the fortification/building of the men of
Surrey'.[9] The date of this list is debatable, and although it probably
belongs to 914 or later, much of the system it describes could have
originated at an earlier date.[10] This system involved the assignment
of a certain number of hides (family units of land) to the defence and
maintenance of about 30 fortified places on or south of the Thames
(not including London). In the case of Southwark, this amounted to
the equivalent of 1,800 hides: the largest after Wallingford, Warwick
and Winchester. According to a formula at the close of the *Burghal
Hidage*, calculating how many people were needed to man the walls
based on assignments of land, this would be enough to garrison
some 7,425 ft (2,263 m) – potentially enough for the whole island
of Southwark, which in the Roman and (probably) early medieval
period was a ridge running up to the south end of London Bridge,
surrounded by tidal marshes.[11] It could have been a major link in the
bristling defensive network created to ward off viking attacks south
of the Thames. Thus far, however, evidence of Southwark's earliest
stages of activity prior to the last third or so of the tenth century has

been limited. It may not even have gone beyond the planning stage.[12] Nothing of the town from the ninth or early tenth century has been found:[13] it may have been meagre in size, or its remains could have been swallowed up by later development. There is some scattered evidence for earlier Anglo-Saxon activity on the southern shore of the Thames, including a papal privilege for a minster at Bermondsey in the early eighth century,[14] but in the tenth century the first datable material comes from a significant defensive ditch which enclosed the northernmost part of the island (about five hectares).[15] A series of excavations have determined that this ran south-east from the Thames, probably eventually making a semicircle. One timber found in the ditch was from a tree felled in AD 953.[16]

On the north side of the Thames the picture is somewhat better, if again built up from fragments. Some the most significant of these were preserved as Londoners cannibalised their own ships and buildings to reclaim land from the river. All sorts of material was used to prop up embankments on the shoreline of the Thames from the late tenth century onwards, dumped into the water behind piles so as to create a filled-in platform. At Queenhithe and Vintners' Place, this infill included something quite remarkable: three substantial pieces of wooden aisled roofing, almost certainly from the same building. In the abstract this sounds unremarkable, but it is a staggeringly rare and important discovery for a period and a city mostly known from the post-holes of long-decayed wooden buildings. The Thames revetments evoke a quite breathtaking building (Figure 6.1).

The jointing and different sizes of the posts indicate they were used on top of each other: that is to say, in a building with at least three tiers of wooden pillars and arcades which reached some 27.5 ft (8.4 m) in height, with a roof probably extending up to 36 ft (11 m). It would have been akin in look and scale to the famous Norwegian stave churches, erected two centuries later. Little more can be known about the Queenhithe building or its purpose. It was certainly high-status – building on this scale needed serious expertise and resources – but could have been either secular or religious. Its timbers were felled sometime between 956 and 979, and reused about a generation later. It also probably stood somewhere nearby, as pieces of wood this size are unlikely to have been carried far.[17]

Figure 6.1. Fragments of an elaborate tenth-century wooden building, reused to shore up the banks of the Thames (Museum of London).

These were not the only unusual pieces of mid-tenth-century buildings repurposed to hold back the waters of the Thames. A smaller piece of plank cut down between 932 and 971 provides another example of something mundane and functional, but again arrestingly rare: a window, triangular in shape, and only about four inches in height. This tiny hole would not have let much light into the building it formed part of. The interior – inevitably damp – would have been all the harder to keep clean of dirt and vermin. But that in a sense was also part of the virtue of little windows such as this: they were small enough to keep out intruders and the worst of the weather in the cold and wet that Londoners of the tenth century would have already loathed.[18]

These fragments of long-gone buildings conjure up some echo of life in the city. Its citizens would peer out at a few grand and lofty edifices through small triangular peepholes as they huddled in the small, single-storey wooden cabins (as they would seem to us) that constituted the bulk of the city's housing stock. London's urban sprawl, such as it was, would have been loose at this stage, distinguished from rural settlement more by quantity than quality. Internally, it would have been divided up into tenements or clusters known in Old English as *hagan*. One did not have to go far, however, to leave the town behind and enter a landscape of fields, streams and marshes. This was true throughout the Anglo-Saxon period (and indeed before and after). As today, there was no hard and fast line where 'urban' met 'rural', since in the tenth century construction would have thinned out even before reaching the Roman walls. There is no evidence that the site of the Roman amphitheatre was anything more than an oval-shaped mound and dip, perhaps often filled with stagnant and insect-infested water.[19]

The situation was similar beyond the walls, and can be perceived thanks to an early charter from Westminster. There had supposedly been a monastery on this site for centuries, although it only comes into view in the time of King Edgar, when it was taken over by St Dunstan, who later became archbishop of Canterbury (959–88) but retained an active interest in Westminster. Thanks to Dunstan's sway with the new king, Westminster was lavished with property, including a large swathe of land to the immediate west of London which surrounded the monastery itself.[20] This extended from where the monastery itself sat, on the site of Westminster Abbey, across Green Park, Buckingham Palace and Piccadilly to join up with Oxford Street (or, as it was known at the time, Watling Street: part of a long Roman road extending from Canterbury to Wroxeter), and eventually east to Farringdon Street and down to the Thames around Blackfriars Station.

This grant of a large tract of two square miles of central London probably dates to 959, although the oldest surviving copy – written out in the distinct and elegant form of tenth-century English script known as 'square minuscule' (Figure 6.2) – comes from a few decades later.[21] Like many Anglo-Saxon charters, it includes a detailed description (in suitably earthy Old English) of the boundaries of the land which the charter concerned (Map 4).

The bounds describe a landscape jarringly different from the London architecture one sees in that area now. Instead of sleek glass and steel mingling with elegant Georgian and Victorian frontages, the charter describes land that runs along a 'boundary stream'

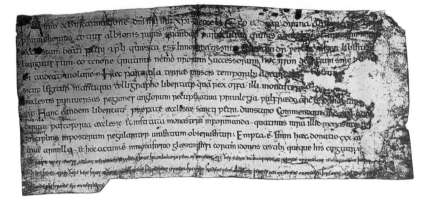

Figure 6.2. Charter from Westminster, probably written in the late tenth century but dated 951 (S 670) (Westminster Abbey).

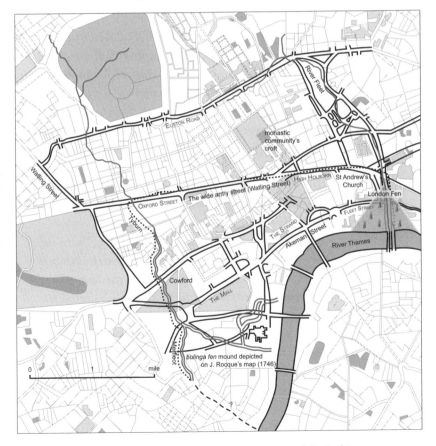

Map 4. The bounds of the Westminster estate delimited in S 670, with lands to the north delimited in S 903.

(*merfleot*), probably part of the Tyburn which now lies submerged beneath Westminster and empties into the Thames near Downing Street. One then encounters a tree stump and *Bulunga* fen before following a ditch to the 'Cowford': the place where the small river Tyburn met Akeman Street, a Roman road that eventually led to *Acemannesceaster*, or Bath (indeed, when the road reaches Heathrow airport, as the A4, it is again called Bath Road). The 'Cowford' was in the vicinity of Buckingham Palace and Green Park Tube station. Next, one followed the Tyburn to a 'wide army-street'. England was criss-crossed with 'army-streets', which were the highways of the day. In this case, it referred to another Roman road: Watling Street/ Oxford Street. At some point along what is now High Holborn (the name of which, incidentally, derives from *holu burna*, Old English for 'stream in the hollow', probably referring to the river Fleet) the charter states that there stood an 'old wooden church of St Andrew'. It may have been on the same site as the current St Andrew Holborn.[22] The final leg of the charter's boundary clause leads us into 'London Fen': an extensive area of marshland following the course of the river Fleet down to the Thames, roughly along Farringdon Street, which still dips down noticeably relative to Ludgate Hill on the east and Fleet Street on the west.[23]

Running the City: Gilds and Bishops

Tenth-century London had one foot firmly in rural life. From the sound of the Westminster charter, a traveller would enter what was effectively a mix of marsh and farmland as soon as they passed the Roman walls and came towards the Fleet. As might be expected, the practical arrangements for running such a city had to be flexible and accommodating, and some aspects of them are preserved in a legal text written down during the reign of Æthelstan (924–39).[24] It is one of several such compositions from his time as king which illustrate the back-and-forth of royal and local legislation that was standard in the tenth century.[25] London is not the only locality represented among Æthelstan's laws – another was produced by the men of Kent, for example – but it is the only town. Already in the 890s the Londoners were thought of as a group contributing to the military effort against the vikings,[26] and in the time of Æthelstan they still held this distinction: London defined its surrounding area to an unusual degree.

London's affairs at this time were protected by a body referred to as a 'peace-gild'. Later medieval guilds particular to specific crafts descend from groups such as this. The role of the tenth-century peace-gild was different, however, and combined the functions of a mutual aid society and a drinking club, with a good dose of vigilante justice.[27] This was a large association, divided up into units of tens and hundreds, and incorporated bishops and reeves – nominated officials – as well as men and women of both noble and humble rank (literally 'earlish or churlish', *ge eorlisce ge ceorlisce*), some of whom were not expected to be wealthy enough to afford a horse. It may have embraced every eligible individual in London, and even some who were not permanent residents: a reference to multiple bishops suggests that all those with property in the town could be counted as members of the peace-gild.[28] The set of rules that this body laid down for itself is mostly concerned with the handling of theft. Its procedure for dealing with infractions was utterly ruthless. The central aim was to secure both material compensation and violent legal satisfaction. Victims could refer to a list of valuations for standard items of livestock: 30 pence for an ox, 20 for a cow, 10 for a pig and 5 for a sheep. A lost slave or horse was worth half a pound (120 pence), unless everyone agreed, based on appearance, that it was not worth so much. Any compensation was to be taken from the goods of the thief him- or herself. The thief would then be killed. There was even an incentive of 12 pence as a reward for whoever did the deed. Killing in pursuit of justice was not only tolerated but encouraged, and anybody who had a problem with it would have to take the matter up with the whole peace-gild instead of a single killer.[29]

Catching any thieves was a challenge, however, and much of the London law is concerned with how a posse would be raised and empowered to track down miscreants. They would start by searching, if necessary, though in that case the compensation automatically jumped up to at least 120 pence even if the goods were worth less – presumably because of the trouble a search entailed. But if a trail could readily be identified, they would set off in pursuit. Much is made of crossing north or south over a boundary – perhaps that of Middlesex – though, if so, it did not slow the chase.[30] The roving band of Londoners, out for blood, had elaborate arrangements in place for how they would handle thieves with the temerity to flee into another jurisdiction. They would demand that the local reeve support them as they continued their pursuit, or he would face punishment himself. Provision was made for shock and awe tactics, in case the Londoners met with resistance in the form of a kindred strong and bold enough to stand up for a thief: they would send for reinforcements from both London and the thief's district, 'as many men as may seem to us suitable in so great a suit, so that the guilty men may stand in greater awe on account of our association'.[31] Again, the aim was to kill the thief 'and those who fight with him and support him, unless they will desert him'.[32] Tense confrontations might ensue as London's upholders of the peace pressed their case wherever it led.

Anglo-Saxon justice was a rough business, in which might generally meant right: if a case could not be proven on the basis of documents or better yet reliable witness statements, whoever brought the most trustworthy men or women to support their case in court would win. Very few circumstances were explicitly allowed to prompt mitigation. At the beginning of their law code, the Londoners spelt out that fatal punishment could be meted out to anyone over the age of 12. This was too much even for tenth-century sensibilities, and a coda at the end of the tract states that 'it seemed too cruel to [the king] that a person should be killed so young, or for so small an offence', and he insisted that the minimum age limit for execution be upped to 15 – though younger boys and girls who resisted, fled or refused to surrender were still liable to execution.[33] In practice, application of the law was somewhat more flexible. A thief who repeated his crime several times in Wiltshire in the years either side of 900 got off with fines or forfeitures thanks to the intervention of powerful allies.[34] Many people would have followed this course of negotiating a settlement in return for paying a fine or giving up some of their property, and might even submit to a period of penal servitude.[35]

It should be stressed that the peace-gild was not a formal governmental or judicial institution as such – it brought criminals to justice, but did not actually deal it out – and was also not the only body of its kind even in London. At least one gild of London *cnihtas* came into being in the time of Edgar, probably composed of men charged with official responsibilities such as thegns or reeves,[36] and there is no more word of London's peace-gild after the law code of Æthelstan's time. Yet that could be because this unusually large and ambitious gild had merged with other assemblies and administrative organs in London, for in European towns of this period protection of shared interests by a gild commonly provided the basis for more formal urban representation or self-government.[37] London's peace-gild was not especially remarkable for the privileges it claimed – any community with enough clout could do so – but it is testimony to the coherence and collective confidence that the Londoners already possessed by the early tenth century.[38] The peace-gild would, in pursuing its goals, have provided a forum in which the city's great and good could come together and police their own. Once a month, the leading members of the organisation were obliged to meet and retire for dinner together.[39] There is a further clue towards the end of the law code describing the peace-gild as overlapping with London's representatives in higher-level gatherings. The final four clauses of the law code are clearly supplements added in light of subsequent decisions made at two meetings held by royal command. The first of these, at Thunderfield in Surrey, was attended by two men named Ælfheah Stybb and Brihtnoth, son of Odda. Their status is not made clear, although since the information they relayed from the royal meeting concerned the duties of reeves in their shires, they may have been the reeves representing London and/or Middlesex;[40] in any case, they were probably prominent members of the gild, as was another powerful individual said to have conveyed the king's wishes from a second meeting at Whittlebury in Northamptonshire to the archbishop (and, by implication, back to London): Theodred, the bishop of London (925×926–951×953).[41]

Theodred stands out as one of the more prominent and influential occupants of the episcopal throne of St Paul's in the Anglo-Saxon era,[42] and continued the important tradition of the bishops of London being close to the king and intimately involved in royal government, as much diplomats and administrators as priests.[43] In the lists of witnesses at the end of royal charters – which were carefully ordered to reflect a combination of prominence and seniority among those who had been present – Theodred rose to a significantly higher rank than was usual for bishops of London in the tenth century.[44] He even accompanied the king on his expedition to fight a combined force of Dublin vikings, men of Alba and Cumbrians in a pivotal battle at an unidentified location named *Brunanburh* in 937,[45] and had first-hand experience of the brutality of tenth-century justice: later writers reported that Theodred felt pangs of guilt after condemning to death thieves who had targeted a saint's shrine – an act that some felt undermined his holy station.[46] All of this points to a bishop who stood unusually high in the king's estimation, and who played a very active role in worldly as well as spiritual life, sometimes to the extent that his actions became questionable. Probably as a temporary measure, he was also appointed bishop over some or all of East Anglia, where he had built up extensive lands and was remembered in later times as a patron of the cult of St Edmund (d.869), the martyred king of the East Angles.[47]

It was Bury St Edmund's that preserved the only surviving copy of Theodred's will, the document that provides most information about him.[48] All the clerics who are named as heirs to his ecclesiastical vestments and treasures bear names that, like 'Theodred', suggest German origins.[49] The bishop may well have been an immigrant himself, or the child of recent immigrants who still possessed strong ties to the homeland. The will also sheds light on Theodred's travels further afield. England in the early tenth century was unusually outward-looking. King Æthelstan married his large collection of sisters off to various foreign kings and princes, and played host to disgruntled exiles from France, Brittany and Norway. Meanwhile, Coenwald, bishop of Worcester (928×929–957/8), toured monasteries in the east Frankish kingdom (what would later become Germany and Switzerland), where he distributed largesse on behalf of the king and picked up a taste for the strict brand of Benedictine monasticism he saw there. But the closest and most cherished ties were those that tied England to Rome, the wellspring of its Christian establishment.[50] There had been constant traffic of Anglo-Saxon visitors across the Alps and back again since the seventh century. One nominee to the archbishopric of Canterbury even froze to death in the Alps in 958 or 959, and a further hazard in the tenth century was posed by the Muslim enclave of La-Garde-Freinet (dép. Var), near Saint-Tropez in the south of France, from which raiders preyed on travellers in the alpine passes.[51]

It was this route that Theodred braved at some point in the period between 942 and his death. His will mentions two chasubles which he picked up at Pavia in northern Italy – quite probably fine and valuable items. An exceptional archaeological discovery at Rome may also relate to this journey. It is the largest of many finds of Anglo-Saxon coins from Rome, and also the best recorded, as it came to light in the course of archaeological excavations on the House of the Vestal Virgins in the Roman Forum in November 1883. Some 830 coins were found, all but six of them from England. Along with them were two silver fasteners or 'hooked tags', which had probably once sealed the bag containing the coins. These are inscribed DOMNO MARINO PAPAE: 'for the lord Pope Marinus'. This must refer to Pope Marinus II (942–6), whose pontificate coincides with the date of the latest coins in the hoard, which were minted after King Edmund had taken control of York (944).[52] These tags are also striking for what they do *not* specify: the name of the donor. This was generally front and centre on other inscribed medieval gift-objects (sometimes to the exclusion of that of the recipient). Having just the name of the recipient is rare, and perhaps indicates that the donor would expect to hand it over in person to someone of higher status.[53]

The Forum Hoard is exceptionally unusual in containing an inscription that identifies the purpose it was destined for. Moreover, that purpose was a prestigious and special one: an offering to the Pope himself. Not every visitor to Rome would expect such a privilege, even though in this case the donation manifestly did not make it to the Pope, or – if it did – failed to remain in his hands. What led to the hoard being buried beneath a building in the Forum remains an enigma. But its contents reveal clues about its background. Among the bulk of the English coins, and especially the more recent portions, the south of England is dominant, and the single best represented mint-town is in fact London. There are even several clusters of up to a dozen coins all stamped with the same dies – a sign that they had seen less attrition through circulation, and had probably stayed together from the time of production, like banknotes with sequential issue numbers.

London issued coins throughout the tenth century. It was one of a dozen mint-places mentioned in a law code of Æthelstan, which assigned it a complement of eight moneyers – the most anywhere in southern England.[54] Winchester was given six and Canterbury seven, while Chester (not named in the law code, which is concerned solely with mints on and south of the Thames) had at least 11.[55] Close analysis of the coins shows that London's position was slightly rocky in the opening years of the tenth century, but became better established by about 920, when its moneyers started producing pennies with elegant busts of Edward the Elder (899–924). Under Æthelstan and his heirs, London was a major player in England's monetary economy, although Canterbury and Winchester were roughly on a par, and further north Chester probably and York maybe surpassed it.[56] In the case of the Forum Hoard, this strong representation of London is therefore important: it was not what one would automatically expect in southern England in the 940s, and points to a London connection somewhere in its past.

The Forum Hoard is exceptional enough without a concrete attachment to a specific individual, and it is too much to hope that evidence will ever materialise to produce any such link. But the particulars of the hoard are suggestive: its connection with London, the likely involvement of a wealthy individual (or institution) who might expect direct contact with the Pope, and the date (probably assembled between 944 and 946) all point to Theodred being a strong contender for its original donor. He had, as mystery novels used to put it, means, motive and opportunity.

Conclusion: London and the Kingdom in the Tenth Century

The tenth century was London's era of consolidation. It probably only developed beyond its Alfredian roots slowly, with fires and floods bringing frequent destruction and rebuilding. Grand buildings could be erected, but might be torn down and recycled in a matter of decades. One did not need to go far before encountering open fields, forests and marshes, which the wealthier and more bellicose Londoners would gamely traverse as the peace-gild pursued suspected thieves. London was firmly integrated into the economy of southern England, and at this stage did most of its business up rather than down the Thames, with inland areas such as Oxfordshire, to judge by the pottery found in the city.[57]

Across the kingdom, fortified nuclei of government and defence multiplied. Some were completely new, but others absorbed various kinds of pre-existing central places such as minsters or élite estates.[58] Although the result was a large complement of what contemporaries called *byrg*, or boroughs, only a portion of them could be described as urban at this stage: that is to say, supporting a relatively large and permanent population engaged in more than just agriculture. Some would come into their own in the later tenth or eleventh century, forming the nuclei of many small towns, but, archaeologically, just a few of the tenth-century boroughs besides London have produced evidence of substantial activity.[59] All had Roman roots, albeit with different fates in the centuries that followed. The group includes a few which had been part of the urban landscape for centuries, such as Canterbury and York,[60] as well as others which had effectively only grown up since the late ninth century, among them Chester, Lincoln and Winchester.[61] All had their own distinct character. London had inherited size and prestige from earlier times, as well as an advantageous location that channelled river and road traffic, whereas Winchester benefited from more consistent and prominent royal presence, as well as two major monastic establishments. York was home to an archbishop, served as a hub of North Sea trade, and was for a long time the centre of a powerful viking kingdom. Chester, in turn, derived much of its success from access to the Irish Sea.

Within this cohort, London's profile was consistently high, as indicated by the number of moneyers it was assigned in comparison to other towns under Æthelstan. It had an unusually strong communal identity, manifested in the peace-gild. One other gauge of its prominence is the presence of London in the royal itinerary. It was occasionally selected for royal gatherings (sometimes known in older literature as meetings of the *witan*): once under Edmund, and with increasing frequency under Edgar.[62] Close to London,

Kingston upon Thames in Surrey emerged as a favoured site for royal ceremonial, including the consecration of several kings from Æthelstan in 925 to Æthelred II in 979.[63] There are other hints at the city's importance on a national level. In a collection of miracle stories put together by a monk named Lantfred at Winchester in the early 970s, London was the most common geographical origin for visitors to the shrine of St Swithun.[64] Elsewhere, 'London Bridge' was the setting for the earliest recorded execution for witchcraft in England, at some point in or shortly before 948. This was long thought to be one of the earliest references to London Bridge,[65] but there is good reason to think that it refers to a bridge near Peterborough where Ermine Street crosses the river Nene, heading towards London.[66] The harrowing details of what transpired are recorded in a charter from Peterborough Abbey.[67] An unnamed widow was deprived of her land at nearby Ailsworth, Northamptonshire, for having stuck iron pins into a likeness of a man named Ælfsige. 'It was discovered', the charter goes on, 'and the deadly image was dragged out of her room'. The widow's son fled and became an outlaw – not the romantic lifestyle associated with Robin Hood, but rather a state in which his life was fair game and outside all legal protection – and the woman herself was drowned at 'London Bridge'. These ugly scenes probably reflect the last act in a longer conflict, climaxing in mob justice and the widow being subjected to the so-called ordeal of cold water: an innocent would sink (and most likely drown) while a witch would float (and probably then be killed anyway).[68] Ælfsige walked away with the land and left it to his son Wulfstan Uccea – Wulfstan 'the swollen' or 'the froggy'.[69] This lurid and grisly story, told very much from the victors' point of view, sheds a sidelight on how London was becoming a more important point of reference in England more widely. This process would speed up rapidly in the last century of Anglo-Saxon England.

CHAPTER 7

Late Anglo-Saxon London

In the troubled opening years of the eleventh century, when viking armies again prowled across England, London lay at the heart of the action. By the spring of 1012, the situation had become dire. The *Anglo-Saxon Chronicle* describes how all the kingdom's chief men congregated in London shortly before Easter, overseen by Ealdorman Eadric. In time, he would come to be known as Eadric Streona, 'the acquisitive', and would defect from the English to the Danish, and back again, in the confused and desperate fighting of 1015–16. But in 1012 he was still King Æthelred II's right-hand man, having been raised by the king from relatively humble origins to become the leading nobleman in the kingdom. At the gathering of worthies in London, Eadric was charged with assembling and handing over one of a series of huge tribute payments which the English were raising to pay off the vikings, in this case amounting to £48,000: a vast sum of money, especially if one considers that Domesday Book records a total annual income from all the king's estates of only a little more than £8,000 in 1066.[1]

While Eadric and the other leaders of the English deliberated and counted their coin in the city, an even more worrying scene unfolded a couple of miles downriver at Greenwich. There, the most senior figure in the Anglo-Saxon church, Ælfheah, archbishop of Canterbury, was the captive of the viking army. He had been taken in September 1011, when the vikings seized Canterbury. The capture of the archbishop sent shockwaves through England: 'there could misery be seen where happiness was often seen before', as the *Chronicle* puts it.[2] Seven months later, the vikings wanted to capitalise on their prestigious prisoner. In addition to the tribute that Eadric was cobbling together, they expected a ransom to be paid for Archbishop Ælfheah (£3,000, according to one source).[3] But the archbishop refused to co-operate, and would not allow any money to be paid for him. The vikings did not take this well. On the Saturday after Easter, they got riotously drunk on wine that had been brought 'from the south' (presumably from what is now mainland Europe), and Ælfheah was hauled in front of a crowd of unruly vikings. Before long, things turned ugly. Despite the protestations of their leader, Thorkell the Tall,[4] the angry vikings pelted the archbishop savagely with bones and ox heads (perhaps detritus from their earlier merriments), and at last one of the vikings – allegedly a man named Thrum, whom the archbishop had confirmed as a Christian the day before – stepped forth and crushed Ælfheah's skull with the blunt end of his axe. Besides Thomas Becket in 1170, Ælfheah is the only archbishop of Canterbury ever to have been murdered, and like Thomas he was soon regarded as a martyr (now most often known as St Alphege). The morning after his death, Ælfheah's body was taken back to London for reverent burial in St Paul's.

At the viking encampment in Greenwich there were other consequences. After the £48,000 had been ferried down from London and dispersed, the army broke up 'as widely as it had been collected'[5] – that is to say, it collapsed into smaller units, which went their separate ways. One large segment of the force, led by Thorkell himself, chose to stay behind and enter the service of their former enemy, King Æthelred. Their motivation is not made clear, but revolt against the murder of the archbishop may have been a strong contributing factor.[6] If so, London was the perfect place to mete out their revenge.

London under Æthelred II (978–1016)

The unpleasant events surrounding Archbishop Ælfheah's death exemplify the significance London held at the beginning of the eleventh century. While London had been an important place for some 400 years, it took on a much more prominent role in the last century or so of the Anglo-Saxon period. The city stands out strongly in the annals of the *Anglo-Saxon Chronicle* for the reign of Æthelred II, especially in the version penned sometime in the period 1018×1023, which describes in lurid detail the misfortunes of the English under

Æthelred that culminated in their defeat and conquest by the vikings.[7] Indeed, London features so much and so positively, that it has been suggested that the writer of this *Chronicle* may himself have been a Londoner.[8]

Although undoubtedly a rich, populous and productive place, it was a combination of the stoutness of its walls (now reinforced with a freshly dug ditch)[9] and the belligerence of its numerous inhabitants that kept London safe. The city's denizens were the heirs of the peace-gild that had roved the surrounding countryside 80 years earlier demanding reparations from all and sundry, and the Londoners of the age of Æthelred were doughty warriors in their own right.[10] In 994, for example, a fleet of 94 ships led by the king of the Danes, Swein Forkbeard (d.1014), mounted an attack on London – 'but there', the *Chronicle* says, 'they [the vikings] suffered more harm and injury than they ever thought any citizens would do to them'.[11] And, with the Virgin Mary watching over them, the Londoners triumphed. Over the course of Æthelred's reign London repulsed at least three more viking assaults, and when Swein came back and took over the kingdom in 1013, London was the last place to submit to him. Militarily, these years presented some of the greatest direct threats to London between Boudicca and the Blitz. The city's martial prominence offers a sharp contrast to the comfortable and unwarlike image one might have of a successful commercial city in modern times. If London and other towns were oases of relative peace and prosperity, it was only because the townsmen were ready to take up arms to defend themselves. England's eleventh-century towns still retained something of the fortress-settlements of Alfred and Edward the Elder's time, and were ready to flex their military as well as economic muscles.[12]

Financially, militarily and administratively, London took on new significance under Æthelred. It was a key node in England's fiscal system, reflected in London's being the place where tribute payment was gathered in 1012. It was also starting to feature more prominently in the movements of the king and his councillors.[13] By the later years of the reign, it had become the king's preferred base of operations. In the opening months of 1016, one English army gathered by Edmund Ironside, Æthelred's eldest surviving son, refused to go to war unless both the king and the citizens of London should

join them, and Æthelred himself died at London and was interred
in St Paul's soon after, in April 1016 – the first English king buried
in London since Sæbbi in the seventh century.[14] Royal burials were
sensitive affairs, laden with as much concern for the future as for the
past.[15] Æthelred's burial in London, and its immediate consequences,
therefore marked a critical time for the city. Whether interment in
London had been Æthelred's long-term intent is not known; certainly
London lay well off the beaten track of burial places for Æthelred's
family. But to those embroiled in the desperate circumstances of
1016, the location of Æthelred's funeral was perhaps less surprising.
It constituted recognition of London's status, its ties to the king, and
the place of the city and its inhabitants at the forefront of the political
scene.[16] It was at this time, and quite probably because of these unique
conditions, that London's citizens and those who assembled there
began to speak for the kingdom as a whole, especially at the tense and
sensitive moments when one king died and another succeeded to the
throne.[17] According to the C, D and E manuscripts of the *Anglo-Saxon
Chronicle*, Æthelred's son Edmund Ironside was chosen as king by
the councillors and citizens (*burhwaru*) of London in the aftermath
of his father's death in April 1016.[18] This particular succession was
especially contested, and the *Chronicle* represents only one of several
versions of events, one which strongly favoured Edmund's claim.
Another, preserved by a twelfth-century historian with access to a
slightly different version of the *Chronicle*, has most of the English
'bishops, abbots [and] ealdormen' agreeing to accept Cnut as king at
Southampton, while Edmund's simultaneous acclamation was the act
of an opposing faction that included the citizens of London.[19] A third
account (highly partisan in its favouring of the Danes) even has Cnut
accepted as king by most Londoners immediately after Æthelred's
death, and says that he entered the city and 'sat on the throne of the
kingdom' (*in solio regni resedit*). But his stay was allegedly brief: Cnut
did not trust the Londoners' loyalty, and so left the city for the Isle of
Sheppey after only a short time – and soon found himself faced by
a new army under Edmund, who had been smuggled out of London
by a dissident group among the city's garrison.[20]

The city was a vital prize in the fierce fighting that ensued,
and London's status as a venue for royal ceremonial and decisions

affecting the whole kingdom solidified during the subsequent decades. Following Cnut's death in 1035, the 'shipmen' or mercenary soldiers based in London were also an important factor in the succession of Harold I (1035–40),[21] and Edward the Confessor's acclamation as king by 'all the people' (*eall folc*) in 1042 likewise took place in London.[22]

The varied takes on the events surrounding the first succession in which London played a part in 1016 reflect its hotly contested nature, yet all agree on London's crucial role. Even if its choice of king was not the only one that had been reached, it could not be ignored. Later in 1016, London was the scene of a dramatic siege, during which Cnut's army carved a ditch all the way around Southwark so that they could bring their ships to the west of London Bridge, and thus surround the whole town.[23] It appears that command of the city was in the hands of Ulfcetel of East Anglia – one of the most respected Anglo-Saxon leaders, with a fearsome reputation among the vikings[24] – and he and the Londoners held out long enough for Edmund to gather an army and rout the Danes. Despite their valiant efforts the vikings would return before long, to be accepted as lords of the city.

London Under the Danes and Edward the Confessor (1016–66)

The climactic Danish attack on London in 1016 was commemorated in a poem written in Old Norse from the perspective of Cnut's men, referred to by modern scholars as *Liðsmannaflokkr* ('the household warriors' poem').[25] Like many other viking poems of the era, *Liðsmannaflokkr* is replete with highly allusive mythological metaphors. Known as kennings, these add rich layers of depth and colour to the poem. They are composed according to strict metrical and alliterative rules, with the result that each verse is like a knot that must be untied twice: once to get the words into the right order; and again to comprehend what they actually mean. One stanza, for instance, includes the lines *Enn á enskra manna / ǫlum gjóð Hnikars blóði*. On the face of, it this means something like 'Again on of Englishmen we nourish the osprey of Hnikarr with blood'. Rearranged into sense order and put into a more idiomatic translation, this is 'let us once again feed the osprey of Hnikarr on the blood of Englishmen'. When put into the mouths of Cnut's warriors, the general meaning of these words is not hard to guess, but grasping all the nuances requires more effort. One must know that Hnikarr, 'the overthrower', is one of over 200 pseudonyms of Odin, and that his 'osprey' was a raven. Hence, feeding the raven meant providing an abundance of corpses: the warriors did not just hope to win, but to triumph in bloody fashion with the one-eyed god watching over them. The poet who put these rich verses together was quite probably a veteran of the battle – this being an era in which poets were expected to live their craft in hardcore fashion – and indeed may have addressed them to an enigmatic woman who was herself present in London during the battle. Other verses elaborate on how the 'victory-keen leader of the Danes' (sigrfíkinn […] Dana vísi), Cnut himself, would lead an attack on the 'men of the city' (karla borgar), in which 'the blood-ice [i.e. sword] clangs against British mail-shirts' (dynr á brezkum brynjum blóðíss); and how 'Hlǫkk of drinking horns' (i.e. the poet's female addressee, likened here to one of the Valkyries) had seen every morning 'the helmet destroyers [i.e. swords] reddened with blood on the banks of the Thames', so that the 'seagull of Hangi' (another pseudonym for Odin and his raven) should not go hungry (Hvern morgin sér horna / Hlǫkk á Tempsar bakka / – skalat Hanga má hungra – / hjalmskóð roðin blóði). Evocative though they are, kennings often serve to obfuscate as well as enthral. This is certainly the case in Liðsmannaflokkr, where they elevate the warrior-poet's account of the action to legendary proportions while also making the details difficult to pin down. But the prowess of both the English and the vikings, as well as the ferocity of their fighting, is inescapable.

After such a hard campaign, it is no surprise that Cnut did not at first show particular favour towards London. It had been the most implacable centre of resistance to him and his men, and never in fact fell to military assault: once England had been divided between Cnut and Edmund in late 1016, London ended up on Cnut's side north of the Thames, and was apparently the first place to which the victorious army retreated after settling terms with Edmund in Gloucestershire.

The citizens 'bought peace for themselves', probably at the point of a sword, and the army then entered London with its ships to wait out the winter. Around this time, London was the venue for a gathering of English bishops and nobles at which many were killed for their disloyalty to Cnut.[26] One can well imagine this being the time when the poet of *Liðsmannaflokkr* triumphantly concluded his composition with the words 'now that these hard battles have been recently concluded, we can settle down […] in beautiful London'.[27]

London's woes were only beginning.[28] Cnut made the citizens pay a heavy toll for their staunch adherence to Æthelred II and Edmund, and when he demanded a final, huge tribute payment in 1018 London was singled out for a supplementary tribute of £10,500, on top of the £72,000 extracted from the rest of the kingdom.[29] The city's chastening also took a religious form. After the martyrdom of Ælfheah at the hands of the vikings at Greenwich in April 1012, his corpse had been brought to St Paul's. St Paul's may at this time have been building a reputation as the go-to church for the commemoration of viking atrocities.[30] Æthelred II's burial there in 1016 might have added to this reputation in a more general way, while between 1009 and 1012 the adjacent church of St Gregory (within the close of St Paul's) had also temporarily hosted the relics of St Edmund (855–69), an East Anglian king martyred by the vikings a century and a half earlier.[31] Cnut put a stop to all this in 1023. According to one version of the *Anglo-Saxon Chronicle*, he came to St Paul's in that year and 'gave full permission' for Ælfheah's body to be removed and taken to Canterbury.[32]

The *Chronicle*, written from a pro-Canterbury perspective, portrays this as a grand and joyous occasion: bishops (though the bishop of London himself is never mentioned) along with the king, earls and others joined a procession that conveyed the body from St Paul's across the Thames, and in Southwark entrusted it to the archbishop of Canterbury. Some 60 years later, in the 1080s, a Canterbury monk named Osbern wrote an altogether different, and much livelier, version of events. He claimed that Cnut's scheme was not welcomed with open arms, at least in London; rather, it was only accomplished as a sort of heist, inspired by a prophecy made to Cnut during his campaign in England many years before. The king was seized with such eagerness to pursue his plan that he raced straight from the bathtub, clad only in a cloak and sandals, to meet the archbishop when he arrived at St Paul's to help in the operation. Cnut's household warriors, the housecarls (Old Norse *húskarlar*), took up position at key points in the city to create a distraction and suppress any resistance, while within the cathedral a pair of Canterbury monks exhibited a miraculous degree of strength in breaking into Ælfheah's tomb and lifting aside its stone covering. Having extracted the holy corpse, Cnut, the archbishop, the monks and the men-at-arms hastened across the Thames by ship and hightailed it out of the city as quickly as possible, so as to escape any hostility from the Londoners.[33] This dramatic text is the product of a good storyteller concerned to validate the status of Anglo-Saxon saints in a fast-changing religious landscape,[34] and its mix of bath-time panic and superhuman heavy lifting cannot of course be taken at face value – yet in its garrulous vivacity Osbern's account does not necessarily present so very much more spin than that of the probably highly selective *Chronicle* author. In any case, both Osbern and the *Chronicle* state that, a few days after being removed from London, Ælfheah was ensconced in his new home on the north side of the altar in Canterbury Cathedral. For these authors the transfer of his relics (known to medieval authors as a 'translation') could be framed as a homecoming, since Ælfheah had been archbishop of Canterbury. At the same time, it provided a chance for Cnut and his family to rewrite their relationship with a popular English saint, and to snub London.[35]

Among the leading cities of England, Cnut showed more favour to Canterbury and especially Winchester,[36] yet could not afford to ignore London completely. It was a rich resource, and served more and more as the focal point of the minting and financial infrastructure of the kingdom. Firm control was therefore a priority. As *Liðsmannaflokkr* implies, London continued to be a base for the king's standing mercenary force of Scandinavian warriors or 'shipmen' (or, in Old Norse, *liðsmenn*), who remained in the city until at least 1051, and were possibly identical with the housecarls who supposedly helped Cnut remove the body of Ælfheah in 1023.[37] The *liðsmenn* were supported by an annual tax known as *heregeld* ('army payment'), which was large enough to give each warrior an attractive pay packet: the precise details are noted bitterly in some annals of the *Anglo-Saxon Chronicle*.[38]

One of these well-paid soldiers may have been commemorated by a famous tombstone found south of St Paul's in 1852 (Figure 7.1). Made c.1025–50, it shows a formidable-looking beast carved in the characteristically Scandinavian 'Ringerike' style and originally painted in several colours. The edge of the stone carries an Old Norse runic inscription, stating that two men named Ginna and Toki had the monument set up, though whom it commemorated is not mentioned.[39] It is known that there was a Danish cemetery somewhere in London around 1040.[40] As well as the unnamed individual commemorated by the St Paul's stone, it probably contained two men named Manna and Swein, who are remembered as having been killed in England and buried in London on a runic inscription that still survives in Lund (now in Sweden, but in the eleventh century part of the Danish kingdom).[41] A further piece of sculpture of a similar style to the St Paul's stone has also been found in London[42] – but it lacks a secure find-spot, and even the St Paul's tombstone was not discovered *in situ*, so St Paul's remains just one of several possibilities

Figure 7.1. Stone grave marker, inscribed with runes and carved in 'Ringerike' style (Museum of London).

for this cemetery's location. Another archaeological legacy of the vikings is a collection of late tenth- or early eleventh-century axe-heads, spearheads, grappling hooks and other weaponry found in the 1920s at the north end of London Bridge (Figure 7.2).[43] The context in which these were deposited is not clear: they could have been lost in the course of one of the many attacks on London Bridge, or have formed part of an arsenal deliberately or accidentally lost in the Thames. Either way, they powerfully symbolise the violent side of London's contact with the vikings.

Like his father Æthelred II, Edward the Confessor (1042–66) spent more time than Cnut in and near London, and made the development of Westminster Abbey into his personal project. London was therefore the setting for some of the most momentous events of Edward's reign, including several of the fraught political confrontations of the early 1050s. Earl Godwine was summoned there to account for himself in September 1051, after a fracas in Dover had escalated into a face-off between a royal army and that of Godwine and his sons. This conflict laid bare simmering tensions between Godwine and his family on one side, and the king and his foreign

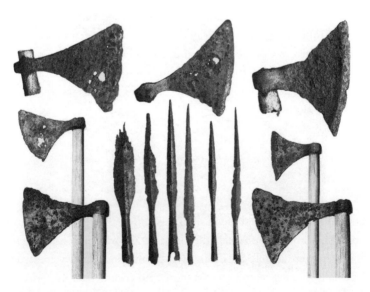

Figure 7.2. Part of a collection of Scandinavian-style weaponry recovered from the north end of London Bridge in the 1920s (Museum of London).

(especially French) appointees on the other. The earl and his sons came to Southwark, but had to slip away once support for their cause began to ebb. For the moment, Edward was victorious. He promoted Robert of Jumièges – one of several Normans who rose to prominence in England under Edward – from bishop of London to archbishop of Canterbury, snubbing the local choice of a kinsman of Earl Godwine's.[44] But the following summer, Godwine and his sons returned by sea and, after winning support from the south coast, made their way up the Thames. At London the king was waiting for them – and for military reinforcements, which were arriving all too slowly. The earl and his followers again approached via Southwark. As the tide rose, they manoeuvred their fleet beneath London Bridge, and drew up their ground forces on the southern shore. They faced the king's fleet on the river, and his men on the north bank. As before, the situation was tense. Godwine and his son Harold asked to be restored to their old positions; Edward initially refused, but when a step towards reconciliation in the form of a hostage exchange was mooted, several of the king's leading men decided to flee the city. Archbishop Robert and Ulf, another Norman and bishop of Dorchester (1049–52), dashed out of the east gate (probably Aldersgate), killing many as they went. The archbishop subsequently fled the country on a clapped-out ship; others retreated to some of the few castles that had been erected by Normans and other Frenchmen in England. Finally, yet another assembly of leading men took place at London, in the course of which Godwine and his sons were restored to their positions of power.[45]

London: Mother of Cities

Disruptive though they were, these events highlight London's status as the focus of political life in the kingdom in the eleventh century. Losing London meant risking the kingdom as a whole. Contemporary observers were acutely conscious of its prominence. They were struck especially by its size, military strength and commercial importance. A Flemish cleric writing in the early 1040s described London as the *metropoli[s] terrae* [...] *populosissima* ('most populous metropolis of the land').[46] By metropolis, he meant the central or 'mother' city in the kingdom.[47] In the immediate aftermath of the Norman Conquest, one Norman writer described London as the place 'where [the English élite] most often held their meetings';[48] another from elsewhere in northern France described it as 'a most spacious city, full of evil inhabitants, and richer than anywhere else in the kingdom. Protected on the left by walls and on the right by the river, it fears neither armies nor capture by guile'.[49] When an anonymous Anglo-Saxon monk of Canterbury Cathedral came to draw the first surviving world map produced in England sometime in the period 1025–50, he included in his stylised representation of Britain – scrunched, as was usual with medieval maps that were centred on Jerusalem or the eastern Mediterranean, into the bottom-left corner – only two cities: London and Winchester.[50]

Whether London was the 'capital city', however, is less clear. Across Europe, this was a time of many 'royal cities', palaces or residences that kings would visit from time to time, but very few capitals in the sense of a permanent base for rulers and their agents.[51] By that measure, London cannot be counted among them. Even when the king was in town, the immediate business of governance was streamlined for mobility's sake. Anglo-Saxon rulers of the tenth and eleventh centuries favoured a peripatetic existence, and moved constantly through the southern and south-western parts of England. They did so in order to exploit their scattered material resources, and, perhaps more importantly, to see and be seen. People of consequence had to go to the king, wherever he might be, rather than expect to find him and his mobile bureaucracy at a fixed location.[52] A wide range of places served as either one-off or repeat venues for royal meetings, including several other towns: Gloucester, Winchester, Windsor and others all figured as prominently in the royal itinerary as London and Westminster.[53] The initial stand-off between king and earl in 1051 took place in Gloucestershire, and Godwine's death in 1053 came while both he and the king were feasting in Winchester. Winchester in particular had a special place in the West Saxon dynasty's heart, and was also favoured by Cnut. Numerous kings were interred in one of the two major churches that dominated the core of the city.[54] Canterbury was – as it remains in the twenty-first century – the seat of the supreme ecclesiastical authority within England, and as such held primacy of a different sort. The transfer of Archbishop Ælfheah's relics from St Paul's to Canterbury Cathedral in 1023 vividly demonstrates the power wielded by Canterbury, and where Cnut's sympathies perhaps lay.

In the eleventh century, London was therefore still a long way from being the capital city. Nowhere really was at this time,[55] but in practice significant steps were being taken to establish London as the most important of the capitals the developing kingdom of England did not have. There is no doubt that London was rising rapidly in profile because of its size, wealth and incipient centrality.[56] A closer look at those aspects of late Anglo-Saxon administration that came to be permanently based in London is called for.

A City of Silver

As a well-connected city, London offered an attractive hub for emergent organs of administration that touched on the whole kingdom. Just as *Lundenwic* had found a niche in being peripheral yet reachable for multiple bases of wealth and power, so the late Anglo-Saxon city profited from its position and network, becoming the key centre for a new and larger kingdom of England. It played a direct part in the increasingly ambitious nature of late Anglo-Saxon royal government, as kings sought to project and solidify certain aspects of their rule. There are many scattered signals of administrative operations moving towards London. Most, however, are just that: signals, which are difficult to fit into a co-ordinated framework. One writ (formalised administrative letter, from the Old English *gewrit*, 'letter') of Edward the Confessor's casually states, when notifying the Londoners that the king has granted rights in the city to the abbot of Chertsey, that it applies 'here' (*her*); in other words, the writ was written in London. It is likely that writs were produced wherever the king happened to be, but at least sometimes this was in London.[57]

There is one major category of material that bucks this trend. Coins have survived in great numbers from throughout the late Anglo-Saxon period – in part thanks to the vikings who ravaged England and received its tribute payments, for most surviving specimens have been found in Scandinavia. Taken as a whole, these coins tell a compelling story of how London, from about 980, took off as a powerhouse of minting and (in some senses) state finance, and over the next few decades became established as the headquarters of the English monetary system (Figure 7.3).

Figure 7.3. A coin from the beginning of London's era of peak minting activity: penny of Æthelred II (978–1016), 'First Hand' type, London mint, moneyer Beornwulf.

Like so much else, the coinage of this period was changing. In the first place, there was more of it. Excavations at places like the Vintry in London have turned up large numbers of late tenth- and eleventh-century silver pennies. A high proportion of these had been cut into halves or quarters to make small change, which was needed as more and more people – especially in a complex urban economy like that of London – dealt in coin.[58] Users of metal-detectors have brought to light thousands of similar finds from across the country, showing how widespread this surge in coin use was.[59] The mechanisms behind the manufacture of these coins were also transforming. The late Anglo-Saxon currency provides a lesson in the strength of the bonds between central and local power after King Edgar instituted a far-reaching reform in the early 970s which standardised the design of coinage nationwide. Under his son Æthelred II there were another five or six such reforms, and they continued under subsequent kings as a way of reaffirming the quality of the coinage and the moral fibre of the kingdom, as well as drumming up income for the king and his agents. The late Anglo-Saxon coinage became a well-oiled machine, integrating the whole kingdom into a tightly controlled network.

From the time of Edgar's reform onwards, every location that issued coins would normally use the same design, and name the maker (moneyer) and mint-place as well as the king.[60]

Over 100 places issued coins in England between the early 970s and the Norman Conquest, with about 40–70 active at any one time. In practice, however, the vast majority of the coinage came from just a few centres. The four largest mint-places in the kingdom between them accounted for half or more of all the coins in circulation, and none more so than London. Moreover, from about 990 London was supplemented by a mint a few hundred yards away across the river at Southwark (Figure 7.4).

Figure 7.4. One of the earliest coins from Southwark: penny of Æthelred II, 'Crux' type, Southwark mint, moneyer Beorhtlaf.

No other two Anglo-Saxon mint-places were so near each other, or so tightly linked. Although there must have been administrative and jurisdictional reasons for minting coins in Southwark, the smaller south-bank mint-town was closely allied with its northern neighbour, and for practical purposes it is reasonable to count London and Southwark together as a single unit which dominated the currency of late Anglo-Saxon England. London far outstripped even the next most productive mint-places in the country for most of this period. This is patent from the sheer number of surviving coins: a series of catalogues of major modern collections of late Anglo-Saxon coins lists 2,635, 2,453 and 1,143 coins from, respectively, York, Lincoln and Winchester – and 4,164 from London (4,422 with Southwark).[61]

While impressive, this figure is also impressionistic; more detail is needed to get a sense of how and why London contributed so much to the currency. The very best gauge of output is a statistical estimate

based on how many dies or minting stamps can be observed in the surviving corpus. How many coins these dies actually would have made
is a more contentious question, though on balance their average was
probably comparable at all the major mint-places, meaning that the
number of dies is a reasonable guide to relative activity. Unfortunately,
London's scale is also its undoing: gathering and studying a complete
corpus is a huge undertaking, and there are so many coins surviving
from London that this has only been accomplished for a few short
periods. One of these, that of Cnut's first coinage, is among the
biggest of the whole late Anglo-Saxon period, and suggests that a
total of almost 1,100 reverse dies of that type were used at London.
About 400 reverse dies are thought to have been used in Edward the
Confessor's first coinage. Similar estimates are available for Lincoln,
Winchester and York, and show that at both these times London was
approximately twice as productive as the next largest mint-place.[62]

One can go some way towards filling in the gaps between these
snapshots of London's minting activity, by assessing how many moneyers the city supported during each coin type. This is not as reliable
a method: there is no guarantee that all moneyers worked at once,
and some were clearly more productive than others, but in the case of
large mint-places like London and its nearest competitors it is likely
that these factors balance out overall, and hence that the number of
moneyers does roughly correspond to the (relative) significance of
the output. At the outset of this period, the number of moneyers
active in London jumped from ten in the reform type of Edgar and
his sons, to 31 in the first part of Æthelred II's 'Hand' type (from
about 980). The number of moneyers peaked in the reign of Cnut:
69 in his first two successive types (79 with Southwark). Even at the
high point of production late in Æthelred's reign and early in Cnut's,
no other mint-town had more than 40 moneyers.[63]

London's truly frenetic phase of activity was c.980–1040, that is
to say, from the resumption of viking raids until roughly the time of
Cnut's sons – a time when armies, heavy taxation and unrest shook
the kingdom repeatedly. A similar trend can be detected at other
large mint-places in England, but it began earlier in London and was
much more pronounced. This was of course also a period when the
city was growing apace. It was a major port, and a key concentration

of wealth and trade. Yet economic importance was emphatically not the only force behind such huge production of coin: if so, there would have been no drop-off in the mid-eleventh century, when all other indicators show London going from strength to strength. Rather, London's phase of spectacularly voluminous minting was the result of demand rather than supply; of a new pressure that was brought to bear on the city. Put simply, London's minting activity was a consequence of being so centrally located and close to the royal regime. The London moneyers' engorged output reflects the reliance placed on it as demands associated with the king and his projects escalated, culminating with the famous series of tribute payments handed over to the vikings that began in 991. The only one of these payments known to have been gathered and paid at a specific location took place at London in 1012. It may well have been the assembly point for earlier collections of tribute as well.[64]

A significant portion of these sums and others that kept the moneyers of London hard at work would have come from the Londoners themselves, but by no means all. One doubts that the whole kingdom was coming to London to pay their share (not least because of the enhanced activity of other mint-places), but, just as unscrupulous landowners could claim their neighbours' property by paying any tax that they could not afford,[65] middlemen could have profited from gathering any exaction locally, perhaps in kind or bullion as well as cash, and having it commuted or minted in London. A large swathe of south-east England may have been prone to such machinations, for London was actually quite distinct for the degree to which it dominated the surrounding area, with no other substantial mint-towns for some distance.[66] London moneyers would also have been poised to mint the pay or plunder of the rich *liðsmenn*, stationed in the city from 1012. The city's moneyers may therefore have been as much beneficiaries as victims of the pressure that was being applied to the English.

Eventually, the pace of London's minting activity started to ease. Around 1040 it had fewer than 30 moneyers in each coin-issue. Numbers recovered somewhat for most of the reign of Edward the Confessor, though they still fell a long way short of the dizzying heights of earlier years. Only around 1060 did London's minting activity drop off precipitously. In the run-up to the Norman Conquest, it had only about 8–12 moneyers, meaning that it was comparable in scale to Lincoln and Winchester, and even a little smaller than York. Figures from Lincoln, Winchester and York suggest that the average output of each moneyer also declined in the mid-eleventh century, a pattern that probably applied at London, too. More broadly, the mid-eleventh century saw smaller and middling mints pick up a larger share of minting. Whereas London alone had sometimes accounted for 40 per cent of all the late tenth- and early eleventh-century pennies recovered as single finds from England (these being the ones most likely to reflect random losses, and therefore the profile of the currency in circulation), and the top five mints up to 75 per cent, after about 1050 the balance shifted in the opposite direction: the other mints collectively came to account for 50–60 per cent of lost single finds. On the whole, this seems to be a matter of London and the other large mint-towns contributing less, while the smaller mint-places held relatively steady. There were both push and pull factors at work here. The push away from the main towns came from the diminution and, in 1051, temporary cessation of the annual tax known as *heregeld*, which had probably skewed minting towards the major centres and shunted a large part of output into the hands of the vikings. The pull factor came when, as minting returned to what might be called a 'natural' state, reflecting local administrative and commercial needs rather than demands for viking tribute, the multiplying and growing small towns of England took on a larger role in the monetary economy.[67]

Despite its changing contribution to the actual minting of coin, by 1066 London was firmly established as the organisational lynchpin for making and distributing the stamps or dies used to make coins: a legacy of its earlier monetary dominance and a sign of its economic and administrative prominence. In a system as tightly controlled as that of late Anglo-Saxon England, the making of dies was a crucial part of the process; dies were, in modern terms, quite literally a licence to make money. Even so, tracing the history of their distribution is difficult. Centralised distribution and more regionalised arrangements alternated in the decades after Edgar's reform in the early 970s. Winchester is usually considered to have been an important source of dies for the kingdom as a whole early in this period, but it is likely that London became a major player as well before the end of the tenth century. When obverse dies were occasionally moved between mint-places, London features prominently as one of the two locations involved: a map of such links drawn for the mid- and later parts of Æthelred II's reign looks very much like a spider's web focused on London.[68] These probably show instances of dies being returned to the minting system's distribution centre after their use had ended in one location, and then being sent out for use elsewhere when they were found still to be in good working order.

From the middle part of Cnut's reign onwards a more settled pattern of nationwide distribution can be identified, continuing down to the Norman Conquest. The centre responsible for these dies can be identified with some confidence as London. Domesday Book states that in 1066 moneyers from Hereford and Worcester had to go to London to obtain their dies at times of recoinage.[69] Some at least of those dies were being made and/or kept a stone's throw from the Thames. Spoil from the redevelopment of a site now known as Thames Exchange (formerly Three Cranes Wharf), near the north end of Southwark Bridge, was taken away and spread out to make a muddy morass which metal-detector users could work over. Any archaeological context was therefore lost. Among the many treasures found in these vats of muck was a group of four coin dies dating to between the early eleventh and mid-twelfth centuries. All were reverse dies naming their associated mint and moneyer. One came from Southwark, the rest from further afield: Northampton, Norwich and Wareham.[70] These four dies could well have come from a building like that found in York which served as a minting workshop in the tenth century.[71] It was to this neighbourhood on the Thames that moneyers from Hereford and Worcester perhaps went to get their dies in 1066.

The Great and the Good: Running Late Anglo-Saxon London

As London became, in practice, one of the nerve centres of English government as well as a key hub of trade, the great and the good of the kingdom sought to acquire property there. London was one of the most important places in the realm in which to have a foothold of some kind, for everyone from the king downwards. A royal palace definitely stood somewhere in the city: it was there, in 1017, that Cnut finally ordered the treacherous Eadric Streona to be killed, and had his corpse thrown over the wall into the ditch.[72] The city was dotted with other estates owned by major churches and aristocrats.[73] This was not in itself unique, but the breadth of London's interests is striking.

These properties served several purposes. They could provide a pied-à-terre during visits, and urban estates could also be a lucrative source of profit. In London these were often structured as a *haga* or (in Latin) *curtis*: a contiguous block of urban land, often enclosed as a distinct unit. Canterbury and Worcester retained such properties from earlier times, and St Paul's in the tenth century became known as *Paulesbyri* (i.e. 'Paul's bury/*burh*'), also denoting a distinct enclosed chunk of land.[74] In the late Anglo-Saxon period, many others got in on the act, some even from outside England: in the eleventh century, and possibly since 918, St Peter's in Ghent had owned land at Greenwich, Lewisham and Woolwich, and in the south-eastern part of the City itself.[75] There was also extensive interest closer to home, including from the abbeys of Chertsey and Ely. The former acquired in the early eleventh century a *curtis* in London with a wharf exempt from toll, situated near a landing-place called 'fish-hythe';[76] the latter was granted a prime estate, later known as *Abboteshai* ('abbot's *haga*'), by one Leofwine, as penance for having fatally struck his mother with a log during a heated argument.[77] Other *hagan* were tied to specific manors outside London: *Stæningahaga*, which Edward the Confessor granted to Westminster Abbey, was linked to Staines in Middlesex,[78] while *Basingahaga* (recorded in the twelfth century) related to Basing in Hampshire.[79] Unfortunately, the famous Domesday survey of England, which compared holdings of land in 1085–6 with those of January 1066, does not cover London: a blank folio comes before the section on Middlesex, which may have once been intended to describe London.[80] Hence knowledge about late Anglo-Saxon landholding in London is patchy, and mostly derives from charters and wills held by major churches elsewhere in England,[81] meaning that much more is known about bishops' and monasteries' property than that of earls and thegns. Nonetheless, enough anecdotal and indirect evidence survives to show that such individuals – including major figures like Earl Godwine and his sons – held extensive land in the city.[82] The area known in subsequent centuries as Aldermanbury (i.e. 'the ealdorman's *burh*'), located near the former Cripplegate fort, may also have once served as a secular enclosed estate, though it is not clear which ealdorman its name referred to,[83] and in any case the fort was probably invisible above ground in the post-Roman period.[84]

Earls and leading thegns operated on a national level, owning land all over England between Yorkshire and the Channel. When they came to London, they did so essentially as visitors. Handling of day-to-day affairs in the city was the responsibility of worthies based closer to home. London's governance was a larger and more complex version of what can be seen in other late Anglo-Saxon towns.[85] While the structure as a whole cannot be grasped, it is in the late Anglo-Saxon period that some elements of the system on which the City of London has been run down to modern times begin to emerge out of the gloom. These elements can be broken down into institutions and positions. Of the former, the Court of Husting is the first to appear in (probably) the late tenth century. It must already have been well established and respected, for the earliest mention comes from a long way from London (Ramsey, Cambridgeshire). At this time the Husting was referred to as an authority on weights of precious metals, though it probably had wider responsibilities: by the end of the twelfth century it was a court of wide-ranging jurisdiction, presided over by the mayor, sheriffs and aldermen.[86] The earliest reference to the Husting is not specifically dated and represents a Latin translation contained in a chronicle put together at the monastery of Ramsey, though there is no obvious reason to doubt its authority.[87] Another, less problematic, document from Canterbury from the 1030s confirms the existence of the Husting by that time.[88] The Court of Husting has traditionally been related to the Scandinavian presence in the city,[89] because the earliest weight it regulated was the mark, originally a Scandinavian unit.[90] However, by the latter part of the tenth century the mark and ora were in widespread use across eastern England,[91] and the derivation of 'husting' is murky: it has often been seen as Old Norse (*húsþing* or *húskarla þing*, 'meeting of housecarls') but Old English is equally plausible, referring to a meeting associated with a house.[92] In addition to the Husting there may also have been a more general assembly of citizens, which a set of laws issued by King Edgar stipulated should meet three times a year.[93] The Folkmoot, which gathered three times a year in St Paul's churchyard, could have been London's form of this meeting: it is not specifically known to have met before the twelfth century, but by that time it was already an archaism.[94] Either the Husting, the Folkmoot or both could have met on the site of the later Guildhall (established in the twelfth century), which was an open area on the site of the Roman amphitheatre.[95] However, recent excavations have not revealed any remnant of substantial activity on the site between the fourth and twelfth centuries, and there is no sign that in the tenth and eleventh centuries it was anything other than a shallow and boggy depression on the northern fringe of the city, which would soon be flattened out by occupation.[96]

London in the late Anglo-Saxon period operated as a sort of shire in miniature – or, perhaps, a very large town which dominated its small shire.[97] The Husting was thus the equivalent of a shire court, and like other shires London had sub-units with their own assemblies in which local grievances were aired. These sub-units were the wards, headed by individuals known as aldermen, and they served a similar purpose to territories known as 'hundreds' in other shires (which were also, according to a law code of Edgar's, overseen by a *hundrodes ealdor*).[98] Already by the early twelfth century there were at least 22 or 23 wards identifiable in a list of St Paul's properties within the city. Indeed, it is likely that the full complement of 24 which existed until 1394 had already come into being.[99] As with the Folkmoot, there is no specific evidence that the wards originated in the Anglo-Saxon period, though given how well established they were by the twelfth century it is likely that they grew up in the eleventh or before, perhaps at the same time that hundreds come into focus elsewhere.

The circumstances that might have given rise to the development of wards are revealed by the history of a body known as the gild of English *cnihtas*. *Cniht* is the origin of the later term 'knight', but in the Anglo-Saxon period its connotations were closer to 'young man' or even 'retainer/servant'.[100] Like other late Anglo-Saxon gilds, it may have started as a social-cum-military association, perhaps formed from the London-based men of powerful lords, or those responsible for local government.[101] The specifically 'English' name of the gild raises the possibility that there may have been comparable bodies for Scandinavian or other groups. A writ of Edward the Confessor – copied so faithfully from an original or early copy around 1400 that even the distinctive calligraphy and abbreviations of the eleventh century were retained – states that the gild had been formed under Edgar,[102] and held extensive lands with various privileges including 'soke': the power to collect fines and exact certain obligations from a given area, held by only a few larger landholders in the city.[103] Importantly, the property of the gild mostly lay outside the north-east portion of the wall, and corresponds to the ward of Portsoken. In the 1120s, this land and all the privileges pertaining to it were given by the descendants of the original gild members to Holy Trinity Priory at Aldgate. All the documents relating to the gild of *cnihtas* were preserved by Holy Trinity. In addition to Edward's writ, the church provided a narrative of the gild's foundation, allegedly by 13 *cnihtas* under Edgar, who had to hold duels in East Smithfield market to confirm their claim, and who determined how much land they owned south of the river by seeing how far a mounted man could throw a spear over it.[104] These more dramatic elements of the story are perhaps embellished, but there is no reason to doubt that the gild was set up under Edgar. London's complicated local geography seems to have resulted from processes of this kind: concessions of lands and rights to individuals, groups or institutions that later became fossilised as administrative and/or ecclesiastical units.

The 15 men who dissolved the gild of English *cnihtas* included some of the most powerful figures in the city: moneyers, goldsmiths, an alderman and a canon of St Paul's.[105] Leadership of London involved multiple overlapping responsibilities, formal and informal, professional and social, and probably always had done.[106] In the Anglo-Saxon period, however, it is more difficult to pin down who these individuals were. Reeves were probably the lynchpins of urban government,[107] and mediated between local and royal administration, particularly in relation to finance and other royal prerogatives. It is possible that the London law code of Æthelstan already refers to a pair of London reeves, in the form of the two otherwise unknown officials who attended the assembly at Thunderfield seemingly targeted at reeves (see Chapter 6).[108] But such figures only begin to

emerge with any clarity in the eleventh century, especially during
the reign of Edward the Confessor, in the context of writs which
addressed officials pertaining to the affected area. Writs relating to
London and Middlesex introduce a series of individuals associated
with the city: most are described as 'port-reeve', and in one case
from the 1040s the portreeve for London had the same name as the
contemporary shire-reeve (i.e. sheriff) of Middlesex.[109] By the early
twelfth century these offices were closely connected, and dominated
by the city.[110] Under Edward there were sometimes at least two portreeves for London;[111] although neither is called a sheriff, it is possible
that this pair of reeves for London mirrored the twelfth-century
arrangement of London nominating two reeves, one each for the
city and for Middlesex.[112] Most of the figures named as portreeves
in eleventh-century London are little more than names. But, like
their twelfth-century descendants among the gild of *cnihtas*, some
probably held other roles and offices in the city as part of a nascent
urban élite. Swetman, named as portreeve in a writ of 1058×1066,
has the same name as a moneyer who issued coins from the end of
Cnut's reign until just after 1066,[113] and a moneyer of the same period
named Deorman seems to have been the patriarch of a family that
became influential after the Norman Conquest.[114]

The reeves were far from the only prominent individuals in the
city, and indeed their responsibilities probably did not extend to
crucial matters like military leadership or presiding at courts. A
few documents mention secular officials named 'stallers' who held
a higher level of authority under Cnut and his successors; two of
them, A(n)sgar and Osgod Clapa, members of the same family, held
power in London and its environs, while another in-law of theirs,
Tofi the Proud, refounded Waltham Abbey in the time of Cnut.[115]
The role of ealdormen or earls – the dominant group of magnates
in the kingdom as a whole – is less clear in London. The city did
not lie within the remit of any of Edward's more prominent earls,
although Middlesex and Hertfordshire were subject to Godwine's
younger son Leofwine in the 1050s and 1060s.[116] Courts in the city
during the tenth and eleventh centuries seem to have been presided
over by the bishop of London and sometimes the 'stallers', supported
by reeves.

The Church in Late Anglo-Saxon London

The bishop headed one of the two most important ecclesiastical institutions in the city. Whatever remains of the Anglo-Saxon incarnation of London's cathedral is obscured by the subsequent post-Conquest and post-Fire building at St Paul's, so that even the exact location of the Anglo-Saxon cathedral is a matter of debate. Most likely it is now covered by the footprint of the present building, and was once a smaller edifice situated in the midst of the enclosure known as *Paulesbyri*.[117] The bishops of London, based at a palace close to St Paul's, were a significant presence in London and the surrounding area during the late Anglo-Saxon era. Several of them fulfilled a long-standing tradition of the London see playing a prominent diplomatic and political role, extending well beyond London itself. In the later Anglo-Saxon period, the bishopric of London repeatedly served as an important stepping stone for ecclesiastics destined for the very highest and most prominent positions. St Dunstan, a monastic reformer and confidant of King Edgar's, was briefly bishop of London before being translated to the archbishopric of Canterbury in 959; and Wulfstan, who wrote numerous law codes and religious tracts and worked closely with Æthelred II and Cnut, was also bishop of London 996–1002 before becoming archbishop of York and bishop of Worcester.[118] Even some of the bishops with less exalted careers were still clearly right-hand men to the king: Bishop Ælfhun was, in 1013, entrusted with the writing of royal diplomas,[119] and later in the same year with the even more sensitive mission of escorting King Æthelred's sons from London to their exile in Normandy.[120] However, the tendency to appoint ambitious and well-connected men had its risks. Several bishops of London were more concerned to polish the reputation of their former monastery, or to enrich themselves, rather than enhance the standing of the see itself. For these reasons it was not an especially rich institution compared to other English dioceses.[121]

The other major ecclesiastical institution which implanted itself rapidly and vigorously onto the London landscape in the tenth and especially eleventh centuries was the abbey of St Peter at Westminster. Later sources claimed that the monastery had been founded in the seventh century, though the tendency towards inventive reimagination of history at later medieval Westminster was so strong that these assertions carry little weight, and have not yet been substantiated by archaeological discoveries.[122] What is clearer is that Westminster was, most likely in the late 950s or after, taken in hand by St Dunstan, and set on a firmer footing. The abbey was constituted as a Benedictine house for 12 monks, supported by a series of new estates that ran from Westminster itself to the north-west.[123] It remained a relatively minor establishment until the eleventh century. Cnut's son Harold I was buried there in 1040, until his corpse was exhumed and thrown into a swamp following the accession of his half-brother,[124] and the abbey came into its own when Edward the Confessor began to lavish largesse upon it. He and other major landowners gave properties all over England, including some in the vicinity of London at places like Claygate, Greenford, Hampstead, Hanwell, Hendon, Leyton, Shepperton, Sunbury and Wanstead.[125] What drew Edward to Westminster was never made explicit, but a hagiographer writing shortly after Edward's death said that he hoped to be buried there,[126] and a church that lay close to London but had not traditionally been the object of major patronage perhaps appealed, as a relatively blank institutional canvas close to a city of rapidly growing importance.[127] The king's generosity seems to have prompted the people of London to follow suit. One of the many forgeries concocted by the monks of Westminster in the twelfth century was a supposed charter of William the Conqueror's from 1067, which guaranteed the monastery's property and showed William's devotion to Edward's favoured church.[128] While the document cannot be taken as a reliable record of William's actions, it contains summaries of many smaller grants that he supposedly confirmed, and these may be more credible. Sixteen are recorded in total, virtually all relating to Londoners giving over small properties in or near the city; many did so in return for association with the monastic community, as was common practice at the time. Four of these donations are said to have originally been made in the time of Edward the Confessor and/or Abbot Eadwine of Westminster (c.1049–1068×1072);[129] three were confirmed or restored by William. The others most likely belong to the same era. A whole parade of small urban property-owners who disposed of houses and wharves comes into view through this Westminster document. Their grants offer an insight into the local piety that moved the prosperous citizens of mid-eleventh-century London. One donor, Godwine Greatsyd, was the chief of the masons who worked on the new abbey church. Another had temporarily held land belonging to the monastery in return for guarding London Bridge. A man who rejoiced in the name Wulfsige Lickestoppe bequeathed his own house on *Westceape* (Westcheap, the western part of the major commercial street of Cheapside), along with several others. This collection must of course be read with care, but probably does contain the remnants of a small cache of records by which William confirmed numerous grants to Westminster by the Londoners.

Westminster's swift build-up of land was impressive enough, but it was the great building project Edward funded that really took observers' breath away. A vast new church was built, about 100 m in length. Edward's team of master-craftsmen, three of them known by name (including Godwine Greatsyd),[130] adopted from Normandy and elsewhere in mainland Europe a new style of building now known as 'Romanesque', which was characterised by grand and sturdy structures adorned with elegant rounded arches. At Westminster, this was combined with native Anglo-Saxon taste for rich surface adornment.[131] Only a few small fragments of this enormous church survive, for it was rebuilt more or less from the ground up by Edward's pious descendant Henry III (1216–72) two centuries later. Elements of Edward's church can be seen in the dormitory undercroft, and in a wooden door – the oldest in England – made from timber felled in the period 1032–64.[132] More fragments of the church have been found in excavations. However, the best impression of its fresh grandeur is conveyed by the representation of it, shortly after completion, on the Bayeux Tapestry (Figure 7.5).

In 1066 Westminster was among the greatest churches in northern Europe, so ambitious that it was barely finished by the time Edward himself went to his deathbed. The consecration of the new church – represented on the Bayeux Tapestry – was his last major act, undertaken on 28 December 1065, just a week before his death.[133] By this time the abbey was also the focal point of what was in effect a suburb of London. Domesday Book recorded that in 1086 Westminster contained a minimum of 86 households beyond the abbey itself,

Figure 7.5. Representation of
Westminster Abbey on the Bayeux Tapestry.

including 61 peasants who rented farmland from the abbot and 25 soldiers or men-at-arms. This agglomeration was treated like any other rural property by the Domesday assessors, though it was clearly a substantial community which was growing in the shadow of the abbey on one side and the city on the other.[134]

Westminster was probably involved only on a limited scale in the provision of pastoral care to the city's populace, and although the bishop of St Paul's was responsible for overseeing the needs of an area that stretched across Essex, Middlesex and part of Hertfordshire, he was not expected to minister directly to the whole territory himself. In the past, pastoral duties had fallen to minsters, each staffed by several clergy collectively responsible for a large area.[135] But in the eleventh century the ecclesiastical landscape of England changed dramatically, as a plethora of small local churches sprang up: the ancestors of the parish churches that still dot the English landscape, both rural and urban. In the context of London, the first flush of local church building sheds valuable light on the city's infrastructure, for its ecclesiastical and secular arrangements were closely related, as seen already in the case of Portsoken ward, the parish of Holy Trinity and the gild of English *cnihtas*.[136] London quickly gained an impressive number of local churches – by far the most of any English city.[137] When William FitzStephen wrote his famous description of London in the late twelfth century, he claimed that it had 126 parish churches,[138] and modern analysis has arrived at a fairly similar figure: John Schofield's magisterial study of city churches surveyed the evidence for 108 of them, most of which can be traced back at least to the twelfth century.[139] Between centuries of rebuilding, fire and bombing, few of London's churches preserve much physical evidence of their earliest history, at least above ground. Only one, All Hallows Barking/All Hallows-by-the-Tower, contains a standing archway that could date to the late Anglo-Saxon period, and even this was only uncovered thanks to bomb damage in the Blitz (Figures 7.6 and 7.7).[140] An early date is supported, however, by a series of fragments of Anglo-Saxon sculpture uncovered in the church around the same time.[141] The sites of two other city churches (St Benet Fink and St John the Baptist upon Walbrook) have also produced pieces of tenth- or eleventh-century sculpture.[142]

Figure 7.6. Archway of possibly Anglo-Saxon date in All Hallows-by-the-Tower.

Figure 7.7. Part of a series of Anglo-Saxon sculptural
fragments from the tenth or eleventh century, found in All
Hallows-by-the-Tower between the 1920s and 1950s.

In total, some 27 of the churches surveyed by Schofield are represented by archaeological traces from before about 1100; tellingly,
hardly any date to before about 1000.[143] London's first generation of
local churches was essentially an eleventh-century phenomenon.[144]
These early churches seem to have originated as small one- or two-
celled constructions made at least in part from reclaimed Roman
remains.[145] One, St Bride's on Fleet Street, lay outside the city walls
just across the river Fleet, probably near to 'London Fen'. This was
a marginal zone, where land met water and the living met the dead:
a pit nearby (on the City side of the Fleet) held 11 bodies but only
three skulls,[146] so may represent criminals or outcasts of some kind
buried sometime around the eleventh century; and St Bride's itself
seems to have grown up around a well. A small cluster of burials
accompanied this first modest stone church of the late Anglo-Saxon
era. Among them was the tiny body of a stillborn baby, carefully laid
to rest in a stone coffin. Although there are no early texts to explain
the circumstances of this or any of the other burials, or indeed the
unusual dedication of the church to the Irish St Brigid, the physical
remains tell a fascinating story of what may have begun as a family
establishment evolving into an eleventh-century parish church.[147]

Only a few other churches are known from references in Anglo-
Saxon-era texts. St Andrew Holborn is, remarkably, referred to in a

charter boundary description of the late tenth century; by this time
it was the 'old wooden church of St Andrew' (*ealde stoccene sancte
andreas cyricean*), though how old it may have been is not clear.[148] It is
one of precious few churches in or near London that predates 1000.
All Hallows Lombard Street (on the corner with Gracechurch Street)
was bequeathed by a man named Brihtmær 'of Gracechurch' (*at
Gerschereche*, 'of the grass/thatch-roofed church') to Christ Church,
Canterbury, at some point in the period between 1052 and 1070.
The document recording this bequest suggests that the church was
built on Brihtmær's own property as a sort of private operation.[149]
This was one of the main ways in which parishes were starting to
emerge in towns as well as the countryside in the tenth and eleventh
centuries, as local landowners or communities built churches that
served their own needs.[150] At least nine other churches, most only
recorded for the first time after the Norman Conquest, have names
that point to their origin as churches of wealthy patrons who could
have been active before 1066.[151] London's numerous churches thus
probably reflect its complicated knot of small, intersecting interests.
Land and involvement in the city had become valuable commodities.

A Growing City

The attractions of coming to London were numerous: access to
markets brought possibilities of employment, and perhaps eventually enrichment, especially to those with resources, contacts or
desirable skills. If later medieval parallels are anything to go by, the
urban population at times of growth would have been in a constant
state of rapid turnover, and there were probably almost as many
stories of migration into the city as there were migrants.[152] Regular
visitors might have graduated from extended sojourns to permanent
settlement. Specialists are more likely to have moved from further
away, relocating from smaller to larger towns. In the age of viking
depredations, London's relative security may have made it a haven for
refugees, as well as a base for numerous warriors. Others might have
come to the city in connection with a lord's business, like the *cnihtas*
who formed the gild discussed earlier. There must often have been

friction between these groups. As discussed above, the *Encomium Emmae reginae* suggests that in 1016 not all the city's population favoured the cause of Edmund Ironside, and that he was spirited out of the city by a minority faction in the army assembled there. The eventful last months of 1066 were another time of contention.[153] But there was enough common interest uniting the people of London (as of other large cities of the day) to create a strong sense of cohesion.[154] Economic opportunities and mutual dependence of one citizen on another would have carried weight at all levels, from members of the élite who wanted a dwelling in the city and a stake in its wealth, to relatively humble peasant migrants.[155]

Not all of the latter who made the move to London were even necessarily free to do so. One large category of peasants in later Anglo-Saxon England consisted of *geburas*, known as *(in)nati* in Latin: both terms reflect that their birth at a specific location entitled the landlord to some claim over them and their labour. In principle this meant they should not be able to relocate, though there is good evidence that they often did so. At Ely in the late tenth century, a list was prepared of *geburas* associated with the estate of Hatfield in Hertfordshire, including many who had moved to other villages, sometimes up to 20 miles away and in a different shire.[156] Some perhaps even did so in groups, such as three young men from Hatfield who had gone together to Clavering in Essex. None of the Ely *geburas* had moved to a town (maybe because it only listed peasants who were still within a day's journey), but it is entirely credible that towns were a magnet to peasants who did not have ready prospects at home.

Policing wayward peasants was a concern both for lords and incipient urban authorities. Towns at this time were emphatically not oases of freedom in which 'feudal' obligations dissolved; on the contrary, they were tightly woven into networks of land and lordship.[157] In what is now Belgium, the earliest medieval town charter (issued for Huy in August 1066) stipulated that anyone entering into the town remained the dependant of their lord, and also that anyone in the town who could be proved to be the slave or peasant of a lord should be returned to them.[158] London and other English towns may have handled the issue of rural–urban migration in a more collaborative way. Domesday Book lists hundreds of examples of urban properties which were tied to rural estates, usually within about 20 miles. The origins and purposes of these 'urban fields' (sometimes also known as 'contributory estates') have been a battleground for scholarship since the nineteenth century. The case has been made that they reflect obligations to maintain town fortifications, or rural lords seeking to invest in urban property.[159] Some were simply the result of predatory landlords taking advantage of whatever opportunities fate presented them. Domesday Book says that in one case a house in Guildford became attached to the bishop of Bayeux's estate of Bramley a couple of miles south simply because it belonged to a widow who had married the estate's reeve.[160] A variety of scenarios undoubtedly lie behind the 'urban fields' in eleventh-century England, and given the existence of documents like the Ely list which show lords keeping close watch on their rights over migrating peasants at an earlier date, it is worth asking whether some of the Domesday 'urban fields' could have come into being when rural tenants relocated to a town. Doing so would have been a win–win situation: lords retained some of the income and privileges that they derived from the tenants, but also gained rights in the relevant town, while tenants could peacefully move to a new home. London, it must be said, was not particularly well provided with 'urban fields'. A total of 150 individuals or urban properties were linked to 11 rural estates. By comparison, Canterbury in 1066 had 291 individuals or properties linked to 16 estates, and Lewes 258 from 35 estates.[161] But the number and extent of 'urban fields' was clearly not directly proportionate to the size or importance of a town (a higher number might indicate more heavy-handed landlords, for example); nor, importantly, is the Domesday record complete, especially regarding London. London may well have welcomed a great many peasant migrants from near and far, over whom lords continued to exert a measure of control.

As immigrants, merchants and other visitors entered and made their way through the streets of late Anglo-Saxon London they would, in some respects, have encountered a city that looked and felt much like *Lundenwic*. It was still dirty and damp, and small by modern standards. But changes were afoot. They would have noticed many new houses springing up and new streets taking shape. Visitors in the eleventh century could also, perhaps for the first time in several centuries, have walked across a rebuilt London Bridge. This would have been a wooden construction, the timbers of which were felled at some point in the period 987–1032. Already by the mid-1010s it was playing a prominent part in descriptions of London's role in the vicious fighting between the English and the vikings.[162] The city was again becoming important as a conduit and access point.

Late Anglo-Saxon London is known archaeologically from a great quantity of material: 150 buildings had been identified by 2010.[163] These for the most part were like the buildings of earlier times in being fairly small, single-storey wooden affairs, in need of frequent replacement and prone to filth and fire.[164] Yet there was growing diversity in their construction and appearance, most likely as a result of different traditions among incoming settlers.[165] There are occasional signs of greater investment and comfort. Some buildings had glass windows, and others, set back from the street fronts, were built with timber cellars, presumably for storing merchandise.[166] But the largest change was in the quantity rather than the quality of new construction. While only a few streets can be traced back to the era of Alfred and his immediate heirs in the early tenth century,[167] a significant proportion of the city's medieval street plan is thought to have originated between the mid-tenth century and the Norman Conquest, pushing north of Cheapside. What emerged was a tendril-like pattern of streets, which branched out from and within the more grid-like pattern of Alfredian London (Map 5).

These are better interpreted as the result of organic growth than of an overarching plan. A group of roads emanating from Cheapside (Westcheap at this time) may have been created and/or named for particular commodities; hence Milk Street, Wood Street, Bread Street and so on.[168] It was not just a matter of new streets springing up: existing ones were becoming more thickly built-up too. Alleyways serving many buildings set back from the street frontage proliferated as the city grew in the eleventh century.[169] The resulting maze of streets, still apparent in the layout of the modern City, owes very little to the Roman cityscape (save the walls), and is essentially a new creation that started to take shape in the later Anglo-Saxon period.[170] There was extensive growth beyond Cheapside into the north-west of the Roman city and east to the vicinity of the Tower.[171]

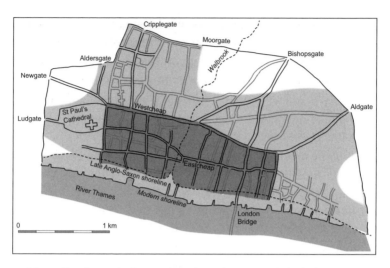

Map 5. London in the late ninth to eleventh centuries. The darker streets and inner area of shading respectively show the probable Alfredian-era layout and approximate extent of substantial settlement; lighter streets and shading show approximate extensions by the mid-eleventh century.

Excavations at 1 Poultry, on Cheapside itself, exemplify this transformation. The site was settled from around the year 900 or even before. Buildings were fairly spread out during its first century or so of activity, however.[172] Towards the end of the tenth century there was a sharp change in the character of the area. Many new buildings went up, lining the street frontage more or less completely. Detritus shows diverse trades in the vicinity: a bone- or metal-worker left practice engravings on scraps of bone and horn; a large number of shoes indicates the presence of a leather worker; and another building operated as a smithy.[173] One of the first inhabitants of this district etched their name – either the male Ælfbeorht or the female Ælfburh – into a piece of decorated bone, which was then lost in a pit in what is now Guildhall Yard,[174] and a churchyard with burials established on the site of the later Guildhall in the mid-eleventh century still lay next to open fields.[175] Layers from 1 Poultry dating to between the mid-eleventh and mid-twelfth centuries threw up even more signs of the vibrant lives of people in this part of London. There was a musical instrument made of horn, and a set of bone ice skates. The latter bring to mind William FitzStephen's lively account of young

Londoners dashing at each other full pelt across the frozen marshes north of the city in the twelfth century.[176] Their great-grandparents a hundred years earlier may have had a similar taste for extreme sports, held on the relatively open ground in the east and north-east of the city that was still without major streets or significant buildings.

Separate and quite distinct processes of expansion were going on elsewhere. Southwark and Westminster blossomed as London's principal suburbs, and a ribbon of habitation started to develop between the latter and the city.[177] Along the Thames waterfront, demand for new land and access to the river stimulated land reclamation just outside the Roman river wall, along the shore of the Thames. The process had to be repeated every few decades or so from the late tenth century onwards as successive generations of revetments needed replacing, which resulted in the reclamation of strips of land stretching down to and into the river from what is now Lower Thames Street (which formerly ran roughly along the shoreline).[178] Rectangular areas would be marked out with rows of wooden piles, and the enclosed area filled with diverse materials: wood, earth and stone, much of it reclaimed from pre-existing contexts such as buildings and ships.[179] By the eleventh century, the narrow strip of land between the river walls and the river had widened enough to accommodate a significant number of buildings, and a collapse of part of the river wall, probably at some point between 1016 and 1066, would have helped to facilitate access to this ribbon of land.[180] Inhabitants of the houses built here enjoyed a relatively comfortable existence: one building produced an impressively wide range of foodstuffs, including wheat, sloe, plum, cherry, blackberry or raspberry, elder, hazelnuts, mammal and fish bones, and even oyster and mussel shells.[181] But it is the revetments and their infills that have proven most revealing. The wooden remains found at Bull Wharf and New Fresh Wharf include parts of several ships that shed light on the types of vessel that frequented London in the tenth and eleventh centuries. They indicate multiple different styles of construction and close contact with the rest of north-west Europe: both construction techniques and some of the actual timbers seem to have originated overseas, particularly in the areas making up modern Scandinavia, the Baltic and the Netherlands. One tenth-century Frisian vessel is known from about 16 timbers cut up and reused at Bull Wharf; it would originally have been at least 18 m in length.[182]

Multiple other sources show that international trading contacts were starting to blossom. In the middle of the twelfth century, the men of Rouen asserted that they had possessed special rights to a wharf in London at Dowgate since the time of Edward the Confessor. If they found anyone else using it, the interlopers had one full and one ebb-tide to make themselves scarce before the Rouennais would displace them by force, without any fear of reprisal.[183] Pottery finds from the city start to include a more appreciable element from continental Europe in the late tenth and eleventh centuries.[184] At the higher end of the market for overseas imports is a beautiful enamel brooch, framed in gold, which was made in Ottonian Germany and found in the nineteenth century at Dowgate Hill, next to Cannon Street Station.[185] Fragments of silk garments dating to the late tenth century were found in refuse on Milk Street. They do not come from an élite setting, and probably represent the possessions of London's prosperous traders and artisans.[186] There are also coins and seals from as far afield as Byzantium, as well as Belgium, Germany, Norway and Ireland.[187]

These foreign connections are further illuminated by a remarkable legal tract known as 'IV Æthelred'. It survives only as part of a collection of Old English laws assembled around 1100 and translated into somewhat idiosyncratic Latin, but is still peppered with vernacular terminology that defeated the translator's capabilities.[188] Since it was edited in 1840 as supposedly Æthelred II's fourth law code, 'IV Æthelred' has been seen as a single unit written to regulate London's trade and minting around 1000, though in reality it is a complicated document spliced together from at least two separate texts, neither of them necessarily from the time of Æthelred.[189] Its second half is in fact probably the older piece of text. It consists of regulations regarding currency crimes, very similar to those of Æthelstan and Edgar. Parts of this text seem to have been drawn on by an earlier law of Æthelred II's probably put together in 997, so that part of it must have been in existence by then. Whether it originated in London or not is a mystery. But the most intriguing part of 'IV Æthelred' is what comes before this currency-related section: a series of regulations on toll payments in London. These explain how much should be paid for various kinds of ship which brought diverse commodities into the city, among them cloth, timber, wool, fish and wine. The list also specifies the nationality of some of the traders bringing these goods. They include visitors from Flanders, Francia (probably the Île-de-France), Normandy and Ponthieu, while merchants from three towns in the Meuse Valley (Huy, Liège and Nivelles) who might be passing through London are singled out for special treatment. Most intriguing of all are a group referred to as 'the men of the [Holy Roman] emperor', who had privileges almost as extensive as those of the Londoners themselves. These 'men of the emperor' could have been merchants from Cologne or other towns in the Rhineland, which was fast becoming an economic powerhouse, and a crucial trading partner for London.[190]

Unusually, the toll list portion of 'IV Æthelred' has several pieces of Old French as well as Old English terminology mixed into its Latin text. The compiler who in around 1100 put together the collection of laws in which it survives was presumably confronted either with a text that swung back and forth between Old English and Old French, or a Latin text which incorporated pieces of Old English and French vocabulary. Neither is likely to have been produced before the Norman Conquest made French into a more prominent language of government and day-to-day life, so this portion of 'IV Æthelred' should probably be seen as a record of the situation in the decades after 1066. Yet there is every reason to believe that the conditions it reflects were the product of years of evolution during the late Anglo-Saxon period.[191]

London's overseas contacts were just one dimension of its economic development in the century before the Norman Conquest. As the coinage indicates, it was ideally placed to capitalise on internal as well as external trade, as a go-between for traders moving in multiple directions within England. The placement of the Bull Wharf site, at the early medieval landing-place known as Æthelred's hythe, in fact suggests that it was primarily intended to accommodate traffic coming down- rather than upriver; that is to say, from the interior of England.[192] Manufactured goods were moving into and out of the city on a large scale. Lead-alloy brooches were made in London in the eleventh century and exported widely. One tranche of half-finished brooches was found while digging a sewer near Bow Church in 1838. Finds of similar brooches illustrate London's links to Lincolnshire and the rest of eastern England, and smaller numbers of London-made pewter brooches have been found even further afield: in Dublin, Germany and the Netherlands. These brooches show that London workshops were at the economic and technological forefront of the industry in the eleventh century.[193] Tenth- and early eleventh-century London's main form of pottery (known as late Saxon shelly ware) illustrates this connection very well, for it was probably manufactured in the area around Oxford, and shipped from there to London and its vicinity in large quantities.[194] This link suggests that bulk movement of goods over fairly long distances had become routine, founded on a burgeoning urban market for these pots and (one presumes) their contents. The chronology of ceramics of this kind is difficult to pin down, as they retained much the same form from c.900 until the mid-eleventh century. It is possible that finds belong to a fairly even spread across that period, but on balance it is more likely that they cluster in the later tenth and eleventh centuries, for other indexes of activity in London point to a significant increase in the tempo of activity within the city at that point.[195]

Conclusion: A City of Connections

The last century of Anglo-Saxon London saw it come closest to the title of this book: a citadel of the Saxons, which took on a leading part in the struggle against viking raids and invasions. Its military prominence was, however, a function of London's larger significance, which derived from the city's large population, prodigious wealth and centrality in the kingdom's government. All of these developments sprang from firm and readily identifiable foundations. The walls were centuries old. Within them, by the tenth century, there were precocious communal institutions, healthy minting and trade, and a relatively substantial population. London from the time of Alfred to Æthelred II was by no means inconsiderable. But it is true that the rapid and interconnected changes which began in the later tenth century left a very different kind of city in its wake.

While London under Æthelstan had been one of several substantial towns of roughly comparable size and status, London at the death of Edward the Confessor was in a league of its own. The transformation that Christopher Brooke and Gillian Keir attributed to 'the period between Alfred and Henry II'[196] (i.e. 871–1189) had its fulcrum in the four-score years leading up to the Norman Conquest. In a very real sense, the late Anglo-Saxon period was a turning point in London's history, when it went from being an important city to a great one.

This turning point is more easily described than explained, but two important factors can be singled out, which mutually supported one another. First, the late tenth and eleventh centuries were in general a favourable time for towns across much of Europe.[197] Long-distance and local commerce was increasing, and London was poised to benefit from both in a unique way. The city combined the attractions of a port with good access to east–west riverine trade and north–south movements across a rebuilt London Bridge, as well as a rich hinterland in the south-east. More circulation of people and goods compounded the impact on London, as it re-energised the advantages the city had enjoyed as a conduit under the Romans and in the age of *Lundenwic*. The redistribution of goods, and in some cases the working of raw materials before sending them on, emerged as one of London's primary attractions. It was there that one could find in abundance the commodities that made medieval England rich, such as wool, probably already important for some time,[198] and perhaps deep-sea fish such as cod and herring, the market for which appears to have blossomed at just the same time as London took off.[199] One could probably also find in the city large quantities of the goods for which these were traded: silver from Germany, wine from France and the Rhineland, silk from further east, and much else besides.

Accessibility also played a central part in the second main factor at work in this period. This was the energy that the late Anglo-Saxon monarchy applied to the running of its kingdom, aided and abetted by local agencies across the land. Scale is important here: Edgar and his heirs sought to impress a high and uniform degree of authority on the core part of their territory, stretching from the south coast to Yorkshire.[200] London's economic centrality gelled with the extending reach and ambition of Anglo-Saxon government. Arrangements for minting, which gradually placed the whole kingdom in London's orbit, exemplify the process, but the growing interest of kings in the city was also crucial. London hosted more and more meetings of the king and his advisers, in the process attracting the interest, investment and often the presence of England's élite – all of which would have further strengthened the economic demand concentrated in London, and drawn to it artisans and merchants from further afield.

A special relationship grew up between the late Anglo-Saxon monarchy and London. Each profited from association with the other, in sharp contrast to the antagonism between crown and city which characterised the later Middle Ages. London's fierce adherence to successive kings from Æthelred II onwards exemplifies the symbiotic connection between commerce and government, especially of the assertive kind practised by late Anglo-Saxon monarchs. It was intrusive and demanding, and not necessarily welcomed by others in the kingdom. In London, however, these connections were profitable enough that they were not only tolerated, but supported. The city regained prominence by capitalising on its networks and connections, whatever form they took and however they intersected.

CHAPTER 8

London in 1066

The Battle of Hastings and After

January of the year 1066 brought little cheer for the Londoners. The king, Edward the Confessor, lay ill at Westminster, having mustered the last of his strength to attend the recent Christmas festivities. He was too ill even to be present at the consecration of the vast new abbey church of Westminster, his long-term personal project, on 28 December 1065. He died a week later, at some point in the night of 4/5 January.

Edward's death set in train a series of momentous events. The king's brother-in-law, Harold Godwineson, immediately took the throne. Being one of the most powerful noblemen in England, and recognised as the late king's last designated successor, Harold seemed poised to take over in relatively seamless fashion. But trouble was brewing in several quarters. Harold's exiled brother Tostig raided the south coast in spring 1066, prompting the new king to set out from London with a large army and fleet. Later that year Tostig joined forces with the king of the Norwegians, Harald Hardrada (an Anglicised form of his epithet, meaning 'hard ruler') (1046–66), and launched an invasion of northern England. Harold raced north to stop them, and on 25 September scored a decisive victory at the battle of Stamford Bridge near York. Both Harald and Tostig were killed. For the moment, Harold seemed to be riding high. But while he was in the north, a second invasion force arrived on the south coast of England. It was led by William, duke of Normandy (duke from 1035; d.1087). William was Edward's cousin, and moreover the old king had felt a close affinity for Normandy, where he spent his youth, including the first six or so years of William's reign. According to the flexible criteria of succession in eleventh-century England,[1]

William definitely had the connections to become king, and by 1066 also possessed the right credentials. He had fought back from the stigma of a low-status mother – hence his other famous epithet, 'the bastard'[2] – and during his early years fended off challenges to his power. By 1066 he was a feared and successful ruler.[3] Moreover, William firmly believed that he was in the right when he assembled a vast fleet to invade England in the course of 1066. Edward may have made some sort of pledge that he would succeed to the English throne, during a brief visit William made to England just after Earl Godwine's temporary expulsion in 1051,[4] and more recently, it was alleged, Harold Godwineson had himself gone on an unforeseen trip to Normandy during which he swore to respect William's claim.[5] By setting himself up as king, Harold had usurped William's rightful place and compromised himself in the eyes of God and of men. In William's view, he was fair game.[6]

What happened next is well known. Harold again hastened across the kingdom, this time to meet a threat at the opposite end of the country. The two forces clashed in the Battle of Hastings on 14 October 1066.[7] After a long, hard fight that swung back and forth over the day, Harold was killed (possibly, though not certainly, by an arrow in the eye), and the English resistance crumbled. William had won the day.[8]

London only enters the story in the confused aftermath of the Battle of Hastings. The city had not been touched by either the northern or southern campaigns of 1066 thus far, and apparently served as a rallying point for the forces Harold marshalled against his brother earlier in 1066. This was entirely in keeping with the strong connections Harold and his family had in the city, and above all with the pre-eminent position London had come to occupy. There was a clear sense that as London went, so went the kingdom, and Duke William's actions after Hastings show that he too knew how crucial it was to secure London.

Following the battle itself, William began what would prove to be a long march through southern England. He began by heading east into Kent, ravaging the countryside for supplies as he went. After meting out bloody revenge to the inhabitants of Romney for slaying a detachment of Norman soldiers who had come ashore there instead of with the main invasion fleet, he met little resistance. Dover submitted without a fight, as did Canterbury – home of the most senior cleric in the land, though the archbishop, Stigand (1052–70), was not present in the town.[9] He, along with the next most senior cleric, Ealdred, archbishop of York (1060–9), was in London, where all was in foment.

The surviving English leadership was given a certain amount of breathing room by William's long progress through Kent, and by an illness that laid the duke low for a month after he seized Canterbury. During this time, the two archbishops, along with Edwin and Morcar, earls of Mercia and Northumbria respectively, and the people of London took matters into their own hands and nominated a new king: Edgar, known as 'the ætheling', meaning 'royal' or 'throne-worthy'.[10] Edgar was King Edward's great-nephew, the grandson of Edmund Ironside. He had come to be in London in 1066 by a thoroughly tortuous saga. Edmund's two sons had been sent out of England in the aftermath of Cnut's conquest in 1016, supposedly so that they could be killed quietly and far from home, but various rulers passed on the task, and by and by the two boys ended up in Hungary. There they prospered, and even married royal brides. One of the two, Edmund, died,[11] but the other son, Edward 'the Exile', lived to father several children. At King Edward's invitation, he was brought back to England in 1057, but died very soon after his return – probably in London, for he was buried in St Paul's.[12] Edgar, the prospective king in the uncertain weeks that followed the Battle of Hastings, was Edward the Exile's one surviving son. Some had high hopes for him, in part simply because he was the choice of London; as a Latin poem recounting the story of the Battle of Hastings and the ensuing events put it, 'the report flew round that London had a king and the English survivors rejoiced'.[13] A newly elected abbot from Peterborough even came to Edgar for confirmation, in the same way as other abbots had turned to earlier kings.[14] But the new king's claim did not rest on the most secure foundations. While Edgar did possess an impeccable bloodline tying him to Edward, Edmund Ironside and Æthelred II, via a prestigious mother of continental origin, he was relatively young (probably about 14), and had no experience ruling as an earl or king. These would have been difficult obstacles to overcome under the best of circumstances, and in the upheaval of late 1066 they were to prove fatal. In characteristically elliptical fashion, the writer of one of the manuscripts of the *Anglo-Saxon Chronicle* laments the disorganised way in which Edgar's claim was prosecuted: 'always the more it ought to have been forward the more it got behind, and the worse it grew from day to day, exactly as everything came to be at the end'.[15]

Such was the situation in London in the latter months of 1066, as the citizens and magnates gathered there scrambled to decide whether it was more opportune to keep up the fight with a new and untested king, or to give in to William's advance. While Edgar's short-lived bid for power took shape, William was circling in for the kill. After recovering from his illness, the duke and his army departed from Canterbury and headed west across Surrey. A detachment of Norman knights separated from the main force and moved north towards London. They drove back an attack from the city's defenders and laid waste Southwark, but did not actually penetrate London itself.[16] Some impression of the daunting citadel the Norman knights found before them is conveyed by William of Poitiers and Guy of Amiens, writers who recounted the events of the Norman Conquest (from a firmly Norman perspective) a few years after their conclusion. In William's words,

> The river Thames flows past this city, carrying foreign riches from a sea port. Although it is inhabited only by citizens, it abounds in a large population famous for their military qualities. At that time, indeed, a crowd of warriors from elsewhere had flocked thither, and the city, in spite of its great size, could scarcely accommodate them.[17]

Guy picked up on much the same qualities:

> The king struck camp and directed his steps to where teeming London shines bright. It is a most spacious city, full of evil inhabitants, and richer than anywhere else in the kingdom. Protected on the left by walls and on the right by the river, it fears neither armies nor capture by guile.[18]

Size, wealth, formidable defences, numerous belligerent inhabitants – these were all qualities that had marked the previous century
of London's history. They are also what led William to approach in
a wary yet resolute fashion: the city was large and dangerous, but, as
the focus of English power and resistance, it could not be bypassed.

Blocked from entering London by the bridge over the Thames,
William and his army swooped further west, and crossed over the
Thames at Wallingford in Berkshire. In December 1066 he came
at London from the north-west. Different sources give significantly
different accounts of what happened next. William of Poitiers states
that Archbishop Stigand was the first major figure to abandon
London and Edgar the Ætheling's cause. He met with William at
Wallingford, and the rest of the city's chief men followed suit as soon
as the Norman army came into sight.[19] The D manuscript of the
Anglo-Saxon Chronicle says nothing about Stigand, but does describe
the other key leaders, including Edgar, leaving the city to meet with
William and submit to him at (Great) Berkhamsted, Hertfordshire,
some 25 miles north-west of London.[20] Guy of Amiens' poem gives
the liveliest and most detailed account of what happened as William
bore down on London (which is not to say that it is necessarily
the most reliable). He claims that the Londoners gathered their
strength for a fight, under the leadership of a grizzled and crippled
veteran named *Ansgardus* who gave orders from a stretcher; this
was probably A(n)sgar the Staller, one of the leading officials in the
city in earlier decades.[21] William, meanwhile, set about preparing
for a siege from a base in Westminster, and issued baleful threats
to the city's stubborn defenders. Another Norman writer, William
of Jumièges, even recorded a fight within the city walls between
an advance unit of the Norman army and the Londoners.[22] But
according to Guy of Amiens, in the event a series of messages was
exchanged between the duke and the garrison, and the city capit-
ulated without a fight.[23]

As always when faced with medieval sources that offer varying
levels of detail, or flat-out contradictions, there is a temptation to pick
and choose between them in order to weave a new master narrative,
ignoring loose or frayed threads from individual texts.[24] The result
is an historical Frankenstein's monster: it is a grand and impressive

achievement, larger than the sum of its parts, but it also lacks the spark, and the specific perspective, that animates each source. The conflicting reports on what transpired when William the Conqueror approached London tell us as much about how a range of authors interpreted the events of 1066 as about what actually happened. There is also a game of 'Chinese whispers' to unravel, as several of the authors had read the work of others, and refashioned it or combined it with other material to create a new take on the events. Above all, none of these writings was produced with modern historians in mind. Each answered to the needs of an eleventh- or twelfth-century author who was thinking of a different audience, and writing in a different genre or tradition. Guy of Amiens' *Carmen de Hastingae Proelio*, for instance, is a poem inspired by the grandeur of classical epics that were all the rage in eleventh-century French schools; it therefore adopts the florid style and taste for vivid scenes associated with its models. Even prose chronicles were written to provide an engaging and digested take on events, usually from a perspective favouring the author or patron.[25]

When there are parts of the story that conflict, one must consider two possibilities: that the authors have chosen to present the same information differently (sometimes by expanding or selectively reporting); or that they had access to different information. These possibilities need to be weighed carefully, with reference to the whole profile of each text – and with the awareness that the events of 1066 were already the stuff of rumour and legend within a few years of their occurrence. Hence the gripping account of the preparations for a siege at London in the *Carmen* should not simply be written off: while some aspects of its testimony are problematic, they can be explained through a combination of literary licence and divergent (sometimes probably distorted) information. In short, it is likely that the Anglo-Saxon leadership did surrender at Berkhamsted rather than Westminster, although preparations for an attack on London may well have been under way on both sides by then, as Guy of Amiens says. But to think only of the key accounts as a stockpile of clues from the scene of a crime committed a thousand years ago is to miss half the point. London, and its place in the story of the Conquest, was on everybody's mind.

Picking Up the Pieces: Dealing with Conquest in 1066

William's entry into London was the end of one story – of the Anglo-Saxon kingdom as such, and of Edgar the Ætheling's bid for power – but the start of another. The Norman Conquest would gradually bring England much more firmly into the cultural and political orbit of western continental Europe, and especially France. It also meant rapid change within England, as a wave of castles and cathedrals rose up, and the ruling secular and ecclesiastical classes became heavily dominated by Normans and other French-speakers.

All of this was still to come when William undertook his first major act as king of the English in London: his coronation. All the principal sources agree on the importance of this ceremony, and place it on Christmas Day in Westminster Abbey. The venue was a very deliberate choice, for it fostered a sense of continuity with Edward the Confessor which William tried to maintain throughout his reign. Guy of Amiens provided a lavish account of William's crown, commissioned specially for the coronation.[26] Even if it is undoubtedly over the top, it gives some flavour of how much significance was attached to ceremonies of this kind in the Middle Ages.

It did not just matter that a coronation took place; it also mattered deeply *how* that coronation took place. Describing a coronation carried off without a hitch could be a point in favour of legitimacy and stability. But highlighting anything that went awry at such a critical moment was a doorway to comment and critique: it implied that a king might not be up to the job, or foreshadowed future events that the writer knew loomed on the horizon.[27] Medieval writers were therefore keenly aware of the potential for signs and omens at such times. In William's case, most contemporary historians did choose just to describe him being crowned, without further comment, leaving the impression that he had been properly recognised as king. In a couple of cases, however, this was not so. William of Poitiers (and Orderic Vitalis, who made heavy use of William's text) told how, as the coronation was taking place, the acclamation of the assembled throng was so enthusiastic that it sparked panic in the surrounding streets.[28] Some of the soldiers stationed nearby to keep order set fire to buildings, and the flames spread in a scene of spiralling chaos. Most of the crowd fled Westminster Abbey, leaving a trembling king to hurry through the coronation with just a few clergy; outside, looters rushed to take advantage of the disorder. Orderic in particular seized on this incident as a portent of the tense and distrustful relationship between the English and the Normans that would dominate William's time as king.[29] This is an example of how individual chroniclers might or might not choose to weave certain incidents into their narrative in order to make a point – again, with London and its environs as the fulcrum for the political life of the kingdom as a whole.

William's first interactions with London reflected above all its role as a focal point for England. It was the objective of his post-Hastings march, and his entry into the city and coronation at Westminster marked a turning point in his establishment as king. But his relations with the city as a distinct political entity are less clear, and the first impressions on both sides cannot have been favourable. The Norman army had left a trail of destruction in its wake that came right up to the Thames. The southern (Surrey) side of the river, and large tracts of the shires surrounding London, still showed signs of the devastation wrought in 1066 in the Domesday survey 20 years later.[30] There may have been detrimental effects on London's trade for many years.[31]

A further sign of how William set about imposing his will on the Londoners as soon as possible was the erection of fortifications to reinforce his grip on the huge, rich and high-walled city. William of Poitiers says that he ordered one castle to be built even before the coronation, and then retired to Barking in order to oversee the construction of several more fortresses in the city.[32] Building castles to secure key towns was a tactic the Normans were to repeat all over England, but it is telling that in London they built several castles so swiftly: the city's size and importance made it a special case. These early castles included the first incarnation of the Tower of London, nestled in the south-east corner of the Roman walls.[33] At this stage, however, it would have been a rough-and-ready operation in 'ring-work' form: two concentric enclosures, forming an inner and outer court (or 'bailey'), which made use of the existing Roman walls for their southern and eastern defences.[34] This was a large castle by the standards of others in English and Norman towns, enclosing about 10 acres of land, no doubt forcibly cleared of existing habitation.

But there was an even larger castle situated on the opposite side of the city, spanning the walls to the west of St Paul's. The ditch and defences of this imposing edifice bisect modern Ludgate Hill and Newgate Street, to enclose about 15 acres; more if the castle extended outside the walls, as may well have been the case. This fortress seems to have been short-lived, and was perhaps destroyed by fire in 1087. Its later remnants were two smaller castles, known as Baynard's and Mountfichet's, which remained important into the twelfth century but are now known only through topography, texts and archaeology.[35] The eastern castle would change too, as the speedily erected fortifications of 1066 gave way to more long-term plans. In this case, the early enclosure was chosen as the site of an especially large and foreboding new stone castle: the White Tower, now the main keep of the Tower of London. Construction began later within William's reign, probably in the 1070s.[36] The White Tower was a symbolic as well as military enterprise. It dominated the eastern part of the city, and as the royal fortress for London formed a counterpart to the royal palace at Westminster. Its looming bulk left all who came up the Thames to reach London in no doubt of whose authority it lay under.[37]

A New Accommodation: The London Writ

In 1066 London reaped what it had sown in earlier decades. The new king stamped his authority onto the city as thoroughly as he did anywhere, and left London under the watchful eyes of its two new castles. But the tension of the last days of 1066 would ease off in due course. Indeed, in the long run London emerged from the Norman Conquest relatively intact. Its élite remained dominated by families of English, or mixed, heritage through the twelfth century,[38] and compared to other cities like York, which was ravaged during revolts against William later in the 1060s,[39] London suffered little violence.

A large part of this can be put down to the pragmatic accommodation that was thrashed out between William and the Londoners at some point early in his reign. The resulting document is the oldest and arguably most cherished muniment in the hands of the City of London Corporation.[40]

Figure 8.1. Writ issued by William the Conqueror to the citizens of
London, probably soon after his coronation on 25 December 1066.

It is a small piece of parchment approximately the size of a cheque,
with two slits cut most of the way through the bottom, so that two
long, thin slivers of parchment dangle from the document (Figure 8.1).
Each sliver served a distinct purpose: one held a wax impression of
the king's seal, and the other could be used to tie the whole document
together. This writ is cast very much in Anglo-Saxon tradition, being
written in Old English and drafted by a scribe who was familiar with
the customs of writs from Edward's time.[41] Drafted within the very
first months of his reign (probably late 1066 or early 1067), it shows
William utilising the administrative infrastructure of late Anglo-
Saxon England and the local language, in this case in order to send a
very concrete message of stability and continuity. Writs had become
a central tool of government under Edward. They served as formal
notifications to local assemblies of important acts or decisions made
by the king, and might subsequently be kept in case of any future
challenge. The London writ was among those kept for posterity, presumably in the hands of city officials. It opens with the words 'King
William sends friendly greetings to Bishop William, Geoffrey the
port-reeve and all the citizens in London, both French and English';
in other words, it directly addressed two key figures in London, the
bishop (a Norman, albeit appointed by King Edward well before
1066) and the portreeve, who was a new Norman appointee, possibly
the Geoffrey de Mandeville who later served as sheriff of Middlesex
and constable of the Tower, and who was ancestor of a powerful line
of London-based aristocrats.[42] The writ's reference to 'French and
English' among the citizens did not necessarily reflect a numerically

large influx of French-speakers into the city; more likely it referred
to the two linguistic communities who now shared responsibility
for upholding the king's laws.[43] In fact, the London writ is one of the
first occurrences of this expression: it may have been coined by the
veteran English chancellor Regenbald for this very occasion, as a way
of recognising the new dynamic in the kingdom.[44]

What the London writ enshrined was a promise on William's part
to recognise and respect the status of the Londoners. In curt but clear
language, he pledged that they would be subject to the same laws as
they had been under King Edward. That message was reinforced
with two further promises: that every son would be his father's heir,
and that no one should do the citizens wrong. These assertions
carried considerable weight at a time when the English landowning
class was in the process of being disinherited and replaced,[45] and
when there was widespread fear – sometimes justified – of Norman
violence against the English.[46] At the very outset of his reign, the
new king had promised the people of London that they would not
be subject to such depredations. By and large, it seems, his promises
were kept. London did not see too much overhaul of its institutions,
the citizens kept their rights and property, and the city as a whole
went from strength to strength under the Norman kings. In return
it remained loyal, whereas other major towns like Exeter and York
became centres of rebellion. By contrast, London institutions did well
out of the new king. In another document written in the Anglo-Saxon
tradition in 1068, William confirmed the recent foundation of the
large collegiate church of St Martin's Le Grand north of St Paul's by
two wealthy brothers, Ingelric and Eirard, and even donated extensive
new lands to it on both sides of Cripplegate.[47] He probably extended
his generosity to Westminster as well, but since the surviving records
are essentially twelfth-century forgeries it is less clear what form his
munificence took.[48]

Like Alfred's 'refoundation' of London in 886, William's conferral
of the crucial writ was one of the scenes chosen for representation by
the Corporation of London in the Royal Exchange murals. In 1898
it was painted by Seymour Lucas, who imagined a suitably grand
scene of finery and fanfare, in which a kneeling Londoner received
the charter from an imperious-looking William (Figure 8.2).

Figure 8.2. Mural of William the Conqueror bestowing his writ on the citizens, in the Royal Exchange, City of London, painted by Seymour Lucas.

The composition had been carefully arranged, with the organising committee even intervening to make sure that the 'bishop standing in front of the portreeve should be placed at the back of him so as to make [the official's] figure more important',[49] and thus put the civic authorities of the city centre stage. In fact, by picturing the portreeve going directly to the king, Lucas had skipped a crucial step that would have pleased the city fathers of the 1890s even more. Writs were probably not received by officials from the hand of the king, but rather conveyed from the king to a local gathering where their contents could be read out and taken in by the assembled worthies: not just the bishop and portreeve, but a gaggle of citizens meeting at an early form of London's Folkmoot.[50] The artist missed the opportunity to show what may well have been the reason that William was willing to concede this early and remarkable set of promises to the Londoners: he needed to be able to count on the city, and if the Tower was the stick, the writ was the carrot. London was too well established to be ignored, and too central to the operation of the kingdom to risk not having it onside.

*   *   *

1066 did not in fact mark a great caesura in London's history. The city's role in the campaign reinforces one of the central conclusions developed in the latter part of this book: that London had become an epicentre of real and symbolic power in England in a process that was inextricably bound to its economic revival. William's actions in heading for London, and his dealings with it after he arrived, encapsulated the status the city had already gained, and secured its position going into the future.

To break off at this point is hence in some ways artificial. For London, the Norman Conquest was a relatively small bump. But it was a much more significant break in the trajectory of the kingdom as a whole. The imposition of a new dynasty and a new ruling élite created a new climate in which there were great opportunities. As a result, London flourished. A Jewish community arose in the city, an offshoot from that of Rouen.[51] Westminster's role as a centre of royal government was magnified, a process magnificently embodied by Westminster Hall, construction of which took place under William II (1087–1100). In the twelfth century, the tribulations of successive rulers gave the Londoners the opportunity to consolidate their autonomy, as the price for material support.[52]

The kingdom, and its impact on London, thus changed more than the city itself. In this respect, the Norman Conquest marks the beginning of a new chapter in London's story, one that would see it grow still larger, richer and more prominent, as well as much more historically visible, thanks to the survival of an ever greater volume of sources from after about 1200. These future developments were founded on the centuries covered here, and this therefore provides a convenient point from which to stand back and recognise how far the city had come since its ruinous state at the beginning of the Anglo-Saxon period. The Roman city itself started as a citadel for the East Saxons, while *Lundenwic* brought commercial prosperity back to the city in the seventh and eighth centuries. Alfred and his heirs had witnessed a move back into the Roman city, and a century of gradual consolidation. But the 80 or so years before the Norman Conquest, beginning with the reign of Æthelred II, were as crucial to London's development as any that have come after. It was during this time that the city's rising economic profile and military prowess meshed with the growing sophistication and demands of the late Anglo-Saxon monarchy. During the century before 1066, London's status as the leading city in the kingdom – citadel of the Anglo-Saxons, indeed of the English – had been secured, and would never again be displaced.

Notes

INTRODUCTION

1 Christopher Brooke and Gillian Keir, *London 800–1216: The Shaping of a City* (London, 1975). For other key overviews, see John Clark, *Saxon and Norman London* (London, 1989); Derek Keene, 'London from the post-Roman period to *c*.1300', in *The Cambridge Urban History of Britain. 1: 600–1540*, ed. D. M. Palliser (Cambridge, 2000), pp. 187–216.

2 Pierre Chaplais, 'The original charters of Herbert and Gervase, abbots of Westminster (1121–1157)', in *A Medieval Miscellany for Doris Mary Stenton*, ed. Patricia M. Barnes and Cecil F. Slade (London, 1962), pp. 89–110; Julia Crick, 'St. Albans, Westminster and some twelfth-century views of the Anglo-Saxon past', *ANS* 25 (2002), 65–183.

3 See Chapter 5. See also John Clark, 'King Alfred's London and London's King Alfred', *London Archaeologist* 9 (1999), 35–8.

4 Philip Grierson, 'Commerce in the Dark Ages: a critique of the evidence', *Transactions of the Royal Historical Society*, 5th series, 9 (1959), 123–40, at 129.

5 See Chapter 4.

6 See Chapter 2.

7 See Chapter 7.

8 Rory Naismith, 'London and its mint *c*.880–1066: a preliminary survey', *British Numismatic Journal* 83 (2013), 44–74; see Chapter 7.

9 Hugh Prince, 'The situation of London', in *The City of London from Prehistoric Times to c.1520*, ed. Mary D. Lobel (Oxford, 1989), pp. 1–5.

10 See Chapter 7.

11 Nicholas Barton and Stephen Myers, *The Lost Rivers of London: A Study of Their Effects Upon London and Londoners, and Those of London and Londoners Upon Them* (Whitstable, 2016).

12 Oliver Rackham, *Ancient Woodland: Its History, Vegetation and Uses in England*, 2nd ed. (Colvend, 2003), pp. 112–13.

13 Henry Clifford Darby and Eila M. J. Campbell, *The Domesday Geography of South-East England* (Cambridge, 1962), pp. 122–5.

14 *ASC* 895.

15 Brooke and Keir, *London 800–1216*, pp. 161–2.

16 Derek Keene, 'Medieval London and its region', *London Journal* 14 (1989), 99–111, at 107; Keene, 'London from the post-Roman period', pp. 188

and 196; Robert Cowie and Lyn Blackmore, *Lundenwic: Excavations in Middle Saxon London, 1987–2000* (London, 2012), p. 116; Robert Cowie, '*Lundenburh*: the archaeology of late Saxon London', in '*Hidden Histories and Records of Antiquity': Essays on Saxon and Medieval London for John Clark, Curator Emeritus, Museum of London*, ed. Jonathan Cotton et al. (London, 2014), pp. 17–26, at 22.

17   Chris Wickham, *Framing the Early Middle Ages: Europe and the Mediterranean, 400–800* (Oxford, 2005), pp. 591–4; Daniel G. Russo, *Town Origins and Development in Early England, c.400–950 A D* (Westport, CT, and London, 1998), pp. 2–21.

18   John Baker, 'The language of Anglo-Saxon defence', in *Landscapes of Defence in Early Medieval Europe*, ed. John Baker, Stuart Brookes and Andrew Reynolds (Turnhout, 2013), pp. 65–90, at 67–72.

19   James Campbell, *Essays in Anglo-Saxon History* (London, 1986), pp. 99–119.

20   See Chapter 4.

21   Grenville G. Astill, 'Towns and town hierarchies in Saxon England', *Oxford Journal of Archaeology* 10 (1991), 95–117; Grenville G. Astill, 'General survey 600–1300', in *Cambridge Urban History*, ed. D. M. Palliser, pp. 27–49, at 34–42; John Blair, 'Small towns 600–1270', ibid., pp. 245–70.

22   Greg Waite, 'The preface to the Old English Bede: authorship, transmission, and connection with the *West Saxon Genealogical Regnal List*', *ASE* 44 (2015), 31–93, at 78–83.

23   John Baker and Stuart Brookes, *Beyond the Burghal Hidage: Anglo-Saxon Civil Defence in the Viking Age* (Leiden, 2013), pp. 64–90.

24   See Chapter 7.

25   Martin Biddle and Derek Keene, 'Winchester in the eleventh and twelfth centuries', in *Winchester in the Early Middle Ages: An Edition and Discussion of the Winton Domesday*, ed. Martin Biddle (Oxford, 1976), pp. 241–448, at 289–92; Martin Biddle and Derek Keene, 'General survey and conclusions', ibid., pp. 449–508, at 465–7.

26   Nicholas Brooks, *The Early History of the Church of Canterbury: Christ Church from 597 to 1066* (Leicester, 1984).

27   Tim Pestell, 'Markets, *emporia, wics*, and "productive" sites: pre-Viking trade centres in Anglo-Saxon England', in *The Oxford Handbook of Anglo-Saxon Archaeology*, ed. David A. Hinton, Sally Crawford and Helena Hamerow (Oxford, 2011), pp. 556–79, at 569–70.

28   Paul Blinkhorn, *The Ipswich Ware Project: Ceramics, Trade and Society in Middle Saxon England* (London, 2012).

29   See Chapters 3–4.

30   See Chapter 4.

31   C. E. Blunt, 'The coinage of Athelstan, king of England 924–939', *British Numismatic Journal* 42 (1974), 35–160; Rory Naismith, *Medieval European Coinage, with a Catalogue of the Coins in the Fitzwilliam Museum, Cambridge. 8: Britain and Ireland c.400–1066* (Cambridge, 2017), p. 209.

32 Alan Thacker, 'Early medieval Chester 400–1230', in *A History of the County of Chester. Volume V, Part I: The City of Chester: General History and Topography*, ed. Christopher P. Lewis and Alan Thacker (London, 2003), pp. 16–33; Letty Ten Harkel, 'Material culture and urbanism: the case of Viking-Age Lincoln', *ASSAH* 18 (2013), 157–73; D. M. Palliser, *Medieval York, 600–1540* (Oxford, 2014), pp. 52–84.
33 Astill, 'General survey', pp. 34–8.
34 Adriaan Verhulst, *The Rise of Cities in North-West Europe* (Cambridge, 1999).
35 See Chapter 4.
36 Richard Reece, 'Satellite, parasite, or just London?', in *Londinium and Beyond: Essays on Roman London and Its Hinterland for Harvey Sheldon*, ed. John Clark et al. (London, 2008), pp. 46–8.

I   ROMAN LONDON AND ITS END:
FIRST TO FIFTH CENTURIES AD

1 *Canterbury Professions*, ed. Michael Richter and T. J. Brown (Torquay, 1973), no. 18.
2 Dominic Perring, 'Recent advances in the understanding of Roman London', in *The Towns of Roman Britain: The Contribution of Commercial Archaeology since 1990*, ed. Michael Fulford and Neil Holbrook (London, 2015) pp. 20–43; Gustav Milne, *Book of Roman London: Urban Archaeology in the Nation's Capital* (London, 1995); Dominic Perring, *Roman London* (London, 1991); Ralph Merrifield, *London: City of the Romans* (London, 1983).
3 Dated AD 65/70–80, and carrying the words *londinio mogontio*: R. S. O. Tomlin, *Roman London's First Voices: Writing Tablets from the Bloomberg Excavations, 2010–14* (London, 2016), pp. 70–1 (cf. pp. 94–5 and 106–7).
4 See Richard Coates, 'A new explanation of the name of London', *Transactions of the Philological Society* 96 (1998), 203–29, at 214–21; Richard Coates and Andrew Breeze, *Celtic Voices, English Places. Studies of the Celtic Impact on Place-Names in England* (Stamford, CT, 2000), p. 27; cf. a similar conclusion reached in Peter Schrijver, *Language Contact and the Origins of the Germanic Languages* (New York, 2013), p. 57. An alternative theory proposes that it is 'the place of Londinos', derived from a personal name of unknown origin (A. L. F. Rivet and Colin Smith, *The Place-Names of Roman Britain* (London, 1979), pp. 396–8).
5 Lacey M. Wallace, *The Origin of Roman London* (Cambridge, 2013), pp. 4–5.
6 Ian Tyers, 'Tree-ring analysis', in *Roman London and the Walbrook Stream Crossing: Excavations at 1 Poultry and Vicinity, City of London*, ed. Julian Hill and Peter Rowsome, 2 vols (London, 2011), pp. 562–7; Wallace, *Origin*, pp. 21–2.

7   Peter Marsden, *Roman London* (London, 1980), pp. 17–19; John Morris, *Londinium: London in the Roman Empire* (London, 1982), pp. 74–112; Martin Millett, 'Evaluating Roman London', *Archaeological Journal* 151 (1994), 427–35; Martin Millett, 'Characterizing Roman London', in *Interpreting Roman London: Papers in Memory of Hugh Chapman*, ed. Joanna Bird, Mark Hassall and Harvey Sheldon (Oxford, 1996), pp. 33–8. Arguments have also been mounted for a military origin: Wallace, *Origin*, ch. 1; Dominic Perring, 'Two studies on Roman London: A. London's military origins – B. Population decline and ritual landscapes in Antonine London', *Journal of Roman Archaeology* 24 (2011), 249–82; Perring, 'Recent advances', pp. 21–3.

8   Tacitus, *Annals*, 14.32 (*Tacitus: The Annals. Vol. 5: Books 13–16*, ed. and trans. John Jackson (London, 1931), pp. 160–1).

9   Ibid.

10   Wallace, *Origin*, pp. 77–8.

11   Lacey M. Wallace, 'The foundation of Roman London: examining the Claudian fort hypothesis', *Oxford Journal of Archaeology* 32 (2013), 275–91, at 278.

12   Perring, 'Recent advances', pp. 21–6.

13   Tomlin, *Roman London's First Voices*, pp. 156–8.

14   Lesley Dunwoodie, Chiz Harward and Ken Pitt, *An Early Roman Fort and Urban Development on Londinium's Eastern Hill: Excavations at Plantation Place, City of London, 1997–2003* (London, 2016).

15   John Creighton, *Britannia: The Creation of a Roman Province* (London, 2006), pp. 93–107.

16   Milne, *Book of Roman London*, p. 56.

17   Tim Williams and Hedley Swain, 'The population of Roman London', in *Londinium and Beyond: Essays on Roman London and Its Hinterland for Harvey Sheldon*, ed. John Clark et al. (London, 2008), pp. 33–40.

18   Trevor Brigham, 'A reassessment of the second basilica in London, A.D. 100–400: excavations at Leadenhall Court, 1984–86', *Britannia* 21 (1990), 53–97; John Wacher, *The Towns of Roman Britain*, 2nd ed. (London, 1995), pp. 91–2.

19   Wallace, *Origin*, pp. 88–91.

20   Merrifield, *London*, pp. 72–7. A later palace may have been in Southwark: Creighton, *Britannia*, p. 106.

21   Perring, 'Two studies'; challenged in Wallace, 'Foundation'.

22   Elizabeth Howe and David Lakin, *Roman and Medieval Cripplegate, City of London: Archaeological Excavations 1992–8* (London, 2004); John Shepherd, *The Discovery of the Roman Fort at Cripplegate, City of London* (London, 2012); Merrifield, *London*, pp. 77–83.

23   See Chapter 7.

24   Nick Bateman, Carrie Cowan and Robin Wroe-Brown, *London's Roman Amphitheatre, Guildhall Yard, City of London* (London, 2008).

25 Cf. a set of Roman baths found at Borough in Southwark: https:// historicengland.org.uk/listing/the-list/list-entry/1422618

26 The evidence for nine temples is described in Douglas Killock et al., *Temples and Suburbs: Excavations at Tabard Square, Southwark* (London, 2015), pp. 250–3.

27 John Shepherd, *The Temple of Mithras, London: Excavations by W. F. Grimes and A. Williams at the Walbrook* (London, 1998).

28 Killock et al., *Temples and Suburbs*.

29 *Britannia* 7 (1976), pp. 378–9.

30 Martin Millett, 'London as capital?', in *Roman London: Recent Archaeological Work*, ed. Bruce Watson (Portsmouth, RI, 1998), pp. 7–12, at 12.

31 https://www.archaeology.co.uk/articles/londons-pompeii.htm.

32 Tomlin, *Roman London's First Voices*.

33 Julian Hill and Peter Rowsome (eds), *Roman London and the Walbrook Stream Crossing: Excavations at 1 Poultry and Vicinity, City of London*, 2 vols (London, 2011).

34 Merrifield, *London*, pp. 152–4; Trevor Brigham, 'The late Roman waterfront in London', *Britannia* 21 (1990), 99–183.

35 Peter Marsden, *Ships of the Port of London* (London, 1994); Gustav Milne, *The Port of Roman London* (London, 1985).

36 Trevor Brigham et al., 'A Roman timber building on the Southwark waterfront, London', *Archaeological Journal* 152 (1995), 1–72.

37 Killock et al., *Temples and Suburbs*, pp. 30–1.

38 Millett, 'London as capital?', pp. 8–10.

39 A. H. M. Jones, *The Later Roman Empire, 284–602: A Social and Administrative Survey* (Oxford, 1964), pp. 712–13.

40 Martin Millett, *The Romanization of Britain* (Cambridge, 1990), pp. 65–126; Adam Rogers, 'The development of towns', in *The Oxford Handbook of Roman Britain*, ed. Martin Millett, Louise Revell and Alison Moore (Oxford, 2016), pp. 741–66.

41 Ray Laurence, Simon Esmonde Cleary and Gareth Sears, *The City in the Roman West, c.250 BC–c.AD 250* (Cambridge, 2011), pp. 65–9.

42 John J. Wilkes, 'The status of Londinium', in *Interpreting Roman London*, ed. Bird, Hassall and Sheldon, pp. 27–31, at 28.

43 Mark Hassall, 'London as a Provincial Capital', in *Interpreting Roman London*, ed. Bird, Hassall and Sheldon, pp. 19–26; Mark Hassall, 'London: the Roman city', in *London Under Ground*, ed. Ian Haynes, Harvey Sheldon and Lesley Hannigan (London, 2000), pp. 52–61, at 53–5.

44 Creighton, *Britannia*, p. 101.

45 Reece, 'Satellite, parasite', p. 46.

46 *RIB* 9 and 23.

47 *RIB* 2445.27.

48 Monique Dondin-Payre and Xavier Loriot, 'Tiberinius Celerianus à Londres: Bellovaque et *Moritix*', *L'Antiquité classique* 77 (2008), 127–69.

49   Hill and Rowsome, *Roman London*, pp. 516–17.

50   R. D. Grasby and R. S. O. Tomlin, 'The sepulchral monument of the procurator C. Julius Classicianus', *Britannia* 33 (2002), 43–75.

51   R. P. Wright, 'Official tile-stamps from London which cite the province of Britain', *Britannia* 16 (1985), 193–6.

52   Hassall, 'London: the Roman city', pp. 56–8. But see R. S. O. Tomlin, 'Was London ever a *colonia*? The written evidence', in *Romanitas: Essays on Roman Archaeology in Honour of Sheppard Frere on the Occasion of his Ninetieth Birthday*, ed. R. J. A. Wilson (Oxford, 2006), pp. 49–63 for the argument that its promotion took place at the time of Hadrian's visit in AD 122.

53   *RIB* 19.

54   Alan Bowman, *Life and Letters on the Roman Frontier: Vindolanda and Its People*, 3rd ed. (London, 2003), pp. 101–2.

55   It is impossible to determine if the language here is metaphorical: Craig A. Williams, *Reading Roman Friendship* (Cambridge, 2012), pp. 160–1.

56   Bowman, *Life and Letters*, pp. 140–1.

57   R. S. O. Tomlin in *Britannia* 44 (2013), 390–1.

58   https://www.archaeology.co.uk/articles/londons-pompeii.htm

59   Wacher, *Towns*, pp. 96–7; Ralph Merrifield, 'Roman London', in *The City of London from Prehistoric Times to c.1520*, ed. Mary D. Lobel (Oxford, 1989), pp. 10–19, at 14–15.

60   Howe and Lakin, *Cripplegate*, pp. 41–7.

61   Perring, 'Recent advances', pp. 33–8.

62   Michael Fulford, '*Imperium Galliarum, imperium Britanniarum*. Developing new ideologies and settling old scores: abandonments, demolitions and new building in south-east Britain, c.AD 250–300', in *Londinium and Beyond*, ed. Clark et al., pp. 41–5.

63   Brigham, 'Reassessment', pp. 77–81.

64   Perring, 'Recent advances', p. 37.

65   James Gerrard, 'New light on the end of Roman London', *Archaeological Journal* 168 (2011), 181–94, at 183. Cf. Millett, *Romanization*, pp. 134–42; Robert Cowie, 'Descent into darkness: London in the 5th and 6th centuries', in *Londinium and Beyond*, ed. Clark et al., pp. 49–53, at 50; Richard MacPhail, Henri Galinié and Frans Verhaeghe, 'A future for Dark Earth?', *Antiquity* 77 (2003), 349–58. For an overview of London's transition between the fourth and seventh centuries, see Gavin Speed, *Towns in the Dark? Urban Transformations from Late Roman Britain to Anglo-Saxon England* (Oxford, 2014), pp. 19–27.

66   Gerrard, 'New light', pp. 182–3.

67   Ibid., pp. 187–90.

68   Hill and Rowsome, *Roman London*, pp. 194–241 and 445. 71 Fenchurch Street was similar: Richard Bluer, Trevor Brigham and Robin Nielsen, *Roman and Later Development East of the Forum and Cornhill: Excavations at Lloyd's Register, 71 Fenchurch Street, City of London* (London, 2006).

69 Simon T. Loseby, 'Power and towns in late Roman Britain and early Anglo-Saxon England', *Memorias de la Real Academia de Buenas Letras de Barcelona* 25 (2000), 319–70, at 322; Chris Wickham, *Framing the Early Middle Ages: Europe and the Mediterranean, 400–800* (Oxford, 2005), pp. 591–692.

70 David Hunt, 'The church as a public institution', in *The Cambridge Ancient History. Volume XIII: The Late Empire, A.D. 337–425*, ed. Averil Cameron and Peter Garnsey (Cambridge, 1998), pp. 238–76, at 250–7.

71 David Sankey, 'Cathedrals, granaries and urban vitality in late Roman London', in *Roman London*, ed. Watson, pp. 78–82.

72 Wacher, *Towns*, p. 98.

73 Perring, 'Recent advances', pp. 33–5.

74 The exact date of this division is contentious: Anthony R. Birley, *The Roman Government of Britain* (Oxford, 2005), pp. 333–6.

75 P. J. Casey, *Carausius and Allectus: The British Usurpers* (New Haven, CT, 1994), pp. 53–4. *Panegyrici Latini* VIII.17 (*In Praise of Later Roman Emperors: The Panegyrici Latini*, ed. and trans. C. E. V. Nixon and Barbara Saylor Rodgers (Berkeley, CA, 1994), p. 138).

76 Pierre Bastien and Catherine Metzger, *Le trésor de Beaurains (dit d'Arras)* (Arras, 1977), pp. 94–5.

77 Ibid., pp. 201–5.

78 Birley, *Roman Government*, pp. 397–401.

79 Hubert J. Cloke, Lee Toone and Adrian B. Marsden, *The London Mint of Constantius & Constantine* (London, 2015). It is sometimes claimed that London was reopened as a mint by Magnus Maximus (383–8), on the basis of coins with the mint-signature AVG (i.e. 'Augusta'). But there are reasons to doubt this attribution: several other places in the north-west of the Roman Empire had a name compatible with this mint-signature, and arguments have been mounted for Senlis and Autun in France: Nicholas Fuentes, 'Augusta which the old timers call Londinium', *London Archaeologist* 6 (1989), 120–5; Nicholas Fuentes, 'London/Augusta – a rejoinder', *London Archaeologist* 8 (1991), 333–8.

80 J. C. Mann, 'The administration of Roman Britain', *Antiquity* 35 (1961), 316–20; Adam Rogers, *Late Roman Towns in Britain* (Cambridge, 2011), pp. 32–3.

81 *Notitia Dignitatum* XI.37 (*Notitia Dignitatum*, ed. Otto Seeck (Berlin, 1876), p. 150).

82 Ammianus Marcellinus, *Res gestae* XX.1.1 (*Ammianus Marcellinus: The Later Roman Empire (AD 354–378)*, trans. Walter Hamilton (London, 1986), p. 185).

83 Michael E. Jones, *The End of Roman Britain* (Ithaca, NY, 1996), pp. 154–5; Birley, *Roman Government*, pp. 403–65.

84 Ammianus Marcellinus, *Res gestae* XXVII.8 (trans. Hamilton, pp. 342–3).

85 For an alternative argument that 'Augusta' derives from association with a legion stationed at London, see Tomlin, 'Roman London', pp. 58–9; Fuentes, 'Augusta'.

86 Simon Esmonde Cleary, 'Britain in the fourth century', in *A Companion to Roman Britain*, ed. Malcolm Todd (Oxford, 2004), pp. 409–27, at 416–17.

87 Simon Esmonde Cleary, *The Ending of Roman Britain* (London, 1989), pp. 131–6.

88 Perring, 'Recent advances', p. 38.

89 Hill and Rowsome, *Roman London*, p. 447.

90 James Gerrard, 'The Drapers' Gardens hoard: a preliminary account', *Britannia* 40 (2009), 163–83; James Gerrard, 'Wells and belief systems at the end of Roman Britain: a case study from Roman London', *Late Antique Archaeology* 7 (2011 for 2009), 551–72.

91 Perring, 'Recent advances', p. 38; Sadie Watson and Kieron Heard, *Development on Roman London's Western Hill: Excavations at Paternoster Square, City of London* (London, 2006), pp. 62–7.

92 Bateman, Cowan and Wroe-Brown, *Amphitheatre*, pp. 87–95.

93 C. Cowan et al., *Roman Southwark Settlement and Economy: Excavations in Southwark, 1973–1991* (London, 2009), pp. 33 and 157–66.

94 Jo Lyon, *Within these Walls: Roman and Medieval Defences North of Newgate at the Merrill Lynch Financial Centre, City of London* (London, 2007), pp. 46–52; John Maloney, 'Recent work on London's defences', in *Roman Urban Defences in the West*, ed. John Maloney and Brian Hobley (London, 1983), pp. 96–117, at 105–11.

95 Maloney, 'Recent work', pp. 112–15; Reece, 'Satellite, parasite', p. 47.

96 Marsden, *Roman London*, pp. 179–80.

97 Perring, 'Recent advances', p. 35; Jones, *End*, pp. 245–6; Birley, *Roman Government*, pp. 452–3. Cf. Esmonde Cleary, *Ending*, p. 46 for a more cautious view.

98 Marsden, *Roman London*, pp. 180. Fifth-century activity may also be visible at Pudding Lane and Peter's Hill: Perring, *Roman London*, p. 128.

99 Perring, 'Recent advances', p. 38.

100 Hedley Swain, 'London's last Roman?', *Current Archaeology* 213 (2007), 35–9.

101 Alison Telfer, 'New evidence for the transition from the Late Roman to the Saxon period at St Martin-in-the-Fields, London', in *Intersections: The Archaeology and History of Christianity in England, 400–1200. Papers in Honour of Martin Biddle and Birthe Kjølbye-Biddle*, ed. Martin Henig and Nigel Ramsey (Oxford, 2010), pp. 49–58.

102 John Stow, *A Survey of London*, with introduction and notes by Charles Lethbridge Kingsford, 2 vols (Oxford, 1908), vol. I, p. 331.

103 Gerrard, 'New light', pp. 183–5.

104 Alistair Douglas, James Gerrard and Berni Sudds, *A Roman Settlement and Bath House at Shadwell: Excavations at Tobacco Dock and Babe Ruth Restaurant, the Highway, London* (London, 2011); David Lakin et al., *The Roman Tower at Shadwell, London: A Reappraisal* (London, 2002).

105 Ammianus Marcellinus, *Res gestae* XIV.5.6 (trans. Hamilton, pp. 44–5).

106 Ibid., XXVIIII.3.3 (trans. Hamilton, p. 357).

107 Zosimus, *Historia nova*, VI.5.2–6 (*Zosime: Histoire nouvelle*, ed. and trans. François Paschoud (Paris, 1989), p. 9; *Zosimus: New History*, trans. Ronald T. Ridley (Sydney, 1982), pp. 128–9).

108 These events have been told and assessed many times. For selected discussion see Thomas Charles-Edwards, *Wales and the Britons 350–1064* (Oxford, 2013), pp. 31–56; Birley, *Government*, pp. 455–63; John F. Matthews, 'Olympiodorus of Thebes and the history of the west (407–425)', *Journal of Roman Studies* 60 (1970), 79–97; E. A. Thompson, 'Britain, AD 406–410', *Britannia* 8 (1977), 303–18; Philip Bartholomew, 'Fifth-century facts', *Britannia* 13 (1982), 261–70; Peter Heather, *The Fall of the Roman Empire* (London, 2005), pp. 191–232.

109 Translated in Birley, *Government*, p. 463.

110 P. S. W. Guest, *The Late Roman Gold and Silver Coins from the Hoxne Treasure* (London, 2005); Catherine Johns, *The Hoxne Late Roman Treasure: Gold Jewellery and Silver Plate* (London, 2010).

111 Richard Hobbs, *Late Roman Precious Metal Deposits, c.AD 200–700: Changes over Time and Space* (Oxford, 2006), p. 54.

112 Rory Naismith, *Medieval European Coinage, with a Catalogue of the Coins in the Fitzwilliam Museum, Cambridge. 8: Britain and Ireland c.400–1066* (Cambridge, 2017), pp. 29–31.

113 Gerrard, 'Drapers' Gardens'. Compare Guest, *Late Roman Gold*, pp. 29–32; with Johns, *Hoxne Late Roman Treasure*, pp. 202–3.

2   AMONG THE RUINS: POST-ROMAN LONDON

1   From *A Choice of Anglo-Saxon Verse*, trans. Richard Hamer, 2nd ed. (London, 2015), p. 5.

2   *The Wanderer* (trans. Hamer, ibid., p. 183).

3   Geoffrey of Monmouth, *De gestis Britonum*, ch. 201 (*Geoffrey of Monmouth: The History of the Kings of Britain*, ed. and trans. Michael D. Reeve and Neil Wright (Woodbridge, 2007), pp. 276–7), with John Clark, 'Cadwallo, king of the Britons, the bronze horseman of London', in *Collectanea Londiniensia: Studies in London Archaeology and History Presented to Ralph Merrifield*, ed. Joanna Bird, Hugh Chapman and John Clark (London, 1978), pp. 194–9.

4   *ASC* 456.

5   E.g. R. E. M. Wheeler, 'London and the Grim's Ditches', *Antiquaries Journal* 14 (1934), 254–63; R. E. M. Wheeler, *London and the Saxons* (London, 1935).

6   Robert Cowie, 'Descent into darkness: London in the 5th and 6th centuries', in *Londinium and Beyond: Essays on Roman London and Its Hinterland for Harvey Sheldon*, ed. John Clark et al. (London, 2008), pp. 49–53, at 50. Cf. James Gerrard, 'New light on the end of Roman London', *Archaeological Journal* 168 (2011), 181–94, at 190–1.

7   N. C. Cook, 'An Anglo-Saxon saucer brooch from Lower Thames Street, London', *Antiquaries Journal* 49 (1969), 395.

8   Robert Cowie and Lyn Blackmore, *Lundenwic: Excavations in Middle Saxon London, 1987–2000* (London, 2012), p. 101, listing Anglo-Saxon artefacts pre-dating the early seventh century from London. Several of these have only vague provenances.

9   Cowie, 'Descent into darkness', p. 50.

10   See Chapter 4.

11   Alison Telfer, 'New evidence for the transition from the Late Roman to the Saxon period at St Martin-in-the-Fields, London', in *Intersections: The Archaeology and History of Christianity in England, 400–1200. Papers in Honour of Martin Biddle and Birthe Kjolbye-Biddle*, ed. Martin Henig and Nigel Ramsey (Oxford, 2010), pp. 49–58; Lyn Blackmore, 'New light on the origins, development and decline of the Middle Saxon trading settlement of Lundenwic', in *The Very Beginning of Europe? Cultural and Social Dimensions of Early-Medieval Migration and Colonisation (5th–8th Century)*, ed. Rica Annaert et al. (Brussels, 2012), pp. 147–58, at 149.

12   Cowie and Blackmore, *Lundenwic*, pp. 106–7.

13   Robert Cowie and Lyn Blackmore, *Early and Middle Saxon Rural Settlement in the London Region* (London, 2008), esp. pp. 125–36; John T. Baker, *Cultural Transition in the Chilterns and Essex Region 350 AD to 650 AD* (Hatfield, 2006).

14   S 1171 (BCS 81).

15   Eilert Ekwall, *The Concise Dictionary of English Place-Names*, 4th ed. (Oxford, 1960), p. 26.

16   Richard Coates, 'A new explanation of the name of London', *Transactions of the Philological Society* 96 (1998), 203–29; Peter Schrijver, *Language Contact and the Origins of the Germanic Languages* (New York, 2013), pp. 53–7. It is debatable whether the first Anglo-Saxon borrowing of *Lūndein* was from Latin or Celtic.

17   The explanation for this change is not clear. See Colin Smith, 'Romano-British place-names in Bede', *ASSAH* 1 (1979), 1–19.

18   Robert Cowie and Charlotte Harding, 'Saxon settlement and economy from the Dark Ages to Domesday', in *The Archaeology of Greater London: An Assessment of Archaeological Evidence for Human Presence in the Area Now Covered by Greater London*, ed. Monica Kendall (London, 2000), pp. 171–206, at 177.

19   Although definitely pre-English, the origin of the name of the Thames is unclear: traditionally it was viewed as Celtic (Eilert Ekwall, *English River-Names* (Oxford, 1928), pp. 402–5), but more recent scholarship has favoured a pre-Celtic origin (Peter R. Kitson, 'British and European river-names', *Transactions of the Philological Society* 94 (1996), 73–118, at 90).

20   Ekwall, *River-Names*, pp. 51–2 and 239–41.

21   Ekwall, *English Place-Names*, p. 361.

22 Bede, *HE* IV.6 (*Bede's Ecclesiastical History of the English People*, ed. and trans. Bertram Colgrave and R. A. B. Mynors (Oxford, 1969) pp. 354–5).

23 Ekwall, *English Place-Names*, p. 100.

24 Cowie and Harding, 'Saxon settlement', pp. 177–82.

25 Barri Jones and David J. Mattingly, *An Atlas of Roman Britain* (Oxford, 1990), pp. 148, 154; Thomas Charles-Edwards, *Wales and the Britons 350–1064* (Oxford, 2013), pp. 314–18; Ken Dark, *Britain and the End of the Roman Empire* (Stroud, 2000), pp. 144–9. For possible continuity of Roman land units within Surrey, see John Hines, 'Sūþre-gē: The foundations of Surrey', in *Aspects of Archaeology and History in Surrey: Towards a Research Framework for the County*, ed. Jonathan Cotton, Glenys Crocker and Audrey Graham (Guildford, 2004), pp. 91–102.

26 For the possibility of larger kingdoms in this period, see Guy Halsall, *Barbarian Migrations and the Roman West 376–568* (Cambridge, 2007), pp. 313–19. Views which lay more stress on smaller kingdoms may be found in *The Origins of Anglo-Saxon Kingdoms*, ed. Steven Bassett (London, 1989).

27 Bryan Ward-Perkins, *The Fall of Rome and the End of Civilization* (Oxford, 2005), pp. 87–121; Simon Esmonde Cleary, 'Britain at the end of Empire', in *The Oxford Handbook of Roman Britain*, ed. Martin Millett, Louise Revell and Alison Moore (Oxford, 2016), pp. 134–47, at 138–40.

28 Debby Banham and Rosamond Faith, *Anglo-Saxon Farms and Farming* (Oxford, 2014), esp. pp. 141–62.

29 Simon Esmonde Cleary, *The Ending of Roman Britain* (London, 1989), esp. pp. 63–85.

30 D. A. Brooks, 'The case for continuity in fifth-century Canterbury re-examined', *Oxford Journal of Archaeology* 7 (1988), 99–114; K. Blockley et al., *Excavations in the Marlow Car Park and Surrounding Areas* (Canterbury, 1995).

31 Roger White and Philip Barker, *Wroxeter: The Life and Death of a Roman City* (Stroud, 1998); but cf. Alan Lane, 'Wroxeter and the end of Roman Britain', *Antiquity* 88 (2014), 501–15.

32 *Anonymous Life of Cuthbert* IV.8 and Bede, *Life of St Cuthbert*, ch. 27 (*Two Lives of Saint Cuthbert*, ed. and trans. Bertram Colgrave (Cambridge, 1940), pp. 122–3 and 242–5).

33 Sheppard Frere, *Verulamium Excavations II* (London, 1983), pp. 212–28; N. Faulkner, 'Verulamium: interpreting decline', *Archaeological Journal* 153 (1996), 79–103; Sheppard Frere, 'The saga of Verulamium building XXVII 2', *Britannia* 42 (2011), 263–74; Stephen Cosh and David Neal, 'The dating of building 2, insula XXVII, at Verulamium: a reassessment', *Antiquaries Journal* 95 (2015), 1–26.

34 Cowie and Harding, 'Saxon settlement', p. 179, hint that different sections could have been built at various times. Colin Bowlt, 'A possible extension to Grim's Dyke', in *Londinium and Beyond*, ed. Clarke et al., pp. 107–11 argues for upholding the traditional late or post-Roman date, though it

is possible that different segments of the dyke were built at various times (see also Dominic Perring, *Roman London* (London, 1991), p. 129).

35   J. N. L. Myres, 'The English settlements', in *Roman Britain and the English Settlements*, R. G. Collingwood and J. N. L. Myres (Oxford, 1936), pp. 325–456, at 407–8; Alan Vince, *Saxon London: An Archaeological Investigation* (London, 1990), pp. 51–2.

36   Richard Sharpe, 'The late antique passion of St Alban', in *Alban and St Albans: Roman and Medieval Architecture, Art and Archaeology*, ed. Martin Henig and Philip Lindley (Leeds, 2001), pp. 30–7.

37   Baker, *Cultural Transition*, esp. pp. 25–31.

38   Giorgio Ausenda, 'Current issues and future directions in the study of early Anglo-Saxon England', in *The Anglo-Saxons from the Migration Period to the Eighth Century: An Ethnographic Perspective*, ed. John Hines (San Marino, 1997), pp. 411–50, at 420–2; James E. Fraser, 'Early medieval Europe: the case of Britain and Ireland', in *The Oxford Handbook of Genocide Studies*, ed. Donald Bloxham and A. Dirk Moses (Oxford, 2010), pp. 259–78.

39   David N. Dumville, 'Origins of the kingdom of the English', in *Writing, Kingship and Power in Anglo-Saxon England*, ed. Rory Naismith and David A. Woodman (Cambridge, 2018), pp. 71–121, at 73–102; Alex Woolf, 'Apartheid and economics in Anglo-Saxon England', in *Britons in Anglo-Saxon England*, ed. N. J. Higham (Woodbridge, 2007), pp. 115–29; Mark G. Thomas et al., 'Evidence for an apartheid-like social structure in early Anglo-Saxon England', *Proceedings of the Royal Society B* 273 (2006), 2651–8.

40   E.g. N. J. Higham, *Rome, Britain and the Anglo-Saxons* (London, 1992). A balance of significant migration and cultural emulation is advocated in Peter Heather, *Empires and Barbarians: Migration, Development and the Birth of Europe* (London, 2009), pp. 266–305.

41   Guy Halsall, *Worlds of Arthur: Facts & Fictions of the Dark Ages* (Oxford, 2013), pp. 228–30.

42   Ibid., pp. 260–5.

43   Esmonde Cleary, 'Britain at the end', pp. 144–6.

44   A. D. Lee, 'The army', in *The Cambridge Ancient History. Volume XIII: The Late Empire, A.D. 337–425*, ed. Averil Cameron and Peter Garnsey (Cambridge, 1998), pp. 211–37, at 214.

45   Halsall, *Barbarian Migrations*, p. 31; Halsall, *Worlds of Arthur*, pp. 34–6. For examples from London, see Perring, *Roman London*, pp. 127–30; Peter Marsden, *Roman London* (London, 1980), p. 181.

46   John Wacher, *The Towns of Roman Britain*, 2nd ed. (London, 1995), p. 108.

47   Malcolm Todd, 'The Germanic peoples', in *Late Empire*, ed. Cameron and Garnsey, pp. 461–86, at 474–8.

48   Halsall, *Barbarian Migrations*; Heather, *Empires and Barbarians*; and Patrick Geary, *The Myth of Nations: The Medieval Origins of Europe* (Princeton, 2003) – though all three take somewhat different approaches.

49 A similar story is told for the region immediately to the north of London: Baker, *Cultural Transition*, ch. 3.

50 Martin Carver, Catherine Hills and Jonathan Scheschkewitz, *Wasperton: A Roman, British and Anglo-Saxon Community in Central England* (Woodbridge, 2009).

51 James Gerrard, *The Ruin of Roman Britain: An Archaeological Perspective* (Cambridge, 2013), pp. 254–5.

52 John-Henry Clay, '*Adventus*, warfare and the Britons in the development of West Saxon identity', in *Post-Roman Transitions: Christian and Barbarian Identities in the Early Medieval West*, ed. Walter Pohl and Gerda Heydemann (Turnhout, 2013), pp. 169–213.

53 Ken Dark, *Civitas to Kingdom: British Political Continuity 300–800* (London, 1994), pp. 97–136; with a more reserved view on the role of towns in the changing political framework in Simon T. Loseby, 'Power and towns in late Roman Britain and early Anglo-Saxon England', *Memoria de la Real Academia de Buenas Letras de Barcelona* 25 (2000), 319–70.

54 *Life of Gregory the Great*, ch. 9 (*The Earliest Life of Gregory the Great*, ed. and trans. Bertram Colgrave (Cambridge, 1985), pp. 90–1).

55 Nicholas Brooks, 'Canterbury, Rome and the construction of English identity', in *Early Medieval Rome and the Christian West: Essays in Honour of Donald A. Bullough*, ed. Julia M. H. Smith (Leiden, 2000), pp. 221–47; Nicholas Brooks, 'Canterbury and Rome: the limits and myth of Romanitas', *Settimane di studio del Centro italiano di studi sull'alto medioevo* 49 (2002), 797–830.

56 Bede, *HE* I.29 (ed. and trans. Colgrave and Mynors, pp. 104–7).

57 Bede, *HE* II.3 (ibid., pp. 142–3).

3 LONDON BETWEEN KINGDOMS: C.600–800

1 *EHD* no. 164; S. E. Kelly, *Charters of St Paul's, London* (Oxford, 2004), pp. 221–3; Pierre Chaplais, 'The letter from Bishop Wealdhere of London to Archbishop Brihtwold of Canterbury: the earliest original "letter close" extant in the West', in *Medieval Scribes, Manuscripts and Libraries: Essays Presented to N. R. Ker*, ed. M. B. Parkes and Andrew G. Watson (London, 1978), pp. 3–23.

2 Dorothy Whitelock, *Some Anglo-Saxon Bishops of London* (London, 1975), pp. 10–11; Kelly, *St Paul's*, p. 14; J. R. Maddicott, 'London and Droitwich, c.650–750: trade, industry and the rise of Mercia', *ASE* 34 (2005), 7–58, at 22–3.

3 Chaplais, 'Letter', pp. 3–4 and 22.

4 A charter issued by Ine of Wessex at an unnamed meeting including the archbishop of Canterbury and Waldhere as well as other bishops from Wessex and Mercia (S 248 (*Glast* 7)) may stem from the meeting at

Brentford (though the presence of the archbishop of Canterbury and the bishop of Dunwich points towards a provincial synod).

5   This construction of early Anglo-Saxon history came into being around 1100: *Henry, Archdeacon of Huntingdon: Historia Anglorum, the History of the English People*, ed. and trans. Diana Greenway (Oxford, 1996), pp. lx–lxi (though the earliest reference to a king as a 'heptarch' is *Herman the Archdeacon and Goscelin of Saint-Bertin: Miracles of St Edmund*, ed. and trans. Tom Licence (Oxford, 2014), p. 6).

6   Catherine Cubitt, *Anglo-Saxon Church Councils c.650–c.850* (London, 1995), pp. 27–39; Nicholas Brooks, *The Early History of the Church of Canterbury: Christ Church from 597 to 1066* (Leicester, 1984), pp. 13–14; Keith Bailey, 'The Middle Saxons', in *The Origins of Anglo-Saxon Kingdoms*, ed. Steven Bassett (Leicester, 1989), pp. 108–22 and 265–9, at 114.

7   Barbara Yorke, 'The kingdom of the East Saxons', *ASE* 14 (1985), 1–36, at 27–31.

8   David N. Dumville, 'Essex, Middle Anglia, and the expansion of Mercia in the south-east Midlands', in his *Britons and Anglo-Saxons in the Early Middle Ages* (Aldershot, 1993), ch. III, pp. 1–30.

9   Simon Keynes, 'Mercia', in *WBEASE*, pp. 311–13.

10 Patrick Sims-Williams, *Religion and Literature in Western England, 600–800* (Cambridge, 1990), pp. 16–53.

11 Bede, *HE* IV.11 (*Bede's Ecclesiastical History of the English People*, ed. and trans. Bertram Colgrave and R. A. B. Mynors (Oxford, 1992), pp. 364–7).

12 The date and purpose of this document remain unclear: John Blair, 'The Tribal Hidage', in *WBEASE*, pp. 473–5.

13 Barbara Yorke, *Kings and Kingdoms of Early Anglo-Saxon England* (London, 1990), pp. 9–15; Cyril Hart, 'The Tribal Hidage', *Transactions of the Royal Historical Society*, 5th ser., 21 (1971), 133–57.

14 Bede, *HE* III.21 (ed. and trans. Colgrave and Mynors, pp. 278–9). Dumville, 'Essex, Middle Anglia', pp. 11–17.

15 Bailey, 'Middle Saxons'.

16 S 65 (*CantCC* 9); Dumville, 'Essex, Middle Anglia', p. 20–1.

17 S. E. Kelly, *Charters of Chertsey Abbey* (Oxford, 2015), p. 5.

18 There is extensive work on these units, known variously as 'multiple estates', *regiones* or 'small shires': James Campbell, *Essays in Anglo-Saxon History* (London, 1986), pp. 95–7 and 108–16; Steven Bassett, 'In search of the origins of Anglo-Saxon kingdoms', in *Origins*, ed. Bassett, pp. 3–27 and 237–45, at 17–23; Rosamond Faith, *The English Peasantry and the Growth of Lordship* (London, 1997), pp. 8–14; John Blair, *The Church in Anglo-Saxon Society* (Oxford, 2005), esp. pp. 153–60. For such units in Surrey (and a possible minster at Bermondsey in the early 700s), see John Blair, *Early Medieval Surrey: Land Holding, Church and Settlement before 1300* (Stroud, 1991), pp. 12–24.

19 Yorke, *Kings and Kingdoms*, p. 105.

20 Maddicott, 'London and Droitwich', p. 16.

21 See Chapter 4.

22 Maddicott, 'London and Droitwich', pp. 16–22.

23 Bede, *HE*, III.7 and 30 (ed. and trans. Colgrave and Mynors, pp. 234–5 and 322–3). See also S 1246 (BCS 87).

24 S 1165 (*Chert* 1).

25 John Blair, 'Frithuwold's kingdom and the origins of Surrey', in *Origins*, ed. Bassett, pp. 97–107 and 263–5, at 107.

26 The Old English word *ge* which denotes 'region/territory' in Surrey is related to the German word *gau*, an ancient term for shire-scale units resurrected in Germany during the Third Reich. See J. E. B. Glover, A. Mawer and F. M. Stenton, *The Place-Names of Surrey* (Cambridge, 1934), pp. 1–2.

27 Dumville, 'Essex, Middle Anglia', pp. 20–5; Kelly, *St Paul's*, p. 14.

28 Blair, 'Frithuwold's kingdom', pp. 98–102.

29 For a contrasting view based on early Anglo-Saxon archaeology see John Hines, '*Sūþre-gē*: The foundations of Surrey', in *Aspects of Archaeology and History in Surrey: Towards a Research Framework for the County*, ed. Jonathan Cotton, Glenys Crocker and Audrey Graham (Guildford, 2004), pp. 91–102.

30 S. E. Kelly, *Charters of St Augustine's Abbey, Canterbury, and Minster-in-Thanet* (London, 1995), pp. 196–8; Yorke, 'East Saxons', pp. 20–1 and 33–4.

31 Kelly, *Chertsey*, pp. 3–4; Whitelock, *Anglo-Saxon Bishops*, pp. 5–10. For reservations, see Yorke, 'East Saxons', p. 15 n. 89.

32 He may have been a particular innovator with regard to use of charters – a very sensible move with so many and such changeable political authorities at work: Blair, *Early Medieval Surrey*, pp. 7–8; Patrick Wormald, *The Times of Bede: Studies in Early English Christian Society and Its Historian*, ed. Stephen Baxter (Oxford, 2006), pp. 142–5. For the possible influence of the earlier Wine, bishop of London, on charter-writing in the south-east, see Kelly, *St Paul's*, pp. 108–9.

33 Hlothhere and Eadric 16–16.3 (*EHD*, no. 30, p. 395).

34 The location of this is not known for sure, though it has been suggested that the street name Lothbury derives from the unusual personal-name element *hloth-*, potentially Hlothhere, king of Kent: Eilert Ekwall, *Street-Names of the City of London* (London, 1954), pp. 194–7.

35 S 235 (BCS 72) (founding of a minster at Farnham, Surrey) and S 1246 (BCS 87) (mention of a grant of land in Surrey to Bishop Eorcenwald). S 1171 (BCS 81) is a charter of an East Saxon ruler called Æthelred, issued sometime in the period 685×693, but most likely during Cædwealla's short reign, for it includes a number of West Saxon witnesses in its witness list.

36 Whitelock, *Anglo-Saxon Bishops*, pp. 7–8.

37 *EHD*, no. 32, p. 399. Eorcenwald may have only been beholden to Ine for Surrey, if by the time this law code was put together (688×694) that area was politically dominated by Ine: Whitelock, *Anglo-Saxon Bishops*, p. 10.

38   Cf. Kelly, *St Paul's*, p. 14, who suggests that western Surrey remained under the bishop of London's jurisdiction because of Eorcenwald's personal connections with Chertsey – which of course no longer applied after his death.

39   Maddicott, 'London and Droitwich', p. 17.

40   S 65 (*CantCC* 9).

41   S 1783 (*LondStP* 2). This charter survives in abbreviated form, so could have originally been a joint grant involving the king of the East Saxons.

42   Bailey, 'Middle Saxons', esp. pp. 111–12; Nicholas Brooks and S. E. Kelly, *The Charters of Christ Church, Canterbury*, 2 parts (Oxford, 2013), pp. 324–5; David N. Dumville, *Wessex and England from Alfred to Edgar: Six Essays on Political, Cultural, and Ecclesiastical Revival* (Woodbridge, 1992), p. 3 n. 16 (emphasising the reign of Coenred (704–9)).

43   F. M. Stenton, 'The supremacy of the Mercian kings', in his *Preparatory to Anglo-Saxon England: Being the Collected Papers of Frank Merry Stenton*, ed. Doris Mary Stenton (Oxford, 1970), pp. 48–66 (originally published in 1918), though the term was current before his time: e.g. Thomas Kerslake, 'Vestiges of the supremacy of Mercia in the south of England, during the eighth century', *Transactions of the Bristol and Gloucestershire Archaeological Society* 3 (1878), 106–67, at 131–9.

44   Simon Keynes, 'Mercia and Wessex in the ninth century', in *Mercia: An Anglo-Saxon Kingdom in Europe*, ed. Michelle P. Brown and Carol Ann Farr (London, 2001), pp. 310–28 (focusing on a slightly later period, but the point is still applicable to the seventh century).

45   Maddicott, 'London and Droitwich', pp. 21–3.

46   D. P. Kirby, *The Earliest English Kings*, 2nd ed. (London, 2000), pp. 109–17.

47   Bede, *HE* V.23 (ed. and trans. Colgrave and Mynors, pp. 558–9).

48   S 89 (BCS 154).

49   Felix, *Life of St Guthlac*, ch. 49 (*Felix's Life of Saint Guthlac*, ed. and trans. Bertram Colgrave (Cambridge, 1956), pp. 148–51). In a later chapter (52, pp. 164–7), Æthelbald pays his respects to the recently deceased Guthlac, and hears a further prophecy about the length and greatness of his reign. Kirby, *Earliest English Kings*, pp. 131–2 suggests that the alliance represented by this text may have been integral to Æthelbald's power.

50   *EHD*, no. 177.

51   Simon Keynes, 'The reconstruction of a burnt Cottonian manuscript: the case of Cotton MS. Otho A. I', *British Library Journal* 22 (1997 for 1996), 113–60; Simon Keynes, 'The kingdom of the Mercians in the eighth century', in *Æthelbald and Offa: Two Eighth-Century Kings of Mercia*, ed. David Hill and Margaret Worthington, British Archaeological Reports: British Series 383 (Oxford, 2005), pp. 1–26, at 8.

52   *ASC* 757.

53   See Chapter 4.

54 Maddicott, 'London and Droitwich', pp. 21–2; Kirby, *Earliest English Kings*, p. 113. See S 100 (*CantCC* 13) for a grant of land in Middlesex. On Surrey under Æthelbald, see Kelly, *St Paul's*, pp. 14–15; Kelly, *Chertsey*, pp. 10–11.

55 Patrick Wormald, 'The age of Bede and Æthelbald', in *The Anglo-Saxons*, ed. James Campbell (London, 1982), pp. 70–100 and 250–1, at 95; Stenton, *Anglo-Saxon England*, p. 204; Simon Keynes, 'England, 700–900', in *The New Cambridge Medieval History II: c.700–c.900*, ed. Rosamond McKitterick (Cambridge, 1995), pp. 18–42, at 30.

56 Keynes, 'Kingdom of the Mercians', pp. 8–18.

57 Patrick Sims-Williams, *Religion and Literature in Western England, 600–800* (Cambridge, 1990), pp. 36–9; S. E. Kelly, *The Charters of Selsey* (Oxford, 1998), pp. lxxx–iv; Brooks, *Early History*, pp. 111–23.

58 Rory Naismith, *Money and Power in Anglo-Saxon England: The Southern English Kingdoms 757–865* (Cambridge, 2012), pp. 53–64.

59 Naismith, *Medieval European Coinage, with a Catalogue of the Coins in the Fitzwilliam Museum, Cambridge. 8: Britain and Ireland c. 400–1066* (Cambridge, 2017), pp. 132–8.

60 Pauline Stafford, 'Political women in Mercia, eighth to early tenth centuries', in *Mercia*, ed. Brown and Farr, pp. 35–49, at 37–40.

61 S. E. Kelly, 'Trading privileges from eighth-century England', *EME* 1 (1992), 3–28, at 25.

62 S 144 (*Pet* 6). The charter is undated, but may belong to the later 780s or after. For *Freoricburna* as Kingston, see Blair, *Early Medieval Surrey*, p. 20.

63 S 127 (*Chert* 5); Kelly, *Chertsey*, pp. 11–12.

64 London: S 168 and 170 (*CantCC* 44–5). Chelsea: S 158 (*Sel* 14).

65 Brooks, *Early History*, pp. 132 and 141–2.

66 See Chapter 4.

67 Thomas F. X. Noble, 'The rise and fall of the archbishopric of Lichfield in English, papal, and European perspective', in *England and Rome in the Early Middle Ages: Pilgrimage, Art, and Politics*, ed. Francesca Tinti (Turnhout, 2014), pp. 291–306; Kelly, *St Paul's*, p. 19; Brooks, *Early History*, pp. 123–7.

68 Noble, 'Rise and fall', pp. 293–6.

69 William of Malmesbury, *Gesta pontificum Anglorum*, ch. 7 (*William of Malmesbury, Gesta Pontificum Anglorum; the History of the English Bishops*, ed. and trans. Michael Winterbottom and Rodney Malcolm Thomson, 2 vols (Oxford, 2007), vol. I, 20–1).

70 *ASC* 794 (796).

71 *EHD*, no. 204.

72 *EHD*, no. 205.

73 Robert Cowie, 'The evidence for royal sites in Middle Anglo-Saxon London', *Medieval Archaeology* 48 (2004), 201–9.

74 See Chapter 5.

4 LUNDENWIC:
'AN EMPORIUM FOR MANY NATIONS'

1   Bede, *HE*, IV.22 (*Bede's Ecclesiastical History of the English People*, ed. and trans. Bertram Colgrave and R. A. B. Mynors (Oxford, 1992), pp. 400–5).

2   Richard Hodges, *Dark Age Economics: The Origins of Towns and Trade, A.D. 600–1000*, 2nd ed. (London, 1989); Stéphane Lebecq, *Marchands et navigateurs frisons du haut Moyen Âge* (Lile, 1983).

3   G. L. Gomme, *The Opening of Kingsway and Aldwych by His Majesty the King, Accompanied by Her Majesty the Queen* (London, 1905). Cf. Robert Cowie and Lyn Blackmore, *Lundenwic: Excavations in Middle Saxon London, 1987–2000* (London, 2008), p. 8; J. E. B. Gover, A. Mawer and F. M. Stenton, *The Place-Names of Middlesex, apart from the City of London* (Cambridge, 1942), pp. 166, 178 and 185.

4   *The Building News and Engineering Journal*, 18 November 1904.

5   R. E. M. Wheeler, 'The topography of Saxon London', *Antiquity* 8 (1934), 290–303 and 443–7, at 290. Cf. R. E. M. Wheeler, *London and the Vikings* (London, 1927), p. 64.

6   Wheeler, 'Topography', p. 297.

7   Francis Haverfield, *The Romanization of Britain*, 3rd ed. (Oxford, 1915), p. 84.

8   F. M. Stenton, *Anglo-Saxon England*, 3rd ed. (Oxford, 1971), p. 56.

9   W. F. Grimes, *The Excavation of Roman and Mediaeval London* (London, 1968), pp. 153–4.

10 Alan Vince, 'In search of Saxon London: the view from the pot shed', *Popular Archaeology* 5 (1983), 33–7.

11 R. E. M. Wheeler, *London and the Saxons* (London, 1935), p. 141.

12 Martin Biddle, 'London on the Strand', *Popular Archaeology* 6 (1984), 23–7. The other scholar at the forefront of the identification of earlier Anglo-Saxon London was Alan Vince: Alan Vince, 'The Aldwych: Saxon London rediscovered?', *Current Archaeology* 8 (1984), 310–12. An elegant telling of this story can be found in Martin Biddle, 'The road to Lundenwic', in '*Hidden Histories and Records of Antiquity*': *Essays on Saxon and Medieval London for John Clark, Curator Emeritus, Museum of London*, ed. Jonathan Cotton et al. (London, 2014), pp. 13–17.

13 Robert Cowie, Robert L. Whytehead and Lyn Blackmore, 'Two Middle Saxon occupation sites: excavations at Jubilee Hall and 21–22 Maiden Lane', *TLAMAS* 39 (1988), 47–163.

14 Cowie and Blackmore, *Lundenwic*, pp. 5–7.

15 Ibid., p. 9 sets out the names applied to London from the seventh to later ninth centuries.

16 David Hill, 'Appendix 2. Gazetteer of possible Anglo-Saxon *wics*', in *Wics: The Early Mediaeval Trading Centres of Northern Europe*, ed. David Hill and Robert Cowie (Sheffield, 2001), pp. 95–103.

17 John Wacher, *The Towns of Roman Britain*, 2nd ed. (London, 1995), p. 14.

18 *Wic* is similar to Modern English 'sheep', in that the plural is the same as the singular.

19 E.g. Bede used it to describe London's commercial function in *HE* II.3 (ed. and trans. Colgrave and Mynors, pp. 142–3).

20 Karl Polanyi, 'Ports of trade in early societies', *Journal of Economic History* 23 (1963), 30–45; Karl Polanyi, 'Trade, markets, and money in the European early Middle Ages', *Norwegian Archaeological Review* 11 (1978), 92–6; Karl Polanyi, *The Great Transformation: The Political and Economic Origins of Our Time* (New York, 1944), pp. 53–4. See also Kenneth G. Hirth, 'Interregional trade and the formation of prehistoric gateway communities', *American Antiquity* 43 (1978), 35–45.

21 J. K. Hyde, 'Medieval descriptions of cities', *Bulletin of the John Rylands Library* 48 (1965–6), 308–40; Donald A. Bullough, 'Social and economic structure and topography in the early medieval city', *Settimane di studio del Centro italiano di studi sull'alto medioevo* 21 (1974), 351–99; Chris Wickham, 'Bounding the city: concepts of urban-rural difference in the West in the early Middle Ages', *Settimane di studio del Centro italiano di studi sull'alto medioevo* 56 (2009), 61–80; Christopher Loveluck, *Europe in the Early Middle Ages, c.AD 600–1150: A Comparative Archaeology* (Cambridge, 2013), pp. 20–2.

22 Alcuin, *The Bishops, Kings and Saints of York* ll. 19–20 (ed. and trans. Peter Godman (Oxford, 1982), pp. 4–5).

23 Richard Hodges, *Towns and Trade in the Age of Charlemagne* (London, 2000), pp. 69–92; Richard Hodges, *Dark Age Economics: A New Audit* (London, 2012), pp. 91–115.

24 Alcuin, *The Bishops, Kings and Saints of York* ll. 35–7 (ed. and trans. Godman, pp. 6–7).

25 James Campbell, *Essays in Anglo-Saxon History* (London, 1986), pp. 105–6; Katharina Ulmschneider, *Markets, Minsters, and Metal-Detectors: The Archaeology of Middle Saxon Lincolnshire and Hampshire Compared* (Oxford, 2000), p. 83; Tim Pestell, 'Markets, *emporia*, *wics*, and "productive" sites: pre-Viking trade centres in Anglo-Saxon England', in *The Oxford Handbook of Anglo-Saxon Archaeology*, ed. David A. Hinton, Sally Crawford and Helena Hamerow (Oxford, 2011), pp. 556–79, at 557–9.

26 Campbell, *Essays*, pp. 99–106.

27 Greg Waite, 'The preface to the Old English Bede: authorship, transmission, and connection with the *West Saxon Genealogical Regnal List*', *ASE* 44 (2015), 31–93, at 81.

28 It is also possible that *vicus* related to a royal estate of some kind in London: Rory Naismith, *Money and Power in Anglo-Saxon England: The Southern English Kingdoms 757–865* (Cambridge, 2012), pp. 114–16.

29 It was apparently only removed in the eleventh and twelfth centuries: see Chapter 7.

30   Robert Cowie, 'Londinium to Lundenwic: early and middle Saxon archaeology
     in the London region', in London Under Ground: The Archaeology of a City,
     ed. Ian Haynes, Harvey Sheldon and Lesley Hannigan (Oxford, 2000),
     pp. 175–205, at 181; Ralph Merrifield, 'The contribution of archaeology to
     our understanding of pre-Norman London', in Medieval Art, Architecture
     and Archaeology in London, ed. Lindy Grant (London, 1990), pp. 1–15,
     at 10.
31   Cowie and Blackmore, Lundenwic, p. 101; Gordon Malcolm, David
     Bowsher and Robert Cowie, Middle Saxon London: Excavations at the
     Royal Opera House 1989–99 (London, 2003), p. 143.
32   Cowie and Blackmore, Lundenwic, p. 8.
33   Malcolm, Bowsher and Cowie, Middle Saxon London.
34   Cowie and Blackmore, Lundenwic, p. 116.
35   J. R. Maddicott, 'London and Droitwich, c.650–750: trade, industry and
     the rise of Mercia', ASE 34 (2005), p. 13.
36   Justine Bayley et al., 'A Saxon brass bar ingot cache from Kingsway, London',
     in 'Hidden Histories', ed. Cotton et al., pp. 121–8.
37   Malcolm, Bowsher and Cowie, Middle Saxon London, pp. 278–84.
     Another find of a similar coin has come to light in Lambeth: PAS LON-
     216EAC.
38   Bernhard Bischoff and Michael Lapidge, Biblical Commentaries from the
     Canterbury School of Theodore and Hadrian (Cambridge, 1995), pp. 5–189.
39   Malcolm, Bowsher and Cowie, Middle Saxon London, pp. 150–8.
40   Cowie and Blackmore, Lundenwic, pp. 108–10; Malcolm, Bowsher and
     Cowie, Middle Saxon London, pp. 145–6.
41   S 1204 (CantCC 91).
42   Malcolm, Bowsher and Cowie, Middle Saxon London, p. 145; Vince, Saxon
     London, p. 16.
43   Cowie and Blackmore, Lundenwic, pp. 156–9; Malcolm, Bowsher and
     Cowie, Middle Saxon London, pp. 168–84.
44   Cowie and Blackmore, Lundenwic, p. 26 (Trafalgar Square); Whytehead,
     Cowie and Blackmore, 'Two Middle Saxon occupation sites', pp. 60–5.
45   Peter Boyer and Lynne Keys, 'Saxon iron smelting in Bermondsey?
     Archaeological investigations at 150–156 Abbey Street', Surrey
     Archaeological Collections 97 (2013), 43–58, esp. 53–4.
46   Cowie and Blackmore, Lundenwic, pp. 149–52; Malcolm, Bowsher and
     Cowie, Middle Saxon London, pp. 160–2.
47   Jim Leary et al., Tatberht's Lundenwic: Archaeological Excavations in Middle
     Saxon London (London, 2004), pp. 10–11 and 38–9.
48   Malcolm, Bowsher and Cowie, Middle Saxon London, pp. 162–4.
49   Leary et al., Tatberht's Lundenwic, pp. 103–4. For another (less readily
     comprehensible) eighth-century runic inscription on a piece of bone from
     the Covent Garden site, see R. I. Page, 'Runes at the Royal Opera House,
     London', Nytt om Runer 12 (1997), 12–13.

50 Lyn Blackmore, Alan Vince and Robert Cowie, 'The origins of Lundenwic? Excavations at 8–9 Long Acre/16 Garrick Street, WC2', *London Archaeologist* 10 (2004), 301–5.

51 Cowie and Blackmore, *Lundenwic*, p. 108; Lyn Blackmore, 'The origins and growth of *Lundenwic*, a mart of many nations', in *Central Places in the Migration and Merovingian Periods: Papers from the 52nd Sachsensymposium, Lund, August 2001*, ed. Birgitta Hårdh and Lars Larsson (Lund, 2002), pp. 273–301, at 277–81.

52 Vera I. Evison, *Catalogue of Anglo-Saxon Glass in the British Museum* (London, 2008), no. 89.

53 Cowie and Blackmore, *Lundenwic*, pp. 117–18. See also Lyn Blackmore, 'Aspects of trade and exchange evidenced by recent work on Saxon and medieval pottery from London', *TLAMAS* 50 (1999), 38–54, at 38–41.

54 Maddicott, 'London and Droitwich', pp. 9 and 11–12.

55 For the location of the estate, see John Blair, 'Frithuwold's kingdom and the origins of Surrey', in *Origins*, ed. Bassett, n. 13; a case for Southwark is made in Tony Dyson, 'London and Southwark in the 7th century and later: a neglected reference', *TLAMAS* 31 (1980), 83–95.

56 S 1246 (BCS 87). This charter is more problematic than that of Chertsey, but probably does preserve the essentials of a seventh-century document.

57 Hodges, *Dark Age Economics*, pp. 50–6 and 189–98; Ann Williams, *Kingship and Government in Pre-Conquest England, c.500–1066* (Basingstoke, 1999), pp. 44–8; Tom Saunders, 'Early medieval *emporia* and the tributary social function', in *Wics*, ed. Hill and Cowie, pp. 7–13.

58 Cowie and Blackmore, *Lundenwic*, pp. 108–10. See also Lyn Blackmore, 'Lundenwic: essor et déclin d'un établissement commercial anglo-saxonne des VIIe–IXe siècles', in *Quentovic: environnement, archéologie, histoire*, ed. Stéphane Lebecq, Bruno Béthouart and Laurent Verslype (Lille, 2010), pp. 329–66, at 340 and 353.

59 *Carolingian Chronicles: Royal Frankish Annals and Nithard's Histories*, trans. Bernhard Walter Scholz and Barbara Rogers (Ann Arbor, MI, 1972), p. 88.

60 Christopher Loveluck and Dries Tys, 'Coastal societies, exchange and identity along the Channel and southern North Sea shores of Europe, AD 600–1000', *Journal of Maritime Archaeology* 1 (2006), 140–69; Robin Fleming, 'Elites, boats and foreigners: rethinking the birth of English towns', *Settimane di studio della Fondazione Centro Italiano di Studi sull'Alto Medioevo* 56 (2009), 393–425; Christopher Loveluck, *Northwest Europe in the Early Middle Ages, c. AD 600–1150: A Comparative Archaeology* (Cambridge, 2013), pp. 178–212.

61 As at Ipswich: Christopher Scull, *Early Medieval (Late 5th–Early 8th Centuries AD) Cemeteries at Boss Hall and Buttermarket, Ipswich* (Leeds, 2009). Cf. Alice Thomas, 'Rivers of gold? The coastal zone between the Humber and the Wash in the Mid Saxon period', *ASSAH* 18 (2013), 97–118.

62 Cf. Christopher Scull, 'Ipswich: development and context of an urban precursor in the 7th century', in *Central Places in the Migration and Merovingian Periods*, ed. Birgitta Hårdh and Lars Larsson, pp. 303–16; Scull, *Boss Hall and Buttermarket*, pp. 305–19.

63 Joachim Henning, 'Early European towns: the development of the economy in the Frankish realm between dynamism and deceleration A D 500–1100', in *Post-Roman Towns, Trade and Settlement in Europe and Byzantium*, ed. Joachim Henning, 2 vols (Berlin, 2007), vol. I, pp. 3–40, at 26–30. For the road layout of *Lundenwic* and its possible link to royal authority, see Malcolm, Bowsher and Cowie, *Middle Saxon London*, pp. 145–6.

64 Michael McCormick, 'Where do trading towns come from? Early medieval Venice and the northern *emporia*', in *Post-Roman Towns*, ed. Henning, vol. I, 41–68, at pp. 44–50.

65 David N. Dumville, 'Essex, Middle Anglia, and the expansion of Mercia in the south-east Midlands', in David N. Dumville, *Britons and Anglo-Saxons in the Early Middle Ages* (Aldershot, 1993), pp. 22–5.

66 McCormick, 'Where do trading towns come from?', pp. 47–52.

67 Bede, *HE*, preface (ed. and trans. Colgrave and Mynors, pp. 4–5).

68 S. E. Kelly, *Charters of St Paul's, London* (Oxford, 2004), p. 17. Nothhelm would eventually become archbishop of Canterbury (735–9).

69 Loveluck, *Northwest Europe*, pp. 17–20 and 204–12.

70 See Chapter 1.

71 Hodges, *Dark Age Economics*, pp. 101–6.

72 Naismith, *Money and Power*, pp. 23–37; Michael McCormick, 'Um 808. Was der frühmittelalterliche König mit der Wirtschaft zu tun hatte', in *Die Macht des Königs: Herrschaft in Europa vom Frühmittelalter bis in die Neuzeit*, ed. Bernhard Jussen (Constance, 2005), pp. 55–71.

73 McCormick, 'Where do trading towns come from?', pp. 58–60.

74 See Chapter 3.

75 No such markets have actually been found: Cowie and Blackmore, *Lundenwic*, p. 171.

76 Cowie and Harding, 'Saxon settlement', pp. 188–9. For the case that St Mary-le-Strand may go back to this period, see T. Dyson, 'Two Saxon land-grants for Queenhithe', in *Collectanea Londiniensia: Studies in London Archaeology and History Presented to Ralph Merrifield*, ed. Joanna Bird, Hugh Chapman and John Clark (London, 1978), pp. 200–15, at 205.

77 John Blair, *The Church in Anglo-Saxon Society* (Oxford, 2005); Robert Cowie and Lyn Blackmore, *Early and Middle Saxon Rural Settlement in the London Region* (London, 2008), pp. 90–100.

78 Derek Keene, 'Alfred and London', in *Alfred the Great: Papers from the Eleventh-Centenary Conferences*, ed. Timothy Reuter (Aldershot, 2003), pp. 236–49, at 236.

79 Paul Blinkhorn, *The Ipswich Ware Project: Ceramics, Trade and Society in Middle Saxon England* (London, 2012).

80   Cowie and Blackmore, *Lundenwic*, pp. 172–5; Malcolm, Bowsher and
     Cowie, *Middle Saxon London*, pp. 225–41. See more generally Lyn
     Blackmore, 'La céramique du Vème au Xème siècle à Londres et dans
     la région londonienne', in *La céramique du Vème au Xème siècle dans
     l'Europe du haut Moyen Age: travaux du Groupe de Recherches et d'Études
     sur la céramique dans le Nord-Pas-de-Calais. Actes du Colloque d'Outreau
     (10–12 avril 1992)*, ed. Daniel Piton (Arras, 1993), pp. 129–50; Lyn
     Blackmore, 'Pottery: trade and tradition', in *Wics*, ed. Hill and Cowie,
     pp. 22–42.
81   Cowie and Blackmore, *Lundenwic*, pp. 177–9; Malcolm, Bowsher and
     Cowie, *Middle Saxon London*, pp. 238–41.
82   Cowie and Blackmore, *Lundenwic*, p. 179. See also Jonathan Parkhouse,
     'The distribution and exchange of Mayen lava quernstones in early medieval
     northwestern Europe', in *Exchange and Trade in Medieval Europe: Papers
     of the 'Medieval Europe Brugge 1997' Conference 1997*, ed. Guy de Boe and
     Frans Verhaeghe (Zellik, 1997), pp. 97–106.
83   John Naylor, 'Emporia and their hinterlands in the 7th to 9th-centuries
     A D: some comments and observations from England', in *Les cultures des
     littoraux au haut Moyen Âge: cadres et modes de vie dans l'espace maritime
     Manche-mer du Nord du IIIe au Xe s.*, ed. Inès Leroy and Laurent Verslype
     (Lille, 2016), pp. 59–67, at 62; Maddicott, 'London and Droitwich', p. 14.
84   John Naylor, 'Coinage, trade and the origins of the English *emporia*, ca. A D
     650–750', in *From One Sea to Another: Trading Places in the European and
     Mediterranean Early Middle Ages. Proceedings of the International Conference,
     Comacchio, 27th–29th March 2009*, ed. Sauro Gelichi and Richard Hodges
     (Turnhout, 2012), pp. 237–66.
85   Helena Hamerow, 'Settlement mobility and the "Middle Saxon shift":
     rural settlements and settlement patterns in Anglo-Saxon England',
     ASE 20 (1991), 1–17; Helena Hamerow, *Rural Settlements and Society in
     Anglo-Saxon England* (Oxford, 2012); John Moreland, 'The significance
     of production in eighth-century England', in *The Long Eighth Century:
     Production, Distribution and Demand*, ed. Inge Lyse Hansen and Chris
     Wickham (Leiden, 2000), pp. 69–104, at 76–87.
86   Naylor, 'Emporia and their hinterlands', p. 65; Malcolm, Bowsher and
     Cowie, *Middle Saxon London*, pp. 186–8.
87   Helena Hamerow, 'Agrarian production and the emporia of mid Saxon
     England, ca. A D 650–850', in *Post-Roman Towns*, ed. Henning, vol. I,
     pp. 219–32, esp. 221–3.
88   Susan Hirst, 'Mucking/East Tilbury: lower Thames meeting place and mart
     in the early and middle Saxon periods?', in *Anglo-Saxon Traces*, ed. Jane
     Roberts and Leslie Webster (Tempe, AZ, 2011), pp. 101–15; Christopher
     Scull, Faye Minter and Judith Plouviez, 'Social and economic complexity
     in early medieval England: a central place complex of the East Anglian
     kingdom at Rendlesham, Suffolk', *Antiquity* 90 (2016), 1594–1612.

89 These sites are widely known as 'productive sites', though the term is not altogether satisfactory, as individual cases could be very different in nature (Julian D. Richards, 'What's so special about "productive" sites? Middle Saxon settlements in Northumbria', *ASSAH* 10 (1999), 71–80). See more generally *Markets in Early Medieval Europe: Trading and 'Productive' Sites, 650–850*, ed. Tim Pestell and Katharina Ulmschneider (Macclesfield, 2003); John Naylor, *An Archaeology of Trade in Middle Saxon England*, British Archaeological Reports: British Series 376 (Oxford, 2004); Pestell, 'Markets, *emporia, wics*'.

90 Mark Gardiner, 'Continental trade and non-urban ports in mid-Anglo-Saxon England: excavations at Sandtun', *Archaeological Journal* 158 (2001), 161–290.

91 Chris Wickham, *Framing the Early Middle Ages: Europe and the Mediterranean, 400–800* (Oxford, 2005), pp. 685–8 and 809–10.

92 Willibald, *Life of St Boniface*, ch. 4 and 5 (*Vitae sancti Bonifatii archiepiscopi Moguntini*, ed. W. Levison, MGH Scriptores rerum Germanicarum in usum scholarum separatim editi 57 (Hanover and Leipzig, 1905), pp. 16 and 20; *The Life of Saint Boniface by Willibald*, trans. George W. Robinson (Cambridge, MA, 1916), pp. 43 and 48–9).

93 Hodges, *Dark Age Economics*; Hodges, *Towns and Trade in the Age of Charlemagne*; Stéphane Lebecq, 'The northern seas (fifth to eighth century)', in *The New Cambridge Medieval History. 1: c.500–c.700*, ed. Paul Fouracre (Cambridge, 2005), pp. 639–59.

94 Wickham, *Framing*, pp. 690–2; Sauro Gelichi et al., 'History of a forgotten town: Comacchio and its archaeology', in *From One Sea to Another*, ed. Gelichi and Hodges, pp. 169–205; Richard Hodges, 'Adriatic sea trade in an European perspective', in *From One Sea to Another*, ed. Gelichi and Hodges, pp. 207–34.

95 For Dorestad, see now *Dorestad in an International Framework: New Research on Centres of Trade and Coinage in Carolingian Times*, ed. Annemarieke Willemsen and Hanneke Kik (Turnhout, 2010). For Quentovic, *Quentovic. Environnement, archéologie, histoire. Actes du colloque international de Montreuil-sur-Mer, Etaples et Le Touquet et de la journée d'études de Lille sur les origines de Montreuil-sur-Mer (11–13 mai 2006 et 1er décembre 2006)*, ed. Stéphane Lebecq, Bruno Béthouart and Laurent Verslype (Lille, 2010); Inès Leroy, 'La localisation et les caractères archéologiques du site portuaire de Quentovic. Étude préliminaire du cadre historique et géographique (littoral et basse-Canche)', *Medieval and Modern Matters* 2 (2011), 121–52.

96 The papers in Hill and Cowie, *Wics* survey the main sites. For York, see D. M. Palliser, *Medieval York 600–1540* (Oxford, 2014), pp. 34–48.

97 Simon Coupland, 'Trading places: Quentovic and Dorestad reassessed', *EME* 11 (2002), 209–32.

98 Søren M. Sindbæk, 'Networks and nodal points: the emergence of towns in early Viking Age Scandinavia', *Antiquity* 81 (2007), 119–32; Søren M.

Sindbæk, 'The small world of the Vikings: networks in early medieval communication and exchange', *Norwegian Archaeological Review* 40 (2007), 59–74.

99 Wihtred 28 and Ine 20 (*Die Gesetze der Angelsachsen*, ed. Felix Liebermann, 3 vols (Halle, 1903–16), vol. I, pp. 14 and 98–9; trans. *EHD*, pp. 398 and 401).

100 *Beowulf* ll. 229–490 (*Klaeber's 'Beowulf'*, ed. R. D. Fulk, Robert E. Bjork and John D. Niles (Toronto, 2007), pp. 10–19).

101 S. E. Kelly, 'Trading privileges from eighth-century England', *EME* 1 (1992), 3–28.

102 S. E. Kelly, *Charters of St Augustine's Abbey, Canterbury, and Minster-in-Thanet* (London, 1995), pp. cxii–cxv.

103 The book has been held by Trinity Hall in Cambridge since 1611, but its donor stipulated that it must be returned to St Augustine's should the monastery ever be refounded (see Kelly, *St Augustine's*, pp. lvii–ix).

104 Kelly, 'Trading privileges', pp. 24–5.

105 S 91 (*CantStA* 51).

106 Maddicott, 'London and Droitwich'.

107 In addition to S 91, these are S 86, 88, 91 and 143 (*CantStA* 49, 50, 52–3). See Kelly, 'Trading privileges', pp. 7–10.

108 S 88 (*Charters of Rochester*, ed. A. Campbell (London, 1973), no. 2).

109 S 103a and 1788 (*LondStP* 7–8). These documents do not say whether they applied just in London, though this is likely given the bishop's location.

110 S 98 (BCS 171).

111 See Chapter 3.

112 S 1785 (*LondStP* 3); Maddicott, 'London and Droitwich', pp. 18–19.

113 William Dugdale, *Monasticon Anglicanum*, 3 vols (London, 1655–73), vol. I, p. 138. These streets cannot be located, and could have been either in *Lundenwic* or the City. Cf. Kelly, *St Paul's*, p. 16.

114 S 133 (BCS 259). For discussion see Hartmut Atsma and Jean Vezin, 'Le dossier suspect des possessions de Saint-Denis en Angleterre revisité (VIIIe–IXe siècle)', in *Fälschungen im Mittelalter. Internationaler Kongreß der Monumenta Germaniae Historica München, 16.–19. September 1986*, 5 vols (Hanover, 1988), vol. IV, pp. 211–36.

115 Neil Middleton, 'Early medieval port customs, tolls and controls on foreign trade', *EME* 13 (2005), 313–58, at 330–49; Kelly, 'Trading privileges', pp. 16–22.

116 Kelly, 'Trading privileges', p. 25.

117 Hodges, *Dark Age Economics*, pp. 103–4.

118 C. H. V. Sutherland, *Anglo-Saxon Gold Coinage in the Light of the Crondall Hoard* (Oxford, 1948), pp. 85–8. It is possible that some of these coins were made outside London, imitating its mint-name.

119 Mark Blackburn, 'Two new types of Anglo-Saxon gold shillings', in *Coinage and History in the North Sea World, c.AD 500–1250: Essays in Honour of*

Marion Archibald, ed. Barrie Cook and Gareth Williams (Leiden, 2006), pp. 127–40.

120 Rory Naismith, 'Money of the saints: church and coinage in early Anglo-Saxon England', in *Studies in Early Medieval Coinage 3: Sifting the Evidence*, ed. Tony Abramson (London, 2014), pp. 68–121, at 91–5.

121 Rory Naismith, *Medieval European Coinage, with a Catalogue of the Coins in the Fitzwilliam Museum, Cambridge. 8: Britain and Ireland c. 400–1066* (Cambridge, 2017), pp. 98–9.

122 Ibid., pp. 63–109; Anna Gannon, *SCBI* 63; D. M. Metcalf, *Thrymsas and Sceattas in the Ashmolean Museum, Oxford*, 3 vols (London, 1993–4).

123 See S 168, 170 and 1436 (*CantCC* 44–5 and 59).

124 Naismith, *Money and Power*, pp. 114–16.

125 Mark Blackburn, '"Productive" sites and the pattern of coin loss in England, 600–1180', in *Markets in Early Medieval Europe*, ed. Pestell and Ulmschneider, pp. 20–36.

126 Naylor, 'Coinage, trade and the origins of the English *emporia*'.

127 Naylor, 'Emporia and their hinterlands', pp. 63–4; Cowie and Blackmore, *Lundenwic*, p. 180.

128 Malcolm, Bowsher and Cowie, *Middle Saxon London*, pp. 148–9.

129 Naismith, *Money and Power*, pp. 90–6.

130 Rory Naismith, 'The coinage of Offa revisited', *British Numismatic Journal* 80 (2010), 76–106; Gareth Williams, 'Minting in Wallingford', in *Transforming Townscapes: From Burh to Borough. The Archaeology of Wallingford*, AD 800–1400, ed. Neil Christie and Oliver Creighton (London, 2013), pp. 343–59, at 344; Naismith, *Medieval European Coinage*, pp. 133 and 143–4.

131 For the map of finds, see Vince, *Saxon London*, pp. 18 and 29; Peter Stott, 'Saxon and Norman coins from London', in *Aspects of Saxo-Norman London: 2. Finds and Environmental Evidence*, ed. Alan Vince (London, 1991), pp. 279–325, at 281 and 288; Cowie and Blackmore, *Lundenwic*, pp. 180 and 206–8; Malcolm, Bowsher and Cowie, *Middle Saxon London*, pp. 285–7; Leary et al., *Tatberht's Lundenwic*, pp. 27 and 102–3.

132 Naylor, 'Coinage, trade and the origins of the English emporia'.

133 Naismith, *Money and Power*, pp. 191–2 and 214–16.

134 Malcolm, Bowsher and Cowie, *Middle Saxon London*, pp. 101–5.

135 Cowie and Blackmore, *Lundenwic*, pp. 108–10.

136 Malcolm, Bowsher and Cowie, *Middle Saxon London*, pp. 118–20; Leary et al., *Tatberht's Lundenwic*, pp. 76–7 and 124–5.

137 Cowie and Blackmore, *Lundenwic*, pp. 115–16 and 211–12.

138 Ibid., pp. 35–43.

139 Cowie and Blackmore, *Early and Middle Saxon Rural Settlement*, pp. 90–100; Gerald C. Dunning and Vera I. Evison, 'The palace of Westminster sword', *Archaeologia* 98 (1961), 123–58.

140 S 208 (BCS 492).

141 See Chapter 5.

142 Naismith, *Medieval European Coinage*, pp. 106–8.

143 Coupland, 'Trading places', pp. 220–6.

144 Richard Hodges and David Whitehouse, *Mohammed, Charlemagne and the Origins of Europe: Archaeology and the Pirenne Thesis* (London, 1983), pp. 163–5; Cowie and Blackmore, *Lundenwic*, pp. 111–12; Naismith, *Money and Power*, pp. 214–16 and 231–9.

5   ALFRED THE GREAT AND THE VIKINGS

1   Clare A. P. Willsdon, *Mural Painting in Britain 1840–1940: Image and Meaning* (Oxford, 2000), pp. 71–2.

2   Simon Keynes, 'The cult of King Alfred the Great', ASE 28 (1999), 225–356; Joanne Parker, *'England's Darling': The Victorian Cult of Alfred the Great* (Manchester, 2007).

3   Asser, *De rebus gestis Ælfredi*, preface (*Alfred the Great: Asser's Life of King Alfred and Other Contemporary Sources*, trans. Simon Keynes and Michael Lapidge (Harmondsworth, 1983), p. 67).

4   Alfred's thought is discussed in impressive detail in David Pratt, *The Political Thought of King Alfred the Great* (Cambridge, 2007).

5   *Old English Pastoral Care*, preface (*Alfred the Great*, trans. Keynes and Lapidge, p. 126).

6   Sarah Foot, 'The making of *Angelcynn*: English identity before the Norman Conquest', *Transactions of the Royal Historical Society*, 6th ser., 6 (1996), 25–49, esp. 26–8; Pratt, *Political Thought*, pp. 105–7. For a more reserved approach, see George Molyneaux, *The Formation of the English Kingdom in the Tenth Century* (Oxford, 2015), esp. pp. 203–6.

7   ASC 886.

8   Derek Keene, 'Alfred and London', in *Alfred the Great: Papers from the Eleventh-Centenary Conferences*, ed. Timothy Reuter (Aldershot, 2003), pp. 235–49, at 241–2.

9   Asser, *De rebus gestis Ælfredi*, ch. 83 (*Alfred the Great*, trans. Keynes and Lapidge, p. 98). Cf. ASC 886.

10 The oaths are reported and written down in Nithard, *Historia* III.5 (*Histoire des fils de Louis le Pieux*, ed. and trans. Philippe Lauer (Paris, 1926), pp. 100–11). See for context Patrick Geary, 'Oathtaking and conflict management in the ninth century', in *Rechtsverständnis und Konfliktbewältigung: Gerechtliche und außergerichtliche Strategien im Mittelalter*, ed. Stefan Esders (Cologne, 2007), pp. 239–54; Rosamond McKitterick, 'The oaths of Strasbourg (842) and their implications in the light of recent scholarship', in *Loyalty in the Middle Ages: Ideal and Practice of a Cross-Social Value*, ed. Jörg Sonntag and Coralie Zermatten (Turnhout, 2015), pp. 141–60.

11 Simon Keynes, 'King Alfred and the Mercians', in *Kings, Currency and Alliances: History and Coinage in Southern England in the Ninth Century*, ed.

Mark Blackburn and David N. Dumville (Woodbridge, 1998), pp. 1–45, at 25.

12   Janet Nelson, 'The political ideas of Alfred of Wessex', in *Kings and Kingship in Medieval Europe*, ed. Anne J. Duggan (London, 1993), pp. 125–58, at 154–7.

13   Martin Biddle, 'The study of Winchester: archaeology and history in a British town, 1961–1983', in *British Academy Papers on Anglo-Saxon England*, ed. Eric Gerald Stanley (Oxford, 1990), pp. 299–341, at 325–32.

14   Asser, *De rebus gestis Ælfredi*, ch. 91 (*Alfred the Great*, trans. Keynes and Lapidge, p. 101).

15   John Baker and Stuart Brookes, *Beyond the Burghal Hidage: Anglo-Saxon Civil Defence in the Viking Age* (Leiden, 2013), pp. 90–106; *The Defence of Wessex: The Burghal Hidage and Anglo-Saxon Fortifications*, ed. David Hill and Alexander Rumble (Manchester, 1996); Martin Carver, *The Birth of a Borough: An Archaeological Study of Anglo-Saxon Stafford* (Woodbridge, 2010), pp. 127–45.

16   Richard Holt, 'The urban transformation in England, 900–1100', *ANS* 32 (2009), 57–78; Grenville G. Astill, 'General survey 600–1300', in *The Cambridge Urban History of Britain. 1: 600–1540*, ed. D. M. Palliser (Cambridge, 2000), pp. 27–49, at 34–7.

17   Greg Waite, 'The preface to the Old English Bede: authorship, transmission, and connection with the *West Saxon Genealogical Regnal List*', *ASE* 44 (2015), 31–93, at 82.

18   *Canterbury Professions*, ed. Michael Richter and Thomas J. Brown (Torquay, 1973), no. 18.

19   Robert Cowie and Lyn Blackmore, *Early and Middle Saxon Rural Settlement in the London Region* (London, 2008), p. 102. Cf. David Bowler, 'Rangoon Street', *Popular Archaeology* 5:6 (1983), 13–18.

20   Julian Ayre and Robin Wroe-Brown, 'The Post-Roman foreshore and the origins of the late Anglo-Saxon waterfront and dock of Æthelred's Hithe: excavations at Bull Wharf, City of London', *Archaeological Journal* 172 (2015), 121–94, at 130–3 and 159–62. Cf. Cowie and Blackmore, *Rural Settlement*, p. 101. For the more general phenomenon of 'deviant burials', see Andrew Reynolds, *Anglo-Saxon Deviant Burial Customs* (Oxford, 2009).

21   John Schofield, *St Paul's Cathedral before Wren* (London, 2011), pp. 51–2 and 54–6; John Schofield, Lyn Blackmore and David Stocker, 'St Paul's Cathedral, AD 604–1087', *London Archaeologist* 12 (2009), 79–86, esp. 81–2. See also Cowie and Blackmore, *Rural Settlement*, p. 102 for a list of artefacts found in the western part of the City of Middle Saxon (i.e. 7th–mid-9th century) date.

22   S. E. Kelly, *Charters of St Paul's, London* (Oxford, 2004), pp. 7–8, who notes that there is no physical evidence for these churches' early origins. Some earlier discussion was more optimistic: Christopher Brooke and Gillian

Keir, *London 800–1216: The Shaping of a City* (London, 1975), pp. 140–1;
Tim Tatton-Brown, 'The topography of Anglo-Saxon London', *Antiquity*
60 (1986), 21–8, at 23.

23 Gustav Milne and Nathalie Cohen, *Excavations at Medieval Cripplegate,
London: Archaeology after the Blitz, 1946–68* (London, 2001), pp. 127–9.

24 Robert Cowie, 'The evidence for royal sites in Middle Anglo-Saxon
London', *Medieval Archaeology* 48 (2004), 201–9. For support of an eighth-
century palace in this location, see (among others) T. Dyson and John
Schofield, 'Saxon London', in *Anglo-Saxon Towns in Southern England*, ed.
Jeremy Haslam (Chichester, 1984), pp. 285–314, at 306–9; Pamela Taylor,
'Ingelric, Count Eustace and the foundation of St Martin-le-Grand', *ANS*
24 (2002),215–37, at 220.

25 See Chapters 3–4. Stenton argued (*Anglo-Saxon England*, 3rd ed. (Oxford,
1971), p. 57) that there may have been several different royal sites in London.

26 James H. Barrett, 'What caused the Viking Age?', *Antiquity* 82 (2008),
671–85.

27 Søren M. Sindbæk, 'Silver economies and social ties: long-distance
interaction, long-term investments – and why the Viking Age happened',
in *Silver Economies, Monetisation and Society in Scandinavia, AD 800–1100*,
ed. James Graham-Campbell, Søren M. Sindbæk and Gareth Williams
(Aarhus, 2011), pp. 41–65.

28 See among others Judith Jesch, *The Viking Diaspora* (London, 2015);
see also *Vikings: Life and Legend*, ed. Gareth Williams, Peter Pentz and
Matthias Wemhoff (London, 2014).

29 David N. Dumville, 'Vikings in the British Isles: a question of sources', in *The
Scandinavians from the Vendel Period to the Tenth Century: An Ethnographic
Perspective*, ed. Judith Jesch (Woodbridge, 2002), pp. 209–50, at 209.

30 The Gersum Project (www.gersum.org).

31 Clare Downham, 'The earliest Viking activity in England?', *EHR* 132
(2017), 1–12.

32 *ASC* 842.

33 *ASC* 851.

34 Keynes, 'King Alfred and the Mercians', pp. 4–11.

35 Shane McLeod, *The Beginning of Scandinavian Settlement in England: The
Viking 'Great Army' and Early Settlers, c.865–900* (Turnhout, 2014).

36 Ben Raffield, 'Bands of brothers: a reappraisal of the Viking Great Army
and its implications for the Scandinavian colonization of England', *EME*
24 (2016), 308–37.

37 *DOE* s.v.; Richard Abels, 'Alfred the Great, the *micel hæðen here* and the
viking threat', in *Alfred the Great*, ed. Reuter, pp. 265–79.

38 Dawn M. Hadley and Julian D. Richards, 'The winter camp of the Viking
Great Army, AD 872–3, Torksey, Lincolnshire', *Antiquaries Journal* 96
(2016), 23–67; Mark Blackburn, *Viking Coinage and Currency in the British
Isles* (London, 2011), pp. 221–64.

39   Nicholas Brooks and James Graham-Campbell, 'Reflections on the Viking-Age silver hoard from Croydon, Surrey', in Nicholas Brooks, *Communities and Warfare 700–1400* (London, 2000), pp. 69–92.

40   *ASC* 872.

41   S 1278 (BCS 534; trans. *EHD*, no. 94).

42   *ASC* 874.

43   F. M. Stenton, *Preparatory to Anglo-Saxon England: Being the Collected Papers of Frank Merry Stenton*, ed. Doris Mary Stenton (Oxford, 1970), pp. 372–3; Keynes, 'King Alfred and the Mercians', pp. 12–19.

44   Rory Naismith, *Medieval European Coinage, with a Catalogue of the Coins in the Fitzwilliam Museum, Cambridge. 8: Britain and Ireland c.400–1066* (Cambridge, 2017), pp. 159–63. The process has much in common with modern acts of quantitative easing undertaken at times of economic pressure.

45   Ibid., pp. 155–7 and 160.

46   Ibid., p. 163; Philip Grierson and Mark Blackburn, *Medieval European Coinage, with a Catalogue of the Coins in the Fitzwilliam Museum, Cambridge. 1: The Early Middle Ages (5th–10th Centuries)* (Cambridge, 1986), p. 311; Adrian W. Lyons and William A. MacKay, 'The coinage of Æthelred I (865–71)', *British Numismatic Journal* 77 (2007), 71–118, at 111–14; Adrian W. Lyons and William A. MacKay, 'The Lunettes coinage of Alfred the Great', *British Numismatic Journal* 78 (2008), 38–110, at 48–51.

47   Simon Keynes, 'The control of Kent in the ninth century', *EME* 2 (1993), 111–31, at 128–30.

48   The extant corpus as of 1998 is catalogued and discussed in Mark Blackburn and Simon Keynes, 'A corpus of the *Cross-and-Lozenge* and related coinages of Alfred, Ceolwulf II and Archbishop Æthelred', in *Kings, Currency and Alliances*, ed. Blackburn and Dumville, pp. 125–50.

49   Keynes, 'King Alfred and the Mercians', p. 16; Marion Archibald in Leslie Webster and Janet Backhouse, *The Making of England: Anglo-Saxon Art and Culture A D 600–900* (London, 1991), p. 284. For a different reading, see Mark Blackburn, 'The London mint in the reign of Alfred', in *Kings, Currency and Alliances*, ed. Blackburn and Dumville, pp. 105–23, at 113–14.

50   Blackburn and Keynes, 'Cross-and-Lozenge', no. 27.

51   Blackburn, 'London mint', pp. 116–20; with Mark Blackburn, 'Alfred's coinage reforms in context', in *Alfred the Great*, ed. Reuter, pp. 199–218, at 212–14.

52   For a preliminary publication of Watlington, see John Naylor and Gareth Williams, *King Alfred's Coins: The Watlington Viking Hoard* (London, 2017).

53   Jeremy Haslam has argued ('King Alfred, Mercia and London, 874–86: a reassessment', *ASSAH* 17 (2011), 120–46, at 123) that London may have ended up on the viking side of the partition in 877, and been under viking control into the 880s.

54 The text of this treaty is translated in *Alfred the Great*, trans. Keynes and
    Lapidge, pp. 171–2. It dates to some point between 878 and Guthrum's
    death in 890, and should be thought of as a temporary arrangement
    rather than a hard and permanent boundary. See R. H. C. Davis, 'Alfred
    and Guthrum's frontier', *EHR* 97 (1982), 803–10; David N. Dumville,
    *Wessex and England from Alfred to Edgar: Six Essays on Political, Cultural,
    and Ecclesiastical Revival* (Woodbridge, 1992), pp. 1–27 (which proposes
    a radical new reading of the text); Keynes, 'King Alfred and the Mercians',
    pp. 31–4.
55 Davis, 'Alfred and Guthrum's frontier', p. 804.
56 The frontier with viking-controlled territory may have lain in Essex
    for some time: Ann Williams, 'The Vikings in Essex, 871–917', *Essex
    Archaeology and History* 27 (1996), 92–101.
57 ASC 883. The event is usually read as a siege, but Keene, 'Alfred and
    London', p. 241 queries whether this must be so: the key verb (*sæton*)
    allows for a broader range of meanings.
58 Stenton, *Anglo-Saxon England*, pp. 254–5 and 258–9; Henry Loyn, *The
    Vikings in Britain* (Oxford, 1994), p. 43; T. Dyson, 'King Alfred and the
    restoration of London', *London Journal* 15 (1990), 99–110, at 100–1.
59 Stenton, *Anglo-Saxon England*, p. 258; *EHD*, p. 197; Keynes and Lapidge,
    Alfred the Great, p. 266 n. 198, among others.
60 Keynes, 'King Alfred and the Mercians', pp. 21–4. Cf. Haslam, 'King
    Alfred', pp. 137–8.
61 Naismith, *Medieval European Coinage*, pp. 170–1; William MacKay, 'The
    London Monogram coinage of Alfred the Great and the Danelaw', *British
    Numismatic Journal* (forthcoming). For date, see Blackburn, 'London mint',
    pp. 120–2.
62 ASC CABD 893.
63 ASC 895.
64 Richard Hodges, *Towns and Trade in the Age of Charlemagne* (London,
    2000), pp. 112–17.
65 Rory Naismith, *The Coinage of Southern England 796–865*, 2 vols (London,
    2011), no. L30a; Rory Naismith, *SCBI* 67, no. 1068.
66 Marion Archibald in Schofield, *St Paul's Cathedral before Wren*, pp. 250–4;
    Naismith, *SCBI* 67, no. 1440.
67 Keene, 'Alfred and London', p. 237 (suggesting there may have been more
    continuity in the ninth century along the Strand itself, which has seen less
    excavation).
68 S 208 (BCS 492; trans. *EHD*, no. 92).
69 Martin Biddle, 'A city in transition: 400–800', in *The City of London from
    Prehistoric Times to c.1520*, ed. Lobel, pp. 20–9, at 29; Alan Vince, *Saxon
    London: An Archaeological Investigation* (London, 1990), p. 20; Keene,
    'Alfred and London', pp. 239–40 (tentatively identifying this estate with
    Somerset House).

70   Ayre and Wroe-Brown, 'Post-Roman foreshore', pp. 134–9 and 162–3.

71   Robin Fleming, *Britain after Rome: The Fall and Rise, 400–1070* (London, 2010), p. 258. See also Gustav Milne, *The Port of Medieval London* (Stroud, 2003), pp. 41–7; Milne and Cohen, *Excavations at Medieval Cripplegate*.

72   Ayre and Wroe-Brown, 'Post-Roman foreshore', p. 146.

73   Hodges, *Towns and Trade in the Age of Charlemagne*, p. 116.

74   Gustav Milne, 'King Alfred's plan for London', *London Archaeologist* 6 (1990), 206–7.

75   Valerie Horsman, Christine Milne and Gustav Milne, *Aspects of Saxo-Norman London 1: Building and Street Development Near Billingsgate and Cheapside* (London, 1988), pp. 28–30 and 112–13; Milne, 'King Alfred's plan'; Dyson, 'King Alfred', p. 106; Keene, 'Alfred and London', p. 245. For 1 Poultry see Phil Treveil and Peter Rowsome, 'Number 1 Poultry – the main excavation: late Saxon and medieval sequence', *London Archaeologist* 8 (1998), 283–91, at 284. For Bow Lane see also John Schofield, Patrick Allen and Colin Taylor, 'Medieval buildings and property development in the area of Cheapside', *TLAMAS* 41 (1990), 39–237, at 153–5. For Botolph Lane, see Horsman, Milne and Milne, *Aspects of Saxo-Norman London* 1, pp. 14–16.

76   Dyson, 'King Alfred', p. 107; Robert Cowie and Charlotte Harding, 'Saxon settlement and economy from the Dark Ages to Domesday', in *The Archaeology of Greater London: An Assessment of Archaeological Evidence for Human Presence in the Area Now Covered by Greater London*, ed. Monica Kendall (London, 2000), pp. 171–206, at 193. On the rebuilding of London Bridge, see Chapter 7. For more optimistic but less convincing arguments that London Bridge had already been rebuilt by the eighth or ninth century, see Martha Carlin, *Medieval Southwark* (London, 1996), p. 12; Jeremy Haslam, 'The development of London by King Alfred: a reassessment', *TLAMAS* 61 (2010), 109–44, at 130–7. For the status of Southwark at this time, see Chapter 6.

77   S 346 (BCS 561) and 1628 (*CantCC* 100).

78   S 1628 (*CantCC* 100). Brooks and Kelly point out that there are some difficulties with the text, which may have been drawn up later than its supposed date, though they still treat its contents as essentially trustworthy.

79   Fleming, *Britain After Rome*, pp. 259–60.

80   J. R. Maddicott, 'London and Droitwich, *c.*650–750: trade, industry and the rise of Mercia', *ASE* 34 (2005), 7–58, at 24–43 traces the establishment of this trade; see also Della Hooke, 'The Droitwich salt industry: an examination of the west midland charter evidence', *ASSAH* 2 (1981), 123–69.

81   Dyson, 'King Alfred', pp. 102–7.

82   Ibid., p. 105; Nicholas Brooks and S. E. Kelly, *The Charters of Christ Church, Canterbury*, 2 parts (Oxford, 2013), pp. 835–6.

83 Different locations for the estates are proposed in Eilert Ekwall, *Street-Names of the City of London* (London, 1954), pp. 38–40; T. Dyson, 'Two Saxon land-grants for Queenhithe', in *Collectanea Londiniensia: Studies in London Archaeology and History Presented to Ralph Merrifield*, ed. Joanna Bird, Hugh Chapman and John Clark (London, 1978), pp. 200–15; with a more reserved reading in Kelly, *St Paul's*, p. 25 n. 81.

84 The growth of the new street layout is a subject of much complexity: see Dyson, 'Two Saxon land-grants'; Tatton-Brown, 'Topography'; Dyson, 'King Alfred'; Milne, 'King Alfred's plan'; Haslam, 'Development of London'.

85 Kelly, *St Paul's*, pp. 26–7, though it is by no means clear that the obligation of other counties to maintain London's walls mentioned by the *ASC* in 1097 (Stenton, *Anglo-Saxon England*, p. 24) goes back to this period. No archaeological evidence has yet emerged for Alfredian-period refurbishment of London's walls: John Schofield, *The Building of London from the Conquest to the Great Fire*, 3rd ed. (Stroud, 1999), p. 24.

86 Cf. John Clark, 'King Alfred's London and London's King Alfred', *London Archaeologist* 9 (1999), 35–8, at 35–6.

87 Roger of Wendover, *Flores historiarum*, in *Rogeri de Wendover Chronica, sive Flores historiarum*, ed. H. O. Coxe, 2 vols (London, 1841–4), vol. 1, p. 345.

88 Keynes, 'King Alfred and the Mercians'; Simon Keynes, 'Edward, king of the Anglo-Saxons', in *Edward the Elder 899–924*, ed. N. J. Higham and D. H. Hill (London, 2001), pp. 40–66; Simon Keynes, 'Anglo-Saxons, kingdom of the', in *WBEASE*, p. 40.

89 Keynes, 'The cult of King Alfred the Great', pp. 233–4, citing the *Mirror of Justices*.

90 R. Blackmore, *Alfred: An Epick Poem in Twelve Books* (London, 1723), p. 448 (book XII).

6   LONDON IN THE TENTH CENTURY: C.900–75

1   *ASC* A 962.

2   *Early Sources of Scottish History A.D. 500 to 1286*, trans. Alan Orr Anderson, 2 vols (London, 1922), vol. I, pp. 439–42. The Latin original can be read in *Acta Sanctorum*, ed. Jean Bolland et al., 68 vols (Antwerp and Brussels, 1643–), vol. VII (March 6), col. 476C–477B. See further David N. Dumville, 'St Cathróe of Metz and the hagiography of exoticism', in *Studies in Irish Hagiography: Saints and Scholars*, ed. John Carey, Máire Herbert and Pádraig Ó Riain (Dublin, 2001), pp. 172–88; Steven Vanderputten, 'Reconsidering religious migration and its impact: the problem of "Irish reform monks" in tenth-century Lotharingia', *Revue d'histoire ecclésiastique* 112 (2017), 588–618.

3   Alan Vince, *Saxon London: An Archaeological Investigation* (London, 1990), pp. 27–8.
4   Alan Vince, 'The development of Saxon London', in *Aspects of Saxo-Norman London: 2. Finds and Environmental Evidence*, ed. Alan Vince (London, 1991), pp. 409–35, at 433–4.
5   Vince, *Saxon London*, p. 27; Julian Hill and Aidan Woodger, *Excavations at 72–75 Cheapside/83–93 Queen Street, City of London* (London, 1999), pp. 24–42.
6   Julian Ayre and Robin Wroe-Brown, 'The Post-Roman foreshore and the origins of the late Anglo-Saxon waterfront and dock of Æthelred's Hithe: excavations at Bull Wharf, City of London', *Archaeological Journal* 172 (2015), 121–94, at 138.
7   Valerie Horsman, Christine Milne and Gustav Milne, *Aspects of Saxo-Norman London 1: Building and Street Development Near Billingsgate and Cheapside* (London, 1988), pp. 113–14.
8   Robert Cowie, '*Lundenburh*: the archaeology of late Saxon London', in '*Hidden Histories and Records of Antiquity*': *Essays on Saxon and Medieval London for John Clark, Curator Emeritus, Museum of London*, ed. Jonathan Cotton et al. (London, 2014), pp. 17–26, at 22.
9   Alexander Rumble, 'An edition and translation of the Burghal Hidage, together with Recension C of the Tribal Hidage', in *The Defence of Wessex: The Burghal Hidage and Anglo-Saxon Fortifications*, ed. David Hill and Alexander Rumble (Manchester, 1996), pp. 14–35, at 28–9; Martha Carlin, *Medieval Southwark* (London, 1996), p. 9; Tony Sharp and Bruce Watson, 'Saxo-Norman Southwark: a review of the archaeological and historical evidence', in *Anglo-Saxon Traces*, ed. Jane Roberts and Leslie Webster (Tempe, AZ, 2011), pp. 273–96, at 276–81. The identification has sometimes been queried, as there are other places in Surrey which could have served the same role: Kingston, for instance (Rob Poulton, 'Saxon Surrey', in *The Archaeology of Surrey to 1540*, ed. Joanna Bird and D. G. Bird (Guildford, 1987), pp. 197–222, at 211), but the association with Southwark is generally accepted. For the suggestion that the text actually refers to London, see John Baker and Stuart Brookes, *Beyond the Burghal Hidage: Anglo-Saxon Civil Defence in the Viking Age* (Leiden, 2013), p. 160.
10 Nicholas Brooks, 'The unidentified forts of the Burghal Hidage', *Medieval Archaeology* 8 (1964), 74–90, at 86–8; R. H. C. Davis, 'Alfred and Guthrum's frontier', *EHR* 97 (1982), 803–10, at 807–9 (who advocated an earlier date); David N. Dumville, *Wessex and England from Alfred to Edgar: Six Essays on Political, Cultural, and Ecclesiastical Revival* (Woodbridge, 1992), pp. 24–7. A substantially different reading is propounded in Jeremy Haslam, 'King Alfred and the vikings: strategies and tactics 876–886 A D', *ASSAH* 13 (2005), 122–54 and subsequent publications by the same author.
11 T. Dyson, 'London and Southwark in the 7th century and later: a neglected reference', *TLAMAS* 31 (1980), 83–95; David Hill, 'Gazetteer of *Burghal*

Hidage sites', in *Defence of Wessex*, ed. Hill and Rumble, pp. 189–231, at 218–19.

12 T. Dyson, 'King Alfred and the restoration of London', *London Journal* 15 (1990), 99–110, at 110.

13 One halfpenny of Alfred the Great has been found, though from a probably residual context: Peter Stott, 'Saxon and Norman coins from London', in *Finds and Environmental Evidence*, ed. Vince, pp. 279–325, no. 71. For coins of Æthelstan, Edmund and Eadred found in Southwark (also without archaeological context), see PAS LON-6E8535, LON-3F3A33, LON-925C32 and LON-706381.

14 John Blair, *Early Medieval Surrey: Land Holding, Church and Settlement before 1300* (Stroud, 1991), pp. 102–3 (with BCS 133); Dyson, 'London and Southwark'; Peter Boyer and Lynne Keys, 'Saxon iron smelting in Bermondsey? Archaeological investigations at 150–156 Abbey Street', *Surrey Archaeological Collections* 97 (2013), 43–58.

15 Bruce Watson, 'Saxo-Norman Southwark: a review of the archaeological and historical evidence', *London Archaeologist* 12 (2009), 147–51, at 149; Baker and Brookes, *Beyond the Burghal Hidage*, pp. 158–60.

16 Sharp and Watson, 'Saxo-Norman Southwark', pp. 281–2.

17 Ayre and Wroe-Brown, 'Post-Roman foreshore', pp. 172–7. See also Damian Goodburn, 'Fragments of a 10th-century timber arcade from Vintner's Place on the London waterfront', *Medieval Archaeology* 37 (1993), 78–92; Damian Goodburn, 'London's early medieval timber buildings: Little known traditions of construction', in *Urbanism in Medieval Europe: Papers of the 'Medieval Europe Brugge 1997' Conference*, ed. Guy de Boe and Frans Verhaeghe (Zellik, 1997), pp. 249–57.

18 Ayre and Wroe-Brown, 'Post-Roman foreshore', p. 177.

19 David Bowsher et al., *The London Guildhall: An Archaeological History of a Neighbourhood from Early Medieval to Modern Times*, 2 vols (London, 2007), vol. II, p. 301.

20 See Chapter 7.

21 S 670 (BCS 1048). It carries the date 951, probably in error for 959, which would fit with it being in the name of Edgar and mentioning Dunstan as archbishop. See Julia Crick, 'St. Albans, Westminster and some twelfth-century views of the Anglo-Saxon past', *ANS* 25 (2002), 65–183, at 76–9; Simon Keynes, 'Wulfsige, monk of Glastonbury, abbot of Westminster (c.900–3), and bishop of Sherborne (c.993–1002)', in *St. Wulfsige and Sherborne: Essays to Celebrate the Millennium of the Benedictine Abbey, 998–1998*, ed. Katherine Barker (Oxford, 2005), pp. 53–94, at 56–7; *The Early Lives of St Dunstan*, ed. and trans. Michael Winterbottom and Michael Lapidge (Oxford, 2012), pp. xlvii–viii. A slightly expanded territory incorporating a newly acquired *berewic / croft* to the north (situated between Oxford Street and Euston Road) is described in similar terms in S 903, dating to 1002 (*Gilbert Crispin,*

Abbot of Westminster, ed. J. Armitage Robinson (Cambridge, 1911), pp. 167–8).

22 David Sullivan, *The Westminster Corridor: An Exploration of the Anglo-Saxon History of Westminster Abbey and Its Nearby Lands and People* (London, 1994), p. 92; C. Barron and J. Roscoe, 'The medieval parish church of St Andrew Holborn', *London Topographical Record* 29 (1980), 31–59, at 34.

23 Margaret Gelling, 'The boundaries of the Westminster Charters', *TLAMAS* new series 11 (1954), 101–4; cf. Tim Tatton-Brown, 'The medieval and early Tudor topography of Westminster', in *Westminster: The Art, Architecture and Archaeology of the Royal Abbey and Palace*, ed. Warwick Rodwell and Tim Tatton-Brown, 2 parts (London, 2015–16), part I, pp. 1–22. The point where the Tyburn empties into the Thames near Westminster Abbey is known, though the limits of the 'Thorney Island' on which it sat remain murky: Desmond Donovan, 'Thorney problem', *Geoscientist Online* (September 2016): www.geolsoc.org.uk/Geoscientist/Archive/September-2016/Thorney-problem.

24 VI Æthelstan (*Die Gesetze der Angelsachsen*, ed. Felix Liebermann, 3 vols (Halle, 1903–16), vol. I, pp. 173–83; trans. *EHD*, no. 37).

25 Simon Keynes, 'Royal government and the written word in late Anglo-Saxon England', in *The Uses of Literacy in Early Medieval Europe*, ed. Rosamond McKitterick (Cambridge, 1990), pp. 226–57, at 235–41; David Pratt, 'Written law and communication of authority in tenth-century England', in *England and the Continent in the Tenth Century: Studies in Honour of Wilhelm Levison*, ed. Conrad Leyser, David Rollason and Hannah Williams (Turnhout, 2010), pp. 331–50; Levi Roach, 'Law codes and legal norms in later Anglo-Saxon England', *Historical Research* 86 (2013), 466–85.

26 See Chapter 5.

27 Derek Keene, 'English urban guilds, c.900–1300: the purposes and politics of association', in *Guilds and Association in Europe, 900–1900*, ed. Ian A. Gadd and Patrick Wallis (London, 2006), pp. 3–26.

28 *Gesetze*, ed. Liebermann, vol. II, p. 116.

29 Tom Lambert, *Law & Order in Anglo-Saxon England* (Oxford, 2017), pp. 227–30.

30 Felix Liebermann, 'Einleitung zum Statut der Londoner Friedensgilde unter Aethelstan', in *Mélanges Graux: Recueil de travaux d'érudition classique dédié à la mémoire de Charles Graux* (Montpellier, 1884–1908), vol. II, 77–103.

31 VI Æthelstan 8.4 (*EHD*, p. 425).

32 VI Æthelstan 8.4 (*EHD*, p. 425). See Lambert, *Law & Order*, pp. 154–5.

33 VI Æthelstan 1.1 and 12.1 (*EHD*, pp. 423 and 427).

34 S 1445 (*CantCC* 104). Simon Keynes, 'The Fonthill letter', in *Words, Texts and Manuscripts: Studies in Anglo-Saxon Culture Presented to Helmut Gneuss on the Occasion of his Sixty-Fifth Birthday*, ed. Michael Korhammer, Karl

Reichl and Hans Sauer (Cambridge, 1992), pp. 53–97 explores the case in minute detail.

35   Alice Rio, *Slavery after Rome, 500–1100* (Oxford, 2017), pp. 67–70; Lambert, *Law & Order*, pp. 283–9.

36   See also Chapter 7.

37   Susan Reynolds, *Kingdoms and Communities in Western Europe 900–1300*, 2nd ed. (Oxford, 1997), p. 70.

38   Ibid., pp. 155–6 and 167–8; Pratt, 'Written law', p. 347.

39   VI Æthelstan 8.1 (*EHD*, p. 426).

40   Keynes, 'Royal government', pp. 239–40. For a slightly different view see Patrick Wormald, *The Making of English Law: King Alfred to the Twelfth Century. Vol. I: Legislation and Its Limits* (Oxford, 1999), p. 298.

41   VI Æthelstan 10 and 12.1 (*EHD*, pp. 426–7).

42   Dorothy Whitelock, *Some Anglo-Saxon Bishops of London* (London, 1975), pp. 17–20 (repr. in her *History, Law and Literature in 10th–11th Century England* (London, 1981), no. II); S. E. Kelly, *Charters of St Paul's, London* (Oxford, 2004), pp. 116–18.

43   Andrew Rabin, 'Wulfstan at London: episcopal politics in the reign of Æthelred', *English Studies* 97 (2016), 186–206, at 188–92.

44   Simon Keynes, *An Atlas of Attestations in Anglo-Saxon Charters c.670–1066* (Cambridge, 2002), nos. XXXVII, XLI and XLIV.

45   William of Malmesbury, *Gesta pontificum Anglorum* II.73.16 (*William of Malmesbury, Gesta pontificum Anglorum/ The History of the English Bishops*, ed. and trans. Michael Winterbottom and Rodney Malcolm Thomson, 2 vols (Oxford, 2007), vol. I, pp. 228–31).

46   Helen Foxhall Forbes, *Heaven and Earth in Anglo-Saxon England: Theology and Society in an Age of Faith* (Farnham, 2013), pp. 177–9 discusses the case and cites relevant texts.

47   Kelly, *St Paul's*, p. 117; Whitelock, *Some Anglo-Saxon Bishops*, pp. 18–19.

48   S 1526 (*LondStP*, pp. 225–8).

49   Kelly, *St Paul's*, p. 116; Whitelock, *Some Anglo-Saxon Bishops*, pp. 19–20.

50   See among others *England and Rome in the Early Middle Ages: Pilgrimage, Art, and Politics*, ed. Francesca Tinti (Turnhout, 2014); *Early Medieval Rome and the Christian West: Essays in Honour of Donald A. Bullough*, ed. Julia M. H. Smith (Leiden, 2000).

51   Mohamad Ballan, 'Fraxinetum: an Islamic frontier state in tenth-century Provence', *Comitatus* 41 (2010), 23–76.

52   Rory Naismith and Francesca Tinti, *The Forum Hoard of Anglo-Saxon Coins/Il ripostiglio dell'Atrium Vestae nel Foro Romano*, Bollettino di numismatica 55–6 (Rome, 2016). The book can be freely consulted online at www.numismaticadellostato.it/web/pns/bollettino.

53   Rory Naismith, 'The Forum Hoard and beyond: money, gift, and religion in the early Middle Ages', *Viator* 47 (2016), 35–56.

54   II Æthelstan 14.2 (ed. Liebermann, vol. I, p. 158; trans. *EHD*, p. 420).

55   Pagan, *SCBI* 64, p. 13.

56   Rory Naismith, 'London and its mint *c*.880–1066: a preliminary survey', *British Numismatic Journal* 83 (2013), 44–74, at 52–3.

57   Derek Keene, 'London from the post-Roman period to *c*.1300', in *The Cambridge Urban History of Britain. 1: 600–1540*, ed. D. M. Palliser (Cambridge, 2000), pp. 187–216, at 191.

58   John Blair, *The Church in Anglo-Saxon Society* (Oxford, 2005), pp. 330–41.

59   Grenville G. Astill, 'Towns and town hierarchies in Saxon England', *Oxford Journal of Archaeology* 10 (1991), 95–117, at 103–9; Richard Holt, 'The urban transformation in England, 900–1100', *ANS* 32 (2009), 57–78.

60   D. M. Palliser, *Medieval York 600–1540* (Oxford, 2014), esp. pp. 23–84; Nicholas Brooks, *The Early History of the Church of Canterbury: Christ Church from 597 to 1066* (Leicester, 1984), pp. 15–36.

61   Chester: Alan Thacker, 'Early medieval Chester 400–1230', in *A History of the County of Chester: Volume 5 Part 1. The City of Chester: General History and Topography*, ed. Christopher P. Lewis and Alan Thacker (London, 2003), pp. 16–33. Lincoln: *The City by the Pool: Assessing the Archaeology of the City of Lincoln*, ed. Michael J. Jones, David Stocker and Alan Vince (Oxford, 2003). Winchester: Martin Biddle, 'The study of Winchester: archaeology and history in a British town, 1961–1983', *Proceedings of the British Library* 69 (1983), 93–135.

62   Levi Roach, *Kingship and Consent in Anglo-Saxon England, 871–978: Assemblies and the State in the Early Middle Ages* (Cambridge, 2013), pp. 239–43.

63   Simon Keynes, 'Kingston-upon-Thames', in *WBEASE*, p. 277.

64   In *The Cult of St Swithun*, ed. and trans. Michael Lapidge (Oxford, 2003), pp. 217–333. Cf. Martin Biddle and Derek Keene, 'General survey and conclusions', in *Winchester in the Early Middle Ages: An Edition and Discussion of the Winton Domesday*, ed. Martin Biddle (Oxford, 1976), pp. 449–508, at 461.

65   Martin Biddle, Daphne M. Hudson and Carolyn M. Heighway, *The Future of London's Past: A Survey of the Archaeological Implications of Planning and Development in the Nation's Capital* (Worcester, 1973), p. 23.

66   David Hill, 'London Bridge: a reasonable doubt', *TLAMAS* 27 (1976), 303–4; Anthony Davies, 'Witches in Anglo-Saxon England', in *Superstition and Popular Medicine in Anglo-Saxon England*, ed. D. G. Scragg (Manchester, 1989), pp. 41–56, at 51.

67   S 1377 (*Pet 17*).

68   Scott T. Smith, *Land and Book: Literature and Land Tenure in Anglo-Saxon England* (Toronto, 2012), pp. 74–6; Davies, 'Witches', pp. 49–51; Roach, *Kingship and Consent*, pp. 132–3; Foxhall Forbes, *Heaven and Earth*, pp. 159–60; also Martin Foys, 'How a widow becomes a witch: land, loss and law in Anglo-Saxon charter S. 1377', *English Studies* (2018).

69 Ælfsige received the land from King Eadred in a charter dated 948 (S 533 (*Pet* 10)), but the complicated and unpleasant circumstances of its acquisition were evidently remembered a generation later.

7   LATE ANGLO-SAXON LONDON

1   Indeed, these sums are so huge – larger than any other English king raised before the thirteenth century – that some modern historians have doubted the veracity of the ASC's figures: Rory Naismith, *Medieval European Coinage, with a Catalogue of the Coins in the Fitzwilliam Museum, Cambridge. 8: Britain and Ireland c.400–1066* (Cambridge, 2017), pp. 253–6, and references cited there. For royal income in 1066, see Stephen Baxter, *The Earls of Mercia: Lordship and Power in Late Anglo-Saxon England* (Oxford, 2007), p. 129.

2   *ASC* CDE 1011.

3   John of Worcester, *Chronicon* 1012 (*The Chronicle of John of Worcester. Volume II: The Annals from 450 to 1066*, ed. R. R. Darlington and P. McGurk, trans. Jennifer Bray and P. McGurk (Oxford, 1995), pp. 470–1).

4   This detail is registered in the account of the event preserved by a contemporary German chronicler: Thietmar of Merseburg, *Chronicon* VII.42–3 (*Die Chronik des Bischofs Thietmar von Merseburg und ihre Korveier Überarbeitung*, ed. Robert Holtzmann, MGH Scriptores rerum Germanicarum: nova series 9 (Berlin, 1935), pp. 448–51). Thietmar's version of events is clearly somewhat mangled, and his testimony should be treated with caution.

5   *ASC* CDE 1012.

6   Simon Keynes, *The Diplomas of King Æthelred 'the Unready' (978–1016): A Study in their Use as Historical Evidence* (Cambridge, 1980), p. 221.

7   This version is represented in three of the surviving manuscripts, traditionally known as C, D and E.

8   Simon Keynes, 'The declining reputation of King Æthelred the Unready', in *Anglo-Saxon History: Basic Readings*, ed. David A. E. Pelteret (New York, 2000), pp. 157–90, at 162–3; Simon Keynes, 'The historical context of the battle of Maldon', in *The Battle of Maldon, AD 991*, ed. D. G. Scragg (Oxford, 1991), pp. 81–113, at 95–8.

9   Jo Lyon, *Within these Walls: Roman and Medieval Defences North of Newgate at the Merrill Lynch Financial Centre, City of London* (London, 2007); Robert Cowie and Charlotte Harding, 'Saxon settlement and economy from the Dark Ages to Domesday', in *The Archaeology of Greater London: An Assessment of Archaeological Evidence for Human Presence in the Area Now Covered by Greater London*, ed. Monica Kendall (London, 2000), pp. 171–206, at 192; and John Clark, *Saxon and Norman London* (London, 1989), p. 21.

10 Christopher Loveluck, *Northwest Europe in the Early Middle Ages, c. AD 600–1150: A Comparative Archaeology* (Cambridge, 2013), pp. 318–19.

11   *ASC* CDE 994.

12   Frederick William Maitland, *Domesday Book and Beyond: Three Essays in the Early History of England* (Cambridge, 1897), pp. 190–1.

13   David Hill, *An Atlas of Anglo-Saxon England* (Toronto, 1981), pp. 90–1 and 94; Simon Keynes, 'Church councils, royal assemblies, and Anglo-Saxon royal diplomas', in *Kingship, Legislation and Power in Anglo-Saxon England*, ed. Gale R. Owen-Crocker and Brian W. Schneider (Woodbridge, 2013), pp. 17–184, at 151–2.

14   *ASC* CDE 1016; Simon Keynes, 'The burial of King Æthelred the Unready at St Paul's', in *The English and Their Legacy: 900–1200. Essays in Honour of Ann Williams*, ed. David Roffe (Woodbridge, 2012), pp. 129–48.

15   Nicole Marafioti, *The King's Body: Burial and Succession in Late Anglo-Saxon England* (Toronto, 2014), pp. 86–93.

16   Ryan Lavelle, *Alfred's Wars: Sources and Interpretations of Anglo-Saxon Warfare in the Viking Age* (Woodbridge, 2010), pp. 260–2.

17   May McKisack, 'London and the succession to the Crown during the Middle Ages', in *Studies in Medieval History Presented to F. M. Powicke*, ed. R. W. Hunt, W. A. Pantin and R. W. Southern (Oxford, 1948), pp. 76–89.

18   *ASC* CDE 1016.

19   John of Worcester, *Chronicon* 1016 (ed. and trans. Darlington and McGurk, pp. 484–5).

20   *Encomium Emmae reginae* II.7 (*Encomium Emmae Reginae*, ed. Alistair Campbell, with introduction by Simon Keynes (Cambridge, 1998), pp. 22–3).

21   *ASC* E 1035.

22   *ASC* E 1042.

23   Tony Sharp and Bruce Watson, 'Saxo-Norman Southwark: a review of the archaeological and historical evidence', in *Anglo-Saxon Traces*, ed. Jane Roberts and Leslie Webster (Tempe, AZ, 2011), pp. 273–96, at 280.

24   Lucy Marten, 'The shiring of East Anglia: an alternative hypothesis', *Historical Research* 81 (2008), 1–27, at 14–16.

25   *Liðsmannaflokkr* (ed. and trans. Russell Poole, '*Liðsmannaflokkr*', in *Poetry from the Kings' Sagas 1: From Mythical Times to c.1035*, ed. Diana Whaley (Turnhout, 2012), pp. 1014–28). All text here is taken from Poole's edition, as is the translation, with minor adaptations. For full discussion of this and other related poems, see also Russell Poole, 'Skaldic verse and Anglo-Saxon history: some aspects of the period 1009–1016', *Speculum* 62 (1987), 265–98, at 280–98.

26   John of Worcester, *Chronicon* 1016 (ed. and trans. Darlington and McGurk, pp. 494–5).

27   *Liðsmannaflokkr* 10 (ed. and trans. Poole, p. 1028).

28   For London's general experience of Cnut's rule see Matthew Firth, 'London under Danish rule: Cnut's politics and policies as a demonstration of power', *Eras Journal* 18 (2016), 1–20.

29   *ASC* CDE 1018.

30   Marafioti, *King's Body*, pp. 93–4.

31   Alan Thacker, 'The cult of saints and the liturgy', in *St Paul's: The Cathedral Church of London, 604–2004*, ed. Derek Keene, Arthur Burns and Andrew Saint (New Haven, CT, and London, 2004), pp. 113–22, at 115.

32   *ASC* D 1023.

33   The text is edited and translated in Alexander Rumble and Rosemary Morris, 'Textual appendix', in *The Reign of Cnut: King of England, Denmark and Norway*, ed. Alexander R. Rumble (London, 1994), pp. 283–315.

34   David Townsend, 'Anglo-Latin hagiography and the Norman transition', *Exemplaria* 3 (1991), 385–433, at 409–12.

35   David Hill, 'An urban policy for Cnut?', in *Reign of Cnut*, ed. Rumble, pp. 101–5, at 103. Cf. Timothy Bolton, *The Empire of Cnut the Great: Conquest and the Consolidation of Power in Northern Europe in the Early Eleventh Century* (Leiden, 2009), pp. 86–9; and M. K. Lawson, *Cnut: England's Viking King*, 2nd ed. (Stroud, 2004), pp. 130–2.

36   Matthew Townend, 'Contextualizing the *Knútsdrápur*: skaldic praise-poetry at the court of Cnut', *ASE* 30 (2001), 145–80.

37   Nicholas Hooper, 'Military developments in the reign of Cnut', in *Reign of Cnut*, ed. Rumble, pp. 89–100, at 97–100; Lawson, *Cnut*, pp. 162–8; Lavelle, *Alfred's Wars*, pp. 244–5. In 1051 (according to *ASC* D) Edward ended – at least temporarily – the *heregeld* which had been established to support the mercenaries in 1012 (Keynes, *Diplomas*, pp. 221–4; Keynes, 'Historical context', pp. 98–102).

38   *ASC* CDE 1040; E 1041.

39   John Schofield, *St Paul's Cathedral before Wren* (London, 2011), pp. 46–9 and 254–65; and Dominic Tweddle et al., *Corpus of Anglo-Saxon Stone Sculpture. 4: South-East England* (Oxford, 1995), pp. 226–8.

40   John of Worcester, *Chronicon* 1040 (ed. and trans. Darlington and McGurk, pp. 530–1).

41   Lis Jacobsen and Erik Moltke, *Danmarks runeindskrifter*, 3 vols (Copenhagen, 1941–2), no. 337.

42   Tweddle et al., *Corpus*, pp. 228–9.

43   R. E. M. Wheeler, *London and the Vikings* (London, 1927), pp. 18–23.

44   Frank Barlow, *Edward the Confessor*, 2nd ed. (New Haven, CT, 1997), pp. 104–5.

45   These events are told in the *ASC* (C, D and E), and by John of Worcester and the *Vita Ædwardi*. See also Barlow, *Edward*, pp. 110–34.

46   *Encomium Emmae reginae* II.7 (ed. Campbell, pp. 22–3).

47   Derek Keene, 'Ideas of the metropolis', *Historical Research* 84 (2011), 379–98.

48   William of Poitiers, *Gesta Guillelmi* II.28 (*The Gesta Guillelmi of William of Poitiers*, ed. and trans. R. H. C. Davis and Marjorie Chibnall (Oxford, 1998), pp. 146–7).

49   Guy of Amiens, *Carmen de Hastingae proelio* 635–40 (*The Carmen de Hastingae Proelio of Guy, Bishop of Amiens*, ed. and trans. Frank Barlow, 2nd ed. (Oxford, 1999), pp. 38–9).

50   London, British Library, Cotton Tiberius B.V, f. 56v.

51   Carlrichard Brühl, *Aus Mittelalter und Diplomatik: Gesammelte Aufsätze*, 3 vols (Hildesheim, 1989–97), vol. I, pp. 69–137.

52   Levi Roach, *Kingship and Consent in Anglo-Saxon England, 871–978: Assemblies and the State in the Early Middle Ages* (Cambridge, 2013), pp. 45–7.

53   Martin Biddle, 'Seasonal festivals and residence: Winchester, Westminster and Gloucester in the tenth to the twelfth centuries', *ANS* 8 (1986), 51–72; cf. Hill, *Atlas*, pp. 90–1 and 94–5; Roach, *Kingship and Consent*, pp. 239–43.

54   Marafioti, *King's Body*, esp. pp. 25–40.

55   Derek Keene, 'Capital cities in medieval England to 1300', in *Lo sguardo lungimirante delle capitali: saggi in onore di Francesca Bocchi*, ed. Rosa Smurra, Hubert Houben and Manuela Ghizzoni (Rome, 2014), pp. 21–60.

56   For an elegant survey of London's development from the tenth to the twelfth centuries, see Judith A. Green, *Forging the Kingdom: Power in English Society, 973–1189* (Cambridge, 2017), pp. 198–220; for economic dimensions of London in the same period, Loveluck, *Northwest Europe*, pp. 315–19.

57   S 1096 (*Chert* 12). See also Simon Keynes, 'Regenbald the chancellor (*sic*)', *ANS* 10 (1988), 185–222, at 214–16.

58   Richard Kelleher and Ian Leins, 'Roman, medieval and later coins from the Vintry, City of London', *Numismatic Chronicle* 168 (2008), 167–240.

59   Rory Naismith, 'The English monetary economy, *c*.973–1100: the contribution of single-finds', *Economic History Review* 66 (2013), 198–225.

60   For a general description of this process, see Naismith, *Medieval European Coinage*, pp. 211–77.

61   These figures refer to the first 51 volumes of the Sylloge of Coins of the British Isles project. Cf. Rory Naismith, 'London and its mint *c*.880–1066: a preliminary survey', *British Numismatic Journal* 83 (2013), 44–74, at 44.

62   Naismith, 'London and its mint', pp. 62–4. Cf. Stewart Lyon, 'Minting in Winchester: an introduction and statistical analysis', in *The Winchester Mint: Coins and Related Finds from the Excavations of 1961–71*, ed. Martin Biddle (Oxford, 2012), pp. 3–54.

63   Naismith, 'London and its mint', pp. 58–62.

64   Cf. Peter Stott, 'Saxon and Norman coins from London', in *Finds and Environmental Evidence*, ed. Vince, no. 71, pp. 296–7.

65   M. K. Lawson, 'The collection of Danegeld and Heregeld in the reigns of Aethelred II and Cnut', *EHR* 99 (1984), 721–38, at 723–5 and 731–4.

66   Anthony Freeman, *The Moneyer and the Mint in the Reign of Edward the Confessor 1042–1066*, British Archaeological Reports: British Series 145 (Oxford, 1985), pp. 182–5.

67 Grenville G. Astill, 'Towns and town hierarchies in Anglo-Saxon England', *Oxford Journal of Archaeology* 10 (1991), 95–117; and Grenville G. Astill, 'Community, identity and the later Anglo-Saxon town: the case of southern England', in *People and Space in the Middle Ages*, ed. Andrew Reynolds, W. Davies and Guy Halsall (Turnhout, 2006), pp. 233–54.

68 Naismith, 'London and its mint', p. 59.

69 GDB 172r and 179r.

70 Marion Archibald, J. R. S. Lang and Gustav Milne, 'Four early medieval coin dies from the London waterfront', *Numismatic Chronicle* 155 (1995), 165–200.

71 E. J. E. Pirie, *Post-Roman Coins from York Excavations, 1971–81* (London, 1986), pp. 33–43.

72 *ASC* CDE 1017. For a possible location near St Paul's, see Derek Keene, 'From conquest to capital: St Paul's c.1100–1300', in *St Paul's*, ed. Keene, Burns and Saint, pp. 17–32, at 18–20. Alan Vince, *Saxon London: An Archaeological Investigation* (London, 1990), pp. 55–6 makes a case for this palace being in the vicinity of Cripplegate.

73 Robin Fleming, 'Rural élites and urban communities in late-Saxon England', *Past & Present* 141 (1993), 3–37.

74 Robert Cowie and Lyn Blackmore, *Early and Middle Saxon Rural Settlement in the London Region* (London, 2008), p. 101; S. E. Kelly, *Charters of St Paul's, London* (Oxford, 2004), p. 145; John Schofield, Lyn Blackmore and David Stocker, 'St Paul's Cathedral, A D 604–1087', *London Archaeologist* 12 (2009), 79–86, at 82

75 Simon Keynes, 'The æthelings in Normandy', *ANS* 13 (1991), 173–205, at 179–80. For the location of the City holdings (at *Wermanecher*), see Eilert Ekwall, *Street-Names of the City of London* (London, 1954), p. 38. Ghent's London property was usurped by Harold Godwineson: Fleming, 'Rural élites', pp. 13–14.

76 S 940 (*Chert* 10). Cf. S 1096 (*Chert* 12).

77 *Liber Eliensis* II.60 (*Liber Eliensis: A History of the Isle of Ely from the Seventh Century to the Twelfth*, trans. Janet Fairweather (Woodbridge, 2005), pp. 156–9).

78 S 1142 (*ASWrits* 98).

79 T. Dyson and John Schofield, 'Saxon London', in *Anglo-Saxon Towns in Southern England*, ed. Jeremy Haslam (Chichester, 1984), pp. 306–7. For other examples in Domesday Book see Maitland, *Domesday*, p. 114.

80 For indirect references to London and its people in Domesday, see Henry Clifford Darby and Elia M. J. Campbell, *The Domesday Geography of South-East England* (Cambridge, 1962), pp. 131–3. See more generally G. H. Martin, 'Domesday London', in *The Middlesex and London Domesday* (London, 1991), pp. 22–32.

81 Kelly, *St Paul's*, pp. 33–4.

82   Fleming, 'Rural élites', pp. 8–10.

83   Dyson and Schofield, 'Saxon London', pp. 306–8; Martin Biddle, 'A city in transition: 400–800', in *The City of London from Prehistoric Times to c.1520*, ed. Mary D. Lobel (Oxford, 1989), pp. 20–9, at 23.

84   Gustav Milne and Nathalie Cohen, *Excavations at Medieval Cripplegate, London: Archaeology after the Blitz, 1946–68* (London, 2001), pp. 127–9.

85   Susan Reynolds, 'Towns in Domesday Book', in *Domesday Studies: Papers Read at the Novocentenary Conference of the Royal Historical Society and the Institute of British Geographers, Winchester, 1986*, ed. James Clarke Holt (Woodbridge, 1987), pp. 295–309.

86   Christopher Brooke and Gillian Keir, *London 800–1216: The Shaping of a City* (London, 1975), pp. 249–51.

87   S 1809 (*Chronicon Abbatiæ Rameseiensis a saec. X usque ad an. circiter 1200*, ed. William Dunn Macray (London, 1886), p. 58 (no. 32)).

88   S 1465 (*CantCC* 153).

89   F. M. Stenton, 'Norman London', in his *Preparatory to Anglo-Saxon England, being the Collected Papers of Frank Merry Stenton*, ed. Doris Mary Stenton (Oxford, 1970), pp. 23–47, at 30–1; Pamela Nightingale, 'The origin of the court of husting and Danish influence on London's development into a capital city', *EHR* 102 (1987), 559–78, esp. 559–63.

90   Naismith, *Medieval European Coinage*, pp. 365–6.

91   Ibid.

92   Peter Sawyer, 'Anglo-Scandinavian trade in the Viking Age and after', in *Anglo-Saxon Monetary History: Essays in Memory of Michael Dolley*, ed. Mark Blackburn (Leicester, 1986), pp. 185–99, at 192; and especially Sara M. Pons-Sanz, *The Lexical Effects of Anglo-Scandinavian Linguistic Contact on Old English* (Turnhout, 2013), pp. 82–4 and 175–7.

93   III Edgar 5.1 (*Die Gesetze der Angelsachsen*, ed. Felix Liebermann, 3 vols (Halle, 1903–16), vol. I, p. 202; trans. *EHD*, p. 433).

94   James Tait, *The Medieval English Borough: Studies on Its Origins and Constitutional History* (Manchester, 1936), pp. 41 and 62–3; Stenton, 'Norman London', pp. 29–30; Susan Reynolds, 'The rulers of London in the twelfth century', *History* 57 (1972), 337–53, at 339; Brooke and Keir, *London 800–1216*, p. 249; John Hudson, *The Oxford History of the Laws of England. Vol. 2: 871–1216* (Oxford, 2012), pp. 818–19. Tait, *Medieval English Borough*, p. 36 suggested the Folkmoot was the successor to the meeting (*gemot*) of VI Æthelstan.

95   E.g. Biddle, 'City in transition', p. 23; Vince, *Saxon London*, p. 56; and Kelly, *St Paul's*, p. 9.

96   David Bowsher et al., *The London Guildhall: An Archaeological History of a Neighbourhood from Early Medieval to Modern Times*, 2 vols (London, 2007), vol. I, pp. 11, 16–18 and 301.

97   Brooke and Keir, *London 800–1216*, p. 170. Tait, *Medieval English Borough*, pp. 60–3 saw it as closer to a hundred.

98 IV Edgar 8.1 and 10 (ed. Liebermann, vol. I, pp. 210–13; trans. *EHD*, p. 436). See George Molyneaux, *The Formation of the English Kingdom in the Tenth Century* (Oxford, 2015), pp. 141–55, seeing them as a tenth-century development.

99 Brooke and Keir, *London 800–1216*, pp. 162–70.

100 *DOE* s.v. *cniht*. See also Derek Keene, 'English urban guilds, *c.*900–1300: the purposes and politics of association', in *Guilds and Associations in Europe, 900–1900*, ed. Ian A. Gadd and Patrick Wallis (London, 2006), pp. 3–26, at 6–9.

101 Kelly, *St Paul's*, pp. 216–19; Jeremy Haslam, 'Parishes, churches, wards and gates in eastern London', in *Minsters and Parish Churches: The Local Church in Transition 950–1200*, ed. John Blair (Oxford, 1988), pp. 35–43; Brooke and Keir, *London 800–1216*, pp. 96–8; F. E. Harmer, *Anglo-Saxon Writs* (Manchester, 1952), pp. 231–4; and Stenton, 'Norman London', pp. 32–3.

102 S 1103 (*LondStP* 32; *ASWrits*, pp. 231–4). The manuscript is Glasgow, University Library, Hunter U.2.6, f. 149r. See further Stenton, 'Norman London', pp. 32–5.

103 Stenton, 'Norman London', pp. 33–5; Brooke and Keir, *London 800–1216*, pp. 155–7. The exact meaning of 'soke' is complicated and debatable: for judicious recent surveys, see Hudson, *Laws*, pp. 56–62; Baxter, *Earls*, pp. 210–11.

104 *The Cartulary of Holy Trinity Aldgate*, ed. G. A. J. Hodgett (London, 1971), no. 871; H. C. Coote, 'The English gild of knights and their *socn*', *TLAMAS* 5 (1881), 477–93.

105 Kelly, *St Paul's*, p. 218; Brooke and Keir, *London 800–1216*, p. 343.

106 See Chapter 6.

107 See more generally Catherine Cubitt, '"As the lawbook teaches": reeves, lawbooks and urban life in the anonymous Old English *Legend of the Seven Sleepers*', *EHR* 124 (2009), 1021–49.

108 VI Æthelstan 9 (ed. Liebermann, vol. I, p. 181; trans. *EHD*, p. 426).

109 S 1119 and 1121 (*ASWrits* 75 and 77).

110 Reynolds, 'Rulers of London'.

111 S 1149–50 (*ASWrits* 105–6).

112 For the eleventh-century reeves more generally, see Brooke and Keir, *London 800–1216*, pp. 193–7.

113 S 1096 (*Chert* 12).

114 Pamela Nightingale, 'Some London moneyers, and reflections on the organization of English mints in the eleventh and twelfth centuries', *Numismatic Chronicle* 142 (1982), 34–50 (repr. in her *Trade, Money, and Power in Medieval England* (Aldershot, 2007), no. V).

115 Brooke and Keir, *London 800–1216*, p. 192; Harmer, *Anglo-Saxon Writs*, pp. 50–2 and 569; Bolton, *Empire of Cnut*, pp. 61–4; Katharin Mack, 'The stallers: administrative innovation in the reign of Edward the Confessor', *Journal of Medieval History* 12 (1986), 123–34.

116 Brooke and Keir, *London 800–1216*, pp. 196–7.

117 Schofield, *St Paul's*, pp. 46–59.

118 Andrew Rabin, 'Wulfstan at London: episcopal politics in the reign of Æthelred', *English Studies* 97 (2016), 186–206.

119 Keynes, 'Burial of King Æthelred', pp. 139–40, with reference to S 931b.

120 *ASC* CDE 1013.

121 Frank Barlow, *The English Church 1000–1066*, 2nd ed. (London and New York, 1979), pp. 219–20.

122 Bernhard Walter Scholz, 'Sulcard of Westminster, "Prologus de construccione Westmonasterii"', *Traditio* 20 (1964), 59–91, at 64–6; more generally Richard Gem, 'The origins of the abbey', in *Westminster Abbey*, ed. C. Wilson (London, 1986), pp. 6–21; Simon Keynes, 'The Anglo-Saxon origins of Westminster Abbey' (forthcoming).

123 Michael Winterbottom and Michael Lapidge (ed. and trans.), *The Early Lives of St Dunstan* (Oxford, 2012), pp. xlvii–xlviii; Simon Keynes, 'Wulfsige, monk of Glastonbury, abbot of Westminster (c.900–3), and bishop of Sherborne (c.993–1002)', in *St. Wulfsige and Sherborne: Essays to Celebrate the Millennium of the Benedictine Abbey, 998–1998*, ed. Katherine Barker (Oxford, 2005), pp. 53–94, at 56–9; David Sullivan, *The Westminster Corridor: An Exploration of the Anglo-Saxon History of Westminster Abbey and Its Nearby Lands and People* (London, 1994).

124 Marafioti, *King's Body*, pp. 144–55.

125 S 1041 and 1043 (*Diplomatarium Anglicum Ævi Saxonici*, ed. Benjamin Thorpe (London, 1865), pp. 400–14). These charters too are thought to be forgeries of the twelfth century, but probably refer to genuine earlier grants.

126 *Vita Ædwardi regis* I.6 and II.9 (*The Life of King Edward Who Rests at Westminster*, ed. and trans. Frank Barlow, 2nd ed. (Oxford, 1992), pp. 66–71 and 110–13).

127 Barlow, *Edward*, pp. 229–32.

128 *Regesta regum Anglo-Normannorum: The Acta of William I (1066–1087)*, ed. David Bates (Oxford, 1998), no. 290 (no. 324 also includes gifts from some denizens of London, mingled with other landowners).

129 David Knowles, C. N. L. Brooke and Vera C. M. London, *The Heads of Religious Houses: England and Wales. I: 940–1216*, 2nd ed. (Cambridge, 2001), p. 76.

130 Richard Gem, 'Craftsmen and administrators in the building of the Confessor's abbey', in *Edward the Confessor: The Man and the Legend*, ed. Richard Mortimer (Woodbridge, 2009), pp. 168–72.

131 Richard Gem, 'The romanesque rebuilding of Westminster Abbey', *ANS* 3 (1981), 33–60, at 40–55; Eric Fernie, 'Edward the Confessor's Westminster Abbey', in *Edward the Confessor*, ed. Mortimer, pp. pp. 139–50.

132 Warwick Rodwell, 'New glimpses of Edward the Confessor's abbey at Westminster', in *Edward the Confessor*, ed. Mortimer, pp. 151–67; Warwick

Rodwell, Daniel Miles, Derek Hamilton and Martin Bridge, 'The dating of the Pyx Door', *English Heritage Historical Review* 1 (2006), 24–7.

133 *Vita Ædwardi regis* II.9 (ed. and trans. Barlow, pp. 110–13).

134 GDB 128r; Gervase Rosser, *Medieval Westminster 1200–1540* (Oxford, 1989), pp. 9–16.

135 Haslam, 'Parishes', makes a case for 'sub-minsters' providing pastoral care in London before smaller parishes developed: in principle this is entirely plausible, though specific examples are difficult to trace.

136 See Chapter 6.

137 John Blair, *The Church in Anglo-Saxon Society* (Oxford, 2005), p. 404.

138 F. M. Stenton (trans.), *Norman London: An Essay* (London, 1934), p. 27.

139 John Schofield, 'Saxon and medieval parish churches in the City of London: a review', *TLAMAS* 45 (1994), 23–145.

140 Schofield, 'Parish churches', pp. 81–2; for a different view see Harold McCarter Taylor and Joan Taylor, *Anglo-Saxon Architecture*, 2 vols (Cambridge, 1965–78), vol. I, pp. 399–400. The method of construction was used from the eighth to thirteenth centuries (Schofield, 'Parish churches', p. 43).

141 Tweddle et al., *Corpus*, pp. 218–24.

142 Ibid., pp. 224–5.

143 Schofield, 'Parish churches', pp. 42–5.

144 Vince, *Saxon London*, pp. 75–6; and Blair, *Church in Anglo-Saxon Society*, pp. 405–6.

145 Schofield, 'Parish churches', pp. 35–44.

146 Andrew Reynolds, *Anglo-Saxon Deviant Burial Customs* (Oxford, 2009), p. 45 (citing the unpublished work of Bill McCann).

147 Gustav Milne, *St Bride's Church, London: Archaeological Research 1952–60 and 1992–5* (London, 1997), esp. pp. 25–6, 92–3 and 100–3.

148 S 670. See Chapter 6.

149 S 1647 (*CantCC* 183).

150 Blair, *Church in Anglo-Saxon Society*, pp. 402–7 and 498–504; and Sarah Hamilton, *Church and People in the Medieval West, 900–1200* (Harlow, 2013), pp. 47–8.

151 Brooke and Keir, *London 800–1216*, p. 138.

152 Regina Schäfer, 'Rural-urban migrations, medieval era', in *The Encyclopedia of Global Human Migration*, ed. Immanuel Ness and Peter Bellwood, 5 vols (Chichester, 2013), vol. IV, pp. 2660–5; Christopher Dyer, *Making a Living in the Middle Ages: The People of Britain 850–1520* (New Haven and London, 2002), pp. 67–8; Edward Miller and John Hatcher, *Medieval England: Towns, Commerce and Crafts, 1086–1348* (London, 1995), pp. 70–1.

153 See Chapter 8.

154 Charles West, 'Urban populations and associations', in *A Social History of England 900–1200*, ed. Julia Crick and Elisabeth Van Houts (Cambridge, 2011), pp. 198–207, at 201–6.

155 Loveluck, *Northwest Europe*, pp. 315–19.
156 David A. E. Pelteret, 'Two Old English lists of serfs', *Mediaeval Studies* 48 (1986), 470–513, at 471–92.
157 Chris Wickham, *Medieval Europe* (New Haven, CT, and London, 2016), p. 130.
158 Edited in André Joris, *La ville de Huy au Moyen Age des origines à la fin du XIVe siècle* (Paris, 1959), pp. 479–84; with discussion in André Joris, *Huy et sa charte de franchise, 1066: antécédents, signification, problèmes* (Brussels, 1966).
159 For the so-called 'garrison theory', see Maitland, *Domesday Book*, pp. 178–88; developed in Adolphus Ballard, *The Domesday Boroughs* (Oxford, 1904), pp. 11–40. One of several important early critiques of this view was published in Charles Petit-Dutaillis, *Studies and Notes Supplementary to Stubbs' Constitutional History Down to the Great Charter*, trans. W. E. Rhodes (Manchester, 1908), pp. 79–83. For more balanced recent analyses, see Henry Clifford Darby, *The Domesday Geography of England* (Cambridge, 1977), pp. 309–12; and David Roffe, 'Domesday now: a view from the stage', in *Domesday Now: New Approaches to the Inquest and the Book*, ed. David Roffe and K. S. B. Keats-Rohan (Woodbridge, 2016), pp. 7–60, at 30–1.
160 GDB 30r.
161 Ballard, *Domesday Boroughs*, pp. 39–40.
162 Derek Keene, 'London Bridge and the identity of the medieval city', *TLAMAS* 51 (2000), 143–56, at 143–4; Bruce Watson, 'Medieval London Bridge and its role in the defence of the realm', *TLAMAS* 50 (1999), 17–22, at 17–18; Bruce Watson, Trevor Brigham and T. Dyson, *London Bridge: 2000 Years of a River Crossing* (London, 2001), pp. 52–82.
163 Robert Cowie, 'Lundenburh: the archaeology of late Saxon London', in *'Hidden Histories and Records of Antiquity': Essays on Saxon and Medieval London for John Clark, Curator Emeritus, Museum of London*, ed. Jonathan Cotton et al. (London, 2014), pp. 17–26, at 24.
164 John Clark, *Saxon and Norman London* (London, 1989), p. 21; Valerie Horsman, Christine Milne and Gustav Milne, *Aspects of Saxo-Norman London 1: Building and Street Development Near Billingsgate and Cheapside* (London, 1988), esp. pp. 100–7.
165 Patrick Ottaway, *Archaeology in British Towns: From the Emperor Claudius to the Black Death* (London, 1992), p. 137.
166 Horsman, Milne and Milne, *Aspects of Saxo-Norman London 1*, pp. 68–70 and 108–9; Julian Ayre and Robin Wroe-Brown, 'The eleventh- and twelfth-century waterfront and settlement at Queenhithe: excavations at Bull Wharf, City of London', *Archaeological Journal* 172 (2015), 195–272, at 208–9 and 212; Robin Fleming, *Britain after Rome: The Fall and Rise, from 400–1070* (London, 2010), pp. 258–9. Cf. Kevin Leahy and Michael Lewis, 'Domestic dwellings, workshops and working buildings', in *The Material Culture of the Built Environment in Anglo-Saxon England*,

ed. Maren Clegg Hyer and Gale R. Owen-Crocker (Liverpool, 2011), pp. 50–75, at 64.

167 See Chapters 5–6.

168 Ekwall, *Street-Names*, pp. 48–9.

169 Horsman, Milne and Milne, *Aspects of Saxo-Norman London 1*, p. 115.

170 Ibid., pp. 110–11; Cowie, 'Lundenburh', pp. 22–3.

171 Vince, *Saxon London*, pp. 124–9; Cowie and Harding, 'Saxon settlement', p. 193; Richard Bluer, Trevor Brigham and Robin Nielsen, *Roman and Later Development East of the Forum and Cornhill: Excavations at Lloyd's Register, 71 Fenchurch Street, City of London* (London, 2006), p. 75.

172 Mark Burch, Phil Treveil and Derek Keene, *The Development of Early Medieval and Later Poultry and Cheapside: Excavations at 1 Poultry and Vicinity, City of London* (London, 2011), pp. 20–5.

173 Ibid., pp. 25–56. A similar range of crafts from the same period can be seen at nearby sites: Julian Hill and Aidan Woodger, *Excavations at 72–75 Cheapside/83–93 Queen Street, City of London* (London, 1999), pp. 37–41.

174 Nick Holder, 'Inscriptions, writing and literacy in Saxon London', *TLAMAS* 49 (1998), 81–98, at 86.

175 Sadie Watson, *Urban Development in the North-West of Londinium: Excavations at 120–122 Cheapside to 14–18 Gresham Street, City of London, 2005* (London, 2015); Bowsher et al., *Guildhall*, vol. I, pp. 11 and 16–18. A site south of Cheapside (Bow Bells House) had been reoccupied by the tenth century (Isca Howell et al., *Roman and Medieval Development South of Cheapside: Excavations at Bow Bells House, City of London, 2005–6* (London, 2013)). For another tenth-century house north-east of London Bridge, see Ian Blair and David Sankey, *A Roman Drainage Culvert, Great Fire Destruction Debris and Other Evidence from Hillside Sites North-East of London Bridge: Excavations at Monument House and 13–21 Eastcheap, City of London* (London, 2007).

176 Burch, Treveil and Keene, *Development of Early Medieval and Later Poultry*, pp. 57–94. For skating, see the translation of William FitzStephen's description of London in Stenton, *Norman London*, p. 31.

177 Sharp and Watson, 'Saxo-Norman Southwark'; Martha Carlin, *Medieval Southwark* (London, 1995), pp. 13–18; David Divers, *A New Millennium at Southwark Cathedral: Investigations into the First Two Thousand Years* (London, 2009), pp. 35–41; Milne, *St Bride's Church*, p. 101.

178 Fleming, *Britain After Rome*, pp. 257–8.

179 See Chapter 6.

180 Ayre and Wroe-Brown, 'Eleventh- and twelfth-century waterfront', pp. 204–5.

181 Ibid., pp. 208–9.

182 Damian Goodburn in Ayre and Wroe-Brown, 'Post-Roman foreshore', pp. 165–70; and in Ayre and Wroe-Brown, 'Eleventh- and twelfth-century waterfront', pp. 234–6.

183 This is recorded in a charter of Henry II (d.1189) as duke, issued in 1150/1: *Regesta regum Anglo-Normannorum*, ed. H. W. C. Davis, Charles Johnson and H. A. Cronne, 4 vols (Oxford, 1913–69), vol. III, no. 729.

184 Vince, *Saxon London*, p. 153. For early eleventh-century London-area pottery from Scotland and Norway, see Derek Hall et al., 'Gone fishing! New dating evidence for the fish trade in the North Sea', in *Pottery and Social Dynamics in the Mediterranean and Beyond in Medieval and Post-Medieval Times*, ed. John Bintliff and Marta Caroscio, British Archaeological Reports: International Series 2557 (Oxford, 2013), pp. 73–8.

185 Now British Museum 1856,0701.1461. See Charles Roach Smith, *Catalogue of the Museum of London Antiquities, Collected by and the Property of, Charles Roach Smith* (London, 1854), pp. 104–5.

186 Loveluck, *Northwest Europe*, pp. 315–16; Vince, *Saxon London*, p. 96.

187 Geoff Egan, 'Byzantium in London? New archaeological evidence for 11th-century links between England and the Byzantine world', in *Material Culture and Well-Being in Byzantium*, ed. Michael Grünbart, Ewald Kislinger, Anna Muthesius and Dionysios C. Stathakopoulos (Vienna, 2007), pp. 111–17; Stott, 'Saxon and Norman coins', p. 320 for other foreign coins.

188 Patrick Wormald, *The Making of English Law: King Alfred to the Twelfth Century. Volume 1: Legislation and Its Limits* (Oxford, 1999), pp. 236–44.

189 *Die Gesetze der Angelsachsen*, ed. Felix Liebermann, 3 vols (Halle, 1903–16), vol. I, pp. 232–7 is the primary scholarly edition; a more convenient version, with English translation, is *The Laws of the Kings of England from Edmund to Henry I*, ed. and trans. Agnes Jane Robertson (Cambridge, 1925), pp. 70–9.

190 Joseph P. Huffman, *Family, Commerce and Religion in London and Cologne: Anglo-German Emigrants, c.1000–c.1300* (Cambridge, 1998), p. 9.

191 Rory Naismith, 'The laws of London? IV Æthelred in context' , *London Journal* (forthcoming). Cf. Loveluck, *Northwest Europe*, pp. 315–19.

192 Fleming, *Britain After Rome*, p. 258.

193 Rosie Weetch, 'Tradition and innovation: lead-alloy brooches and urban identities in the 11th century', in *The Archaeology of the 11th Century: Continuities and Transformations*, ed. Dawn M. Hadley and Christopher Dyer (Abingdon, 2017), pp. 263–82.

194 Vince, *Saxon London*, pp. 102–3.

195 Brooke and Keir, *London 800–1216*, p. 128; Vince, *Saxon London*, pp. 27–8.

196 Brooke and Keir, *London 800–1216*, p. 361.

197 Chris Wickham, *The Inheritance of Rome: A History of Europe from 400 to 1000* (London, 2009), pp. 543–9; Wickham, *Medieval Europe*, pp. 130–7; Loveluck, *Northwest Europe*, pp. 328–42; Adriaan Verhulst, *The Rise of Cities in North-West Europe* (Cambridge, 1999), pp. 68–118.

198 Peter Sawyer, *The Wealth of Anglo-Saxon England* (Oxford, 2013), p. 105.

199 James H. Barrett, 'Medieval sea fishing, AD 500–1550: chronology, causes and consequences', in *Cod & Herring: The Archaeology & History of Medieval Sea Fishing*, ed. James H. Barrett and David C. Orton (Oxford, 2016), pp. 250–72, at 254; David C. Orton et al., 'Fish for London', ibid. pp. 205–14, at 206–7 and 211.

200 Molyneaux, *Formation*, esp. ch. 5. See also James Campbell, *The Anglo-Saxon State* (London, 2000), pp. 1–53 and 201–25.

8   LONDON IN 1066: THE BATTLE
OF HASTINGS AND AFTER

1 The succession debate in Edward's reign is extremely complicated. For selected surveys see Frank Barlow, *Edward the Confessor*, 2nd ed. (New Haven, CT, 1997), pp. 214–39; Stephen Baxter, 'Edward the Confessor and the succession question', in *Edward the Confessor: The Man and the Legend*, ed. Richard Mortimer (Woodbridge, 2009), pp. 77–118; Tom Licence, 'Edward the Confessor and the succession question: a fresh look at the sources', *ANS* 39 (2016), 113–27.

2 'Bastard' at this stage was more an insult to the mother's status than a condemnation of illegitimacy as such: Sara McDougall, *Royal Bastards: The Birth of Illegitimacy, 800–1230* (Oxford, 2016), pp. 116–20.

3 For a superb new study of William's life and rule, see David Bates, *William the Conqueror* (New Haven, CT, and London, 2016).

4 ASC D 1051. This visit, along with the Norman account of Edward pledging the succession to William via intermediaries at this time, has been extensively discussed: in addition to the references in n. 1, see Bates, *William*, pp. 112–15.

5 Bates, *William*, pp. 108–19 and 191–200.

6 George Garnett, *Conquered England: Kingship, Succession, and Tenure, 1066–1166* (Oxford, 2007), esp. pp. 4–9.

7 Two key volumes are *The Battle of Hastings: Sources and Interpretations*, ed. Stephen Morillo (Woodbridge, 1996) and M. K. Lawson, *The Battle of Hastings 1066*, 3rd ed. (privately published, 2016), https://www.academia. edu/24234095/The_Battle_of_Hastings_1066.

8 Bates, *William*, pp. 243–4; Lawson, *Battle of Hastings*, pp. 92 and 203–13.

9 For William's march through Kent see *The Gesta Guillelmi of William of Poitiers*, ed. and trans. R. H. C. Davis and Marjorie Chibnall (Oxford, 1998), pp. 142–5.

10 Nicholas Hooper, 'Edgar the ætheling: Anglo-Saxon prince, rebel and crusader', *ASE* 14 (1985), 197–214. For the status of *ætheling*, see David N. Dumville, 'The ætheling: a study in Anglo-Saxon constitutional history', *ASE* 8 (1979), 1–33.

11 Simon Keynes, 'The Crowland Psalter and the sons of King Edmund Ironside', *Bodleian Library Record* 11 (1982–5), 359–70.

12 M. K. Lawson, 'Edward Ætheling', in *Oxford Dictionary of National Biography*, ed. H. C. G. Matthew and Brian Harrison, 61 vols (Oxford, 2004), vol. XVII, pp. 896–7.

13 *The Carmen de Hastingae Proelio of Guy, Bishop of Amiens*, ed. and trans. Frank Barlow, 2nd ed. (Oxford, 1999), pp. 38–9.

14 *ASC* E 1066. Hooper, 'Edgar', pp. 203–4.

15 *ASC* D 1066.

16 *Gesta Guillelmi*, ed. and trans. Davis and Chibnall, pp. 146–7.

17 Ibid.

18 *Carmen*, ed. and trans. Barlow, pp. 38–9.

19 *Gesta Guillelmi*, ed. and trans. Davis and Chibnall, pp. 146–7. See also Janet L. Nelson, 'The rites of the Conqueror', *ANS* 4 (1982), 117–32 and 210–21 (cited from her *Politics and Ritual in Early Medieval Europe* (London, 1986), pp. 373–401, at 375–6).

20 *ASC* D 1066. Historically there has been some uncertainty over whether Great or Little Berkhamsted was meant; for a convincing case in favour of Great Berkhamsted (and references to earlier literature), see Edward Impey, 'London's early castles and the context of their creation', in *The White Tower*, ed. Edward Impey (New Haven, CT, 2008), pp. 14–26, at 17–18.

21 See Chapter 7.

22 *The Gesta Normannorum Ducum of William of Jumièges, Orderic Vitalis, and Robert of Torigni*, ed. and trans. Elisabeth van Houts, 2 vols (Oxford, 1992–5), vol. II, pp. 170–3.

23 *Carmen*, ed. and trans. Barlow, pp. 38–45.

24 Cf. Impey, 'London's early castles', pp. 17–18.

25 The *Carmen* is one of the more problematic and debated sources. Its author is not specified in surviving manuscripts, but the text is thought to be a poem about the battle by Guy of Amiens which was referred to in the early twelfth century by another Anglo-Norman writer, Orderic Vitalis. Although an argument has been made that it dates from the twelfth century and is therefore of more limited authority (R. H. C. Davis, 'The Carmen de Hastingae Proelio', *EHR* 93 (1978), 241–61), it is still generally accepted as one of the earliest and most important accounts of the Norman Conquest (see, among others, Elisabeth van Houts, 'Latin poetry and the Anglo-Norman court, 1066–1135: the Carmen de Hastingae proelio', *Journal of Medieval History* 15 (1989), 39–62; *Carmen*, ed. and trans. Barlow, esp. pp. lxxxvii–xc; Lawson, *Battle of Hastings*, pp. 75–9).

26 *Carmen*, ed. and trans. Barlow, pp. 44–7.

27 For an insightful study on this theme, see Philippe Buc, *The Dangers of Ritual: Between Early Medieval Texts and Social Scientific Theory* (Princeton, 2001).

28 *Gesta Guillelmi*, ed. and trans. Davis and Chibnall, pp. 150–1; *The Ecclesiastical History of Orderic Vitalis*, ed. Marjorie Chibnall, 6 vols (Oxford, 1969–80), vol. II, pp. 182–5.

29 Bates, *William*, pp. 256–7; Nelson, 'Rites', pp. 385–6.

30 John Blair, 'An introduction to the Surrey Domesday', in *The Surrey Domesday*, ed. Ann Williams and R. W. H. Erskine (London, 1989), pp. 1–17, at 5; J. J. N. Palmer, 'The Conqueror's footprints in Domesday Book', in *The Medieval Military Revolution*, ed. Andrew Ayton and J. L. Price (London, 1998), pp. 23–44.

31 Pamela Nightingale, *A Medieval Mercantile Community: The Grocers' Company & the Politics & Trade of London 1000–1485* (New Haven, CT, 1995), p. 20.

32 *Gesta Guillelmi*, ed. and trans. Davis and Chibnall, pp. 148–9 and 160–3.

33 Impey, 'London's early castles'; Christopher Brooke and Gillian Keir, *London 800–1216: The Shaping of a City* (London, 1975), p. 30.

34 Impey, 'London's early castles', pp. 19–22.

35 Ibid., pp. 22–6; Derek Keene, 'From conquest to capital: St Paul's c.1100–1300', in *St Paul's: The Cathedral Church of London, 604–2004*, ed. Derek Keene, Arthur Burns and Andrew Saint (New Haven, CT, and London, 2004), pp. 18–20.

36 Roland B. Harris, 'The structural history of the White Tower, 1066–1200', in *The White Tower*, ed. Impey, pp. 29–93, at 38–43; Roland B. Harris, 'Recent research on the White Tower: reconstructing and dating the Norman building', in *Castles and the Anglo-Norman World: Proceedings of a Conference Held at Norwich Castle Museum in 2012*, ed. John A. Davies, Angela Riley, Jean-Marie Levesque and Charlotte Lapiche (Oxford, 2016), pp. 177–89.

37 Impey, 'London's early castles', p. 26; Oliver Creighton, *Castles and Landscapes: Power, Community and Fortification in Medieval England* (London, 2002), pp. 65–88.

38 Susan Reynolds, 'The rulers of London in the twelfth century', *History* 57 (1972), 337–53, at 339; Ann Williams, *The English and the Norman Conquest* (Woodbridge, 1995), pp. 205–6.

39 D. M. Palliser, *Medieval York, 600–1540* (Oxford, 2014), pp. 89–91 (with reservations about how severe the impact may have been).

40 *Regesta regum Anglo-Normannorum: The Acta of William I (1066–1087)*, ed. David Bates (Oxford, 1998), no. 180.

41 T. A. M. Bishop and Pierre Chaplais, *Facsimiles of English Royal Writs to A.D. 1100: Presented to Vivian Hunter Galbraith* (Oxford, 1957), pl. XIV.

42 Brooke and Keir, *London 800–1216*, p. 372; Katherine Keats-Rohan, *Domesday People: A Prosopography of Persons Occurring in English Documents, 1066–1166. 1: Domesday Book* (Woodbridge, 1999), pp. 226–7.

43 Richard Sharpe, 'Peoples and languages in eleventh- and twelfth-century Britain and Ireland: reading the charter evidence', in *The Reality Behind Charter Diplomatic in Anglo-Norman Britain*, ed. Dauvit Broun (Glasgow, 2011), pp. 1–119, at 3–16.

44 Garnett, *Conquered England*, pp. 12–13. For Regenbald see Simon Keynes, 'Regenbald the chancellor (sic)', *ANS* 10 (1988), 185–222, at 214–18.

45   Williams, *English and the Norman Conquest*, esp. pp. 7–23.

46   Bates, *William*, pp. 351–5. For fear of rape among English women, see Elisabeth van Houts, 'Intermarriage in eleventh-century England', in *Normandy and Its Neighbours, 900–1250: Essays for David Bates*, ed. David Crouch and Kathleen Thompson (Turnhout, 2011), pp. 237–70, at 251–6

47   *Acta of William I*, ed. Bates, nos 181–2; Simon Keynes, 'Church councils, royal assemblies, and Anglo-Saxon royal diplomas', in *Kingship, Legislation and Power in Anglo-Saxon England*, ed. Gale R. Owen-Crocker and Brian W. Schneider (Woodbridge, 2013), pp. 17–184, at 134–5; Brooke and Keir, *London 800–1216*, pp. 310–12; W. H. Stevenson, 'An Old English charter of William the Conqueror in favour of St. Martin's-Le-Grand, London, A.D. 1068', *EHR* 11 (1896), 731–44.

48   *Acta of William I*, ed. Bates, no. 290.

49   Clare A. P. Willsdon, *Mural Painting in Britain 1840–1940: Image and Meaning* (Oxford, 2000), p. 71.

50   See Chapter 7.

51   Joe Hillaby, 'The London Jewry: William I to John', *Jewish Historical Studies* 33 (1992–4), 1–44.

52   Judith A. Green, *Forging the Kingdom: Power in English Society, 973–1189* (Cambridge, 2017), pp. 205–11; Brooke and Keir, *London 800–1216*, pp. 234–57.

Select Bibliography

Archibald, Marion, J. R. S. Lang and Gustav Milne, 'Four early medieval coin dies from the London waterfront', *Numismatic Chronicle* 155 (1995), 165–200

Ayre, Julian, and Robin Wroe-Brown, 'The eleventh- and twelfth-century waterfront and settlement at Queenhithe: excavations at Bull Wharf, City of London', *Archaeological Journal* 172 (2015), 195–272

—— 'The Post-Roman foreshore and the origins of the late Anglo-Saxon waterfront and dock of Æthelred's Hithe: excavations at Bull Wharf, City of London', *Archaeological Journal* 172 (2015), 121–94

Bailey, Keith, 'The Middle Saxons', in *The Origins of Anglo-Saxon Kingdoms*, ed. Steven Bassett (Leicester, 1989), pp. 108–22 and 265–9

Baker, John, *Cultural Transition in the Chilterns and Essex Region 350 AD to 650 AD* (Hatfield, 2006)

Biddle, Martin, 'Seasonal festivals and residence: Winchester, Westminster and Gloucester in the tenth to the twelfth centuries', *ANS* 8 (1986), 51–72

Blackburn, Mark, 'The London mint in the reign of Alfred', in *Kings, Currency and Alliances: History and Coinage in Southern England in the Ninth Century*, ed. Mark Blackburn and David N. Dumville (Woodbridge, 1998), pp. 105–23

Blackmore, Lyn, 'The origins and growth of *Lundenwic*, a mart of many nations', in *Central Places in the Migration and Merovingian Periods: Papers from the 52nd Sachsensymposium, Lund, August 2001*, ed. Birgitta Hårdh and Lars Larsson (Lund, 2002), pp. 273–301

Blair, John, *Early Medieval Surrey: Land Holding, Church and Settlement before 1300* (Stroud, 1991)

—— 'Frithuwold's kingdom and the origins of Surrey', in *The Origins of Anglo-Saxon Kingdoms*, ed. Steven Bassett (London, 1989), pp. 97–107

Bowsher, David, et al., *The London Guildhall: an Archaeological History of a Neighbourhood from Early Medieval to Modern Times*, 2 vols (London, 2007)

Brooke, Christopher, and Gillian Keir, *London 800–1216: the Shaping of a City* (London, 1975)

Brooks, Nicholas, and James Graham-Campbell, 'Reflections on the Viking-Age silver hoard from Croydon, Surrey', in Nicholas Brooks, *Communities and Warfare 700–1400* (London, 2000), pp. 69–92

Burch, Mark, Phil Treveil and Derek Keene, *The Development of Early Medieval and Later Poultry and Cheapside: Excavations at 1 Poultry and Vicinity, City of London* (London, 2011)

Carlin, Martha, *Medieval Southwark* (London, 1996)

Chaplais, Pierre, 'The letter from Bishop Wealdhere of London to Archbishop Brihtwold of Canterbury: the earliest original "letter close" extant in the West', in *Medieval Scribes, Manuscripts and Libraries: Essays Presented to N. R. Ker*, ed. M. B. Parkes and Andrew G. Watson (London, 1978), pp. 3–23

Clark, John, *Saxon and Norman London* (London, 1989)

Clark, John, et al. (ed.), *Londinium and Beyond: Essays on Roman London and its Hinterland for Harvey Sheldon* (London, 2008)

Cowie, Robert, 'The evidence for royal sites in Middle Anglo-Saxon London', *Medieval Archaeology* 48 (2004), 201–9

——'Lundenburh: the archaeology of late Saxon London', in *'Hidden Histories and Records of Antiquity': Essays on Saxon and Medieval London for John Clark, Curator Emeritus, Museum of London*, ed. Jonathan Cotton et al. (London, 2014), pp. 17–26

Cowie, Robert, and Lyn Blackmore, *Early and Middle Saxon Rural Settlement in the London Region* (London, 2008)

——*Lundenwic: Excavations in Middle Saxon London, 1987–2000* (London, 2008)

Cowie, Robert, and Charlotte Harding, 'Saxon settlement from the Dark Ages to Domesday', in *The Archaeology of Greater London: an Assessment of Archaeological Evidence for Human Presence in the Area Now Covered by Greater London*, ed. Monica Kendall (London, 2000), pp. 171–206

Cowie, Robert, Robert L. Whytehead and Lyn Blackmore, 'Two Middle Saxon occupation sites: excavations at Jubilee Hall and 21–22 Maiden Lane' *TLAMAS* 39 (1988), 47–163

Cubitt, Catherine, *Anglo-Saxon Church Councils c.650–c.850* (London, 1995)

Dyson, T., 'King Alfred and the restoration of London', *London Journal* 15 (1990), 99–110

——'London and Southwark in the 7th century and later: a neglected reference', *TLAMAS* 31 (1980), 83–95

——'Two Saxon land-grants for Queenhithe', in *Collectanea Londiniensia: Studies in London Archaeology and History Presented to Ralph Merrifield*, ed. Joanna Bird, Hugh Chapman and John Clark (London, 1978), pp. 200–15

Dyson, T., and John Schofield, 'Saxon London', in *Anglo-Saxon Towns in Southern England*, ed. Jeremy Haslam (Chichester, 1984), pp. 285–314

Egan, Geoff, 'Byzantium in London? New archaeological evidence for 11th-century links between England and the Byzantine world', in *Material Culture and Well-Being in Byzantium*, ed. Michael Grünbart, Ewald Kislinger, Anna Muthesius and Dionysios C. Stathakopoulos (Vienna, 2007), pp. 111–17

Ekwall, Eilert, *Street Names of the City of London* (Oxford, 1954)

Gelling, Margaret, 'The boundaries of the Westminster charters', *TLAMAS* new series 11 (1954), 101–4

Gem, Richard, 'The origins of the abbey', in *Westminster Abbey*, ed. Christopher Wilson (London, 1986), pp. 6–21

——, 'The romanesque rebuilding of Westminster Abbey', *ANS* 3 (1981), 33–60

Gerrard, James, 'New light on the end of Roman London', *Archaeological Journal* 168 (2011), 181–94

Goodburn, Damian, 'Fragments of a 10th-century timber arcade from Vintner's Place on the London waterfront', *Medieval Archaeology* 37 (1993), 78–92

Haslam, Jeremy, 'The development of London by King Alfred: a reassessment', *TLAMAS* 61 (2010), 109–44

—— 'King Alfred, Mercia and London, 874–86: a reassessment', *ASSAH* 17 (2011), 120–46

—— 'Parishes, churches, wards and gates in eastern London', in *Minsters and Parish Churches: the Local Church in Transition 950–1200*, ed. John Blair (Oxford, 1988), pp. 35–43

Haynes, Ian, Harvey Sheldon and Lesley Hannigan (ed.), *London under Ground: the Archaeology of a City* (Oxford, 2000)

Horsman, Valerie, Christine Milne and Gustav Milne, *Aspects of Saxo-Norman London I: Building and Street Development Near Billingsgate and Cheapside* (London, 1988)

Huffman, Joseph P., *Family, Commerce and Religion in London and Cologne: Anglo-German Emigrants, c.1000–c.1300* (Cambridge, 1998)

Impey, Edward, 'London's early castles and the context of their creation', in *The White Tower*, ed. Edward Impey (New Haven, CT, 2008), pp. 14–26

Keene, Derek, 'Alfred and London', in *Alfred the Great: Papers from the Eleventh-Centenary Conferences*, ed. Timothy Reuter (Aldershot, 2003), pp. 236–49

—— 'Capital cities in medieval England to 1300', in *Lo sguardo lungimirante delle capitali: saggi in onore di Francesca Bocchi*, ed. Rosa Smurra, Hubert Houben and Manuela Ghizzoni (Rome, 2014), pp. 21–60

—— 'From conquest to capital: St Paul's c.1100–1300', in *St Paul's: the Cathedral Church of London, 604–2004*, ed. Derek Keene, Arthur Burns and Andrew Saint (New Haven, CT, and London, 2004), pp. 17–32

—— 'London Bridge and the identity of the medieval city', *TLAMAS* 51 (2000), 143–56

—— 'London from the post-Roman period to c.1300', in *The Cambridge Urban History of Britain. 1: 600–1540*, ed. D. M. Palliser (Cambridge, 2000), pp. 187–216

Kelly, S. E. (ed.), *Charters of St Paul's, London* (Oxford, 2004)

Keynes, Simon, 'The burial of King Æthelred the Unready at St Paul's', in *The English and their Legacy: 900–1200. Essays in Honour of Ann Williams*, ed. David Roffe (Woodbridge, 2012), pp. 129–48

—— 'King Alfred and the Mercians', in *Kings, Currency and Alliances: History and Coinage in Southern England in the Ninth Century*, ed. Mark Blackburn and David N. Dumville (Woodbridge, 1998), pp. 1–45

Leary, Jim, et al., *Tatberht's Lundenwic: Archaeological Excavations in Middle Saxon London* (London, 2004)

Lobel, Mary D. (ed.), *The City of London from Prehistoric Times to c.1520* (Oxford, 1989)

Maddicott, J. R., 'London and Droitwich, *c*.650–750: trade, industry and the rise of Mercia', *ASE* 34 (2005), 7–58

Malcolm, Gordon, David Bowsher and Robert Cowie, *Middle Saxon London: Excavations at the Royal Opera House 1989–99* (London, 2003)

Marsden, Peter, *Ships of the Port of London* (London, 1994)

Martin, G. H., 'Domesday London', in *The Middlesex and London Domesday* (London, 1991), pp. 22–32

McKisack, May, 'London and the succession to the Crown during the Middle Ages', in *Studies in Medieval History Presented to F. M. Powicke*, ed. R. W. Hunt, W. A. Pantin and R. W. Southern (Oxford, 1948), pp. 76–89

Merrifield, Ralph, *London: City of the Romans* (London, 1983)

Milne, Gustav, *Book of Roman London: Urban Archaeology in the Nation's Capital* (London, 1995)

—— *The Port of Medieval London* (Stroud, 2003)

—— *St Bride's Church, London: Archaeological Research 1952–60 and 1992–5* (London, 1997)

Naismith, Rory, 'London and its mint *c*.880–1066: a preliminary survey', *British Numismatic Journal* 83 (2013), 44–74

Naismith, Rory, and Francesca Tinti, *The Forum Hoard of Anglo-Saxon Coins/ Il ripostiglio dell'Atrium Vestae nel Foro Romano*, Bollettino di numismatica 55–6 (Rome, 2016)

Nightingale, Pamela, *A Medieval Mercantile Community: the Grocers' Company & the Politics & Trade of London 1000–1485* (New Haven, CT, 1995)

—— 'The origin of the court of husting and Danish influence on London's development into a capital city', *EHR* 102 (1987), 559–78

—— 'Some London moneyers, and reflections on the organization of English mints in the eleventh and twelfth centuries', *Numismatic Chronicle* 142 (1982), 34–50

Perring, Dominic, *Roman London* (London, 1991)

Russo, Daniel G., *Town Origins and Development in Early England, c.400–950 A D* (Westport, CT, and London, 1998)

Schofield, John, *St Paul's Cathedral before Wren* (London, 2011)

—— 'Saxon and medieval parish churches in the City of London: a review', *TLAMAS* 45 (1994), 23–145

Sharp, Tony, and Bruce Watson, 'Saxo-Norman Southwark: a review of the archaeological and historical evidence', in *Anglo-Saxon Traces*, ed. Jane Roberts and Leslie Webster (Tempe, AZ, 2011), pp. 273–96

Stevenson, W. H., 'An Old English charter of William the Conqueror in favour of St. Martin's-Le-Grand, London, A.D. 1068', *EHR* 11 (1896), 731–44

Stocker, David, 'St Paul's Cathedral, A D 604–1087', *London Archaeologist* 12 (2009), 79–86

Tatton-Brown, Tim, 'The topography of Anglo-Saxon London', *Antiquity* 60 (1986), 21–8

Telfer, Alison, 'New evidence for the transition from the Late Roman to the Saxon period at St Martin-in-the-Fields, London', in *Intersections: the Archaeology and History of Christianity in England, 400–1200. Papers in Honour of Martin Biddle and Birthe Kjølbye-Biddle*, ed. Martin Henig and Nigel Ramsey (Oxford, 2010), pp. 49–58

Tomlin, R. S. O., *Roman London's First Voices: Writing Tablets from the Bloomberg Excavations, 2010–14* (London, 2016)

Vince, Alan, *Saxon London: an Archaeological Investigation* (London, 1990)

Vince, Alan (ed.), *Aspects of Saxo-Norman London: 2. Finds and Environmental Evidence* (London, 1991)

Watson, Bruce, 'Medieval London Bridge and its role in the defence of the realm', *TLAMAS* 50 (1999), 17–22

—— 'Saxo-Norman Southwark: a review of the archaeological and historical evidence', *London Archaeologist* 12.6 (2009), 147–51

Watson, Bruce, Trevor Brigham and Tony Dyson, *London Bridge: 2000 Years of a River Crossing* (London, 2001)

Weetch, Rosie, 'Tradition and innovation: lead-alloy brooches and urban identities in the 11th century', in *The Archaeology of the 11th Century: Continuities and Transformations*, ed. Dawn M. Hadley and Christopher Dyer (Abingdon, 2017), pp. 263–82

Wheeler, R. E. M., *London and the Vikings* (London, 1927)

—— *London and the Saxons* (London, 1935)

Whitelock, Dorothy, *Some Anglo-Saxon Bishops of London* (London, 1975)

Williams, Ann, 'The Vikings in Essex, 871–917', *Essex Archaeology and History* 27 (1996), 92–101

Yorke, Barbara, 'The kingdom of the East Saxons', *ASE* 14 (1985), 1–36

Where to See Anglo-Saxon London

Seeing Anglo-Saxon London is largely a matter of looking for a few artefacts and many fossils in the form of streets and buildings which follow layouts that have persisted for a millennium. There is just one place in the city, at All Hallows by the Tower, where a standing piece of (probably) Anglo-Saxon architecture can be seen.

This short guide is intended for anyone who might wish to visit any of the key locations where traces of Anglo-Saxon London survive. It is not exhaustive: a great many other places could have been included, especially in modern Greater London. The emphasis here, however, is on the much smaller and more central area which the Anglo-Saxons themselves identified as London. Some of the places mentioned here offer only a faint tie to the first millennium, being little more than a name. But with the application of some imagination, it is entirely possible to get more of a feel for the early city.

Museums

London is abundantly provided with world-class museums, but there are only a handful that hold a substantial quantity of material from Anglo-Saxon England. The **British Museum** is of course in a league of its own. Pride of place in its early medieval gallery justifiably goes to the treasures from Sutton Hoo, deposited in Suffolk in the seventh century. These are surrounded by a rich array of other artefacts. But while breath-taking, it must be said that these exhibits communicate a better sense of the Anglo-Saxon era as a whole than of the Anglo-Saxon era in London. To obtain some sense of what Anglo-Saxon London was like, and to see artefacts from it set in context, it is essential to visit the **Museum of London**. This holds some of the key items discussed on earlier pages, not least the St Paul's tombstone and tenth-century wooden remains from the Thames shorefront. Items of Anglo-Saxon date, including a beautiful eighth-century sword, can also be seen in the **Jewel Tower** near Westminster Abbey.

Churches

For most of the early Middle Ages, London was a staunchly Christian city, and as such its churches played a central part in the lives of early Londoners. It is likely that dozens of the City of London's modern churches have Anglo-Saxon roots. **St Paul's Cathedral**, for instance, is known to have been founded in 604, while **St Andrew Holborn** was already an 'old wooden church' in the mid-tenth century and **Southwark Cathedral** allegedly originated as a pre-Conquest church. However, in all three cases there is no known evidence, standing or archaeological, for the pre-1066 buildings.

Several churches bear little external resemblance to their medieval forebears, but contain the remnants of earlier buildings, or have been found to sit on top of them. **All Hallows-by-the-Tower**, also known as All Hallows Barking, looks from the outside like a seventeenth-century building, augmented and restored in modern times – which is essentially what it is, following an explosion in 1650 and severe damage during the Blitz in 1940. But the twentieth-century destruction and restoration brought to light remnants of what must have been some of the earliest chapters in the church's history: an archway of reused Roman tiles which probably dates to the late Anglo-Saxon period (certainly from the twelfth century or before), and several fragments of late Anglo-Saxon sculpture. The latter are, as of 2018, on display in a museum beneath the church, which also contains Roman artefacts and objects from the church's later history. All Hallows-by-the-Tower has the richest Anglo-Saxon remains of any London church.

Only tiny fragments remain above ground of Edward the Confessor's church at **Westminster Abbey**, which was demolished and rebuilt in the thirteenth century. However, some of the abbey's Anglo-Saxon artefacts and documents can be seen on display in the Queen's Diamond Jubilee Galleries. Elements of Roman and Anglo-Saxon foundations can be seen in a few other churches, such as in the crypt museum beneath **St Bride's** on Fleet Street. In most cases, however, such remains are below ground and inaccessible (as is, for instance, the case with the important late Roman and early Anglo-Saxon cemetery at **St Martin-in-the-Fields**).

Streets and Sites

In an important sense, the whole City of London, along with Westminster and the West End, are relics of the Anglo-Saxon era. Elements of their layout and even some street names (especially in the City) go back to the early Middle Ages.

Drury Lane, running from Aldwych past Covent Garden up to High Holborn, is now the domain of theatres and cafés, but can claim to be one of the oldest streets in London: it was the original Aldwych ('Drury' refers to a prominent family who lived there in the fifteenth and sixteenth centuries), and was probably a street of *Lundenwic*. It is possible that the **Strand** too – a Roman road ('Akeman Street') – was a thoroughfare of *Lundenwic*, running along what was the north bank of the Thames, while **Oxford Street** to its north formed part of the Roman 'Watling Street', and was in the tenth century referred to as a 'wide army street'. The modern **Aldwych** is a creation of the Edwardian period, as is nearby **Covent Garden**, which originated as a walled garden belonging to Westminster Abbey. But it sat on top of the heart of *Lundenwic*, and the reconstruction of the **Royal Opera House** in the 1990s facilitated one of the most important archaeological excavations for this period; so too did work on the nearby **London Transport Museum**. These discoveries are not immediately apparent to the casual visitor, but are recognised in plaques and museum exhibits elsewhere in the city.

In the City itself, a large number of streets are thought to have originated between the ninth and eleventh centuries. Only a few can be mentioned here, alongside those highlighted in Chapters 5, 6 and 7. **Cheapside** (medieval Westcheap) marked the effective northern edge of Alfredian London. Unusually, it and a few other streets extending from it, such as Newgate Street, followed the Roman street layout, which most other routes in the later Anglo-Saxon city did not. **Gracechurch Street** referred to a church with a grass (i.e. thatched) roof (All Hallows Lombard Street), which was mentioned in a document composed around the time of the Norman Conquest. The origin of **Cripplegate** (and Cripplegate Street) is debated, but could relate to the Old English word *crypel*, meaning either 'cripple' or 'burrow, narrow passage' (perhaps referring to the state of the gate itself at an early stage).

Commemorations of Anglo-Saxon London

The Anglo-Saxon past of London has not traditionally been a prominent part of its heritage – in part because of the lack of obvious monuments in the city as it stands. Yet as this book shows, there is a wealth of historical, institutional and even geographical heritage that modern London owes to the time between the Romans and the Norman Conquest. Some of these features have been celebrated in modern times, and form part of the public artworks erected across the city. The **Royal Exchange** in the heart of the City contains a cycle of 24 murals painted between the 1890s and the mid-twentieth century to illustrate key moments in London's history. The first represents the city's refoundation by Alfred the Great in 886, and the second William the Conqueror bestowing a writ on the citizens of London immediately after the Norman Conquest. A large and lively open-air mosaic marks the spot where **Queenhithe** (Old English *Æðeredeshyd*) was excavated. Created in 2014 and setting the site in its long-term historical perspective, this complements a much more modest plaque erected soon after the excavations in the 1980s.

There are other monuments to the Anglo-Saxon era in London, though these tend to be more focused on the country as a whole than the city itself – such as several paintings and murals in the **Palace of Westminster** which depict the exploits of Alfred the Great.

Index

Unless otherwise stated, local place names or street names (e.g. Gracechurch Street, Wanstead) are in modern Greater London. Old English names beginning Æ are indexed as 'Ae'.